Prophecy and the
Fundamentalist Quest

Prophecy and the Fundamentalist Quest

An Integrative Study of Christian and Muslim Apocalyptic Religion

FARZANA HASSAN

Foreword by John S. Niles

McFarland & Company, Inc., Publishers
Jefferson, North Carolina, and London

LIBRARY OF CONGRESS CATALOGUING-IN-PUBLICATION DATA

Shahid, Farzana Hassan.
  Prophecy and the fundamentalist quest : an integrative study
of Christian and Muslim apocalyptic religion / Farzana Hassan ;
foreword by Dr. John S. Niles.
      p.   cm.
  Includes bibliographical references and index.

  ISBN 978-0-7864-3300-1
  softcover : 50# alkaline paper ∞

  1. Eschatology, Islamic.   2. Eschatology — Biblical teaching.
3. Armageddon — Biblical teaching.   4. Eschatology — Comparative
studies.   5. Apocalyptic literature — History and criticism.   I. Title.
BP166.8.S42 2008
231.7'45 — dc22   2007049731

British Library cataloguing data are available

Cover image ©2008 Shutterstock

Manufactured in the United States of America

*McFarland & Company, Inc., Publishers
  Box 611, Jefferson, North Carolina 28640
  www.mcfarlandpub.com*

To my husband, Shahid.
For his unwavering love and
support through life's sorrows
and joys.

Acknowledgments

I am deeply grateful to my friend Peter Robbins for reviewing the full manuscript meticulously, and to the Rev. John Niles for writing the Foreword.

I must thank my family: My brother Saleem, for sharing his knowledge and research on Madrassahs; my mother Parveen, my sisters Irfana and Saadiya, and my children, Aamir, Ali, Amna and Maryam, for providing editorial help.

And Abujan, though he is no longer with us, for being a constant source of inspiration to me in my quest for learning.

Table of Contents

Foreword by John S. Niles

In a time when the world is shaken by "wars and rumors of wars" and the two largest religions are expressing apocalyptic visions of the future, there is a clear need for insight. Relevant analysis of the apocalyptic literature within the Quran and Bible is in order. Given that so much has been written about the Christian view of the coming apocalypse and so little about the Islamic view, it is particularly important that Westerners arrive at a reasoned understanding of Islamic prophecy and how it may affect events in today's world.

Farzana Hassan is the perfect person to lead us to that understanding.

She has wisely said, "Among the adherents of Islam there is a prevalent view that their faith will eventually prevail over others as a religious ideology. It is a belief embedded in both the Quran and Hadith and therefore deserves our attention as a subject of analysis."

With great insight she explores the dimensions of Islamic prophecy, making comparisons where needed with the biblical view. Her side-by-side examination of the apocalyptic views of Islam and Christianity is truly groundbreaking. May it lead to greater understanding between the two faiths — an understanding that may bring healing to a world in conflict.

Dr. John S. Niles, MSM, is senior minister at St. Andrew's United Church, Toronto, Ontario

Preface

The world has always been riddled with pockets of conflict: ethnic disputes, linguistic wars, and religious skirmishes simmer in limited areas around the globe. In recent years, however, a far broader and more ominous cloud has emerged over the length and breadth of the earth as a battle between the adherents of its two largest religions: Christianity and Islam. Although the conflict between Christendom and the Muslim world is not in fact strictly religious, the battle over people's hearts and minds is nonetheless steeped in religious rhetoric, with both sides invoking scripture to validate their respective stances. Although the conflict encompasses many aspects, such as the fight for political control, access to economic resources and cultural supremacy, its irrefutable underlying religiosity makes it that much more complex and impervious to change. Deriving its inspiration and thrust from scriptural sources — whether the Bible, the Quran, or Hadith literature — the conflict has attained an unshakable sanctity in the minds of the faithful, as it purports to link itself with the Divine, with its concomitant associations with ultimate power, goodness and glory.

Some assert that the conflict is only political in nature and not religiously inspired. The Arab-Israeli conflict, for instance, is a war for territory, control and hegemony in the region. All these aspects are of course crucial, but the warring parties perceive themselves first as religious entities distinct from their adversaries. It is religious differences that are at the foundation of this political struggle. A more religiously homogenous Middle East might not have witnessed the kind of blood bath the holy land has endured for so long. These identities are further solidified as conflicts take longer to resolve. For example, Israel questions the Palestinian right to return because of fears that the country will lose its Jewish character or even be reduced to a state where Jews will once again become a minority — a scenario dreadful to both Israelis and Diaspora Jews. But religious people from among both Palestinians and Jews lay claim to the land based on their respective understanding of scripture. Many from other parts of the world who have no direct stake in the conflict have also aligned themselves with the main players on the stage of global conflict based on religious, political or economic affiliation.

To date, much has been written about biblical prophecy, but the western world has yet to be introduced to the dimensions and implications of Islamic prophecy. And while this book includes Bible prophecy as a subject, it also attempts to deconstruct and analyze Islamic prophecy largely contained in Islam's secondary source of spiritual guidance, known as Hadith. Perhaps at times as graphic as the scenarios presented in the Book of Revelation or the eschatological predictions contained in Daniel, Hadith paints a vivid picture of future events that lends credence to the prophetic gifts of the old prophets and soothsayers of Islam. The implications are so palpable among the faithful that candid analysis is not only warranted, but has become crucial for understanding the dynamics governing relations between the two faiths.

Christianity and Islam, seen as the only two proselytizing faiths in the world, remain pitted against each other in a struggle for ascendancy, driven by presentiments of world glory and domination. The hopefuls on either side wish to impose their brand of religious ideology on the rest of the world, either through force or through persuasion. Thus evangelism and *Tabligh* or *D'awa* (the propagation of the message of Islam) are viewed increasingly by adherents as legitimate means of acquiring more market space for their respective ideologies. With a literalist approach towards understanding scriptural precepts and prophecy, fundamentalism has emerged with full gusto within both Islam and Christianity, manifested in umbrella organizations and localized groups. These movements strive to achieve their utopian ideals by distributing literature and propagating their world view through all the latest media outlets. Through such means as the network of Madrassahs in Pakistan and the "televangelism" of the Christian Coalition in the United States, fundamentalist groups have also infiltrated politics in order either to gain direct control over seats of power or to influence policy through lobbying and interest groups.

Among the adherents of Islam there is a prevalent view that their faith will eventually prevail over others as a religious ideology. It is a belief embedded in both the Quran and Hadith and therefore deserves our attention as a subject of analysis. Hence the book will also explore this dimension of prophecy, making comparisons where needed with a biblical view. I hope that an examination of these hitherto largely unexplored parallels will in some way engender a greater understanding of many of the current conflicts in our embattled world.

While investigating apocalyptic religion, I have drawn heavily from the popular commentaries on prophetic literature available on various websites. Such sites tend to represent popular rather than academic views. Popular belief determines the tide of religions and must be accounted for in any analysis of religious movements. Most of this book's deconstructed prophecies, therefore, have been chosen from these sources even though they may be at odds with the learned opinions of those schooled in theology. Though mainstream biblical and quranic scholarship will question many of the conclusions of these commentaries, the purpose of the current inquiry is to delve deep into the dynamics of the religion of the laity and how those dynamics shape religious movements. A case in point is the anticipated arrival of the Mahdi within Muslim apocalyptic thought. Though serious Islamic scholarship doubts the validity of the numerous Hadith predicting the advent of a "rightly guided one" who will redeem the world of Islam in the end times, Muslim masses seem to have embraced this notion and eagerly await his arrival. Similarly, although the considered opinions of many mainstream Bible scholars may be at variance with the opinions of authors like Tim LaHaye and Hal Lindsey, these authors nonetheless wield considerable influence on the masses.

But tussles within religious traditions are commonplace. The book will touch upon certain aspects of this phenomenon as well, particularly as it influences the interplay between fundamentalist and moderate Muslims. I hope that an analysis of these dynamics will bring us somewhat closer to understanding the devoutly religious mindset and how it shapes popular religious movements.

Since prophecies discussed in this book are largely focused on end-time scenarios, and since many religious people believe we are indeed living in the end times, an analysis of world politics today is also provided in the last two chapters in order to determine possible concordances between prophecy and political reality. That analysis includes a look at contemporary world alliances, particularly relationships between countries and non-state entities such as the Hezbollah and Taliban. The existence of such groups and the insurmountable challenges they pose towards achieving peace are also examined.

Deeply entrenched religious ideologies that have emerged in recent times have complicated matters further. The latter half of the book also explores how the apocalyptic vision has manifested itself in evangelical and jihadist movements as part of an unshakable religious mindset.

CHAPTER ONE

Sources of Christian and Islamic Prophecy

Often considered a window into the unseen future, prophecy has been used by prophets, sages and saints as a tool to forecast events, mostly to warn of dire consequences if a civilization refuses to mend its errant ways. Prophecy forms a significant part of the admonitions to mankind contained in scripture. Warnings of impending disasters, wars, and mass destruction of life and property — as well as promises of redemption — constitute the bulk of prophetic literature in both ancient and modern religious texts.

The prophetic mindset strives to attain insight into the future. The revelations that may come about through the prophetic quest have intrigued humanity from time immemorial. As a subject, prophecy has inspired debates and research, all adding to the plethora of predictions about times to come and the impact they will have on people's lives both as individuals and as members of communities. Primary and secondary sources of prophecy include various scriptures and their commentaries. Christian and Islamic prophecy are found in these sources.

Non-religious prophetic literature does exist and does inspire curiosity in the general public; the predictions of Jean Dixon and Sylvia Browne are examples. It is, however, religious prophetic work that receives the most attention, as it is perceived as emanating from divine authority. The subject of this investigation therefore is the Bible and the Islamic canon (the Quran and Hadith), as well as the popular commentaries on these sources.

The Holy Bible is replete with prophetic content, to such an extent that meticulous "Bible codes" have been extrapolated from it, purporting to predict the exact times, dates and outcomes of various global events. So great is the public's interest in such books that they often make the bestseller lists with sales ranging in the millions. The codes deal with end-time scenarios such as the coming of the prophet Elijah (awaited by the Jews), Satan's ultimate downfall and Armageddon. Although Bible codes also involve other topics, it is around apocalyptic events that they surface most prominently.

Prophecy is interspersed throughout the various books of the Bible, but those containing the most prophetic material include Jeremiah, Daniel, and Ezekiel from the Old Testament and the gospel of Mark, the Acts of the Apostles, Timothy, and the Book of Revelation in the New Testament. These books contain the most graphic accounts of the end of the world described with intricate detail.

The book of Daniel perhaps deserves special mention as a major canonical work among the prophetic books of the Old Testament. Although traditional scholarship places the book at 580 BCE, contemporary Bible scholars have challenged that view, pointing out that the book of Daniel is more an account of events already passed than a book of prophecy. They prefer to date it to approximately 160 BCE. Nonetheless popular religion continues to draw inspiration from it to support its apocalyptic agenda. It recounts the dreams and visions of the prophet Daniel about events at the end of days. Many believe it was Daniel who provided the numerical data to estimate the arrival of the apocalypse, and it is from his dating methods that Jehovah's Witnesses and Seventh-day Adventists calculate the awaited second coming of the Messiah. A crucifixion, the tribulation, Armageddon, the apocalypse and the destruction of the Temple are said to be predicted with great accuracy as a result.

Ezekiel dates back to 595 BCE and appeared during the Babylonian exile. The most remarkable feature of Ezekiel is the vision, described in its first chapter, of Jehovah's throne being carried around by four cherubs. Ezekiel sees the vision after eating the pages of a strange book. During the vision, God commands Ezekiel to enjoin righteousness on his countrymen if they are to be delivered from Nebuchadnezzar's tyranny. The book contains end-time prophecies, especially about the construction of the Third Temple in Jerusalem.

Jeremiah, another Hebrew prophet who lived around 600 BCE, also made several predictions. He suffered great persecution at the hands of his own countrymen, who destroyed his first work of prophecy by shredding it to pieces and then burning it. The primary reason for such treatment was his dire predictions of doom for his people if they refused to mend their ways.

The Apocalypse of St. John, also known as the Book of Revelation, ranks high among the prophetic books of the Bible as well. St. John, like his precursor Ezekiel, eats the pages of a mysterious book, which enables him to catch a glimpse of future events. The account contains numerological references and is often interpreted as containing exact information about eschatological occurrences. There are many parallels between the two books in passages predicting the rapture, the tribulations and the final lasting peace that will ensue.

The thirteenth chapter of the gospel of Mark speaks vividly about the apocalypse. Jesus, standing on the Mount of Olives, describes to his apostles the political and social conditions that will occur before his second advent. He informs them that several wars, earthquakes and false messiahs will precede his return to earth.

Christian denominations and sects placing much emphasis on prophecy include the evangelists, Jehovah's Witnesses and Seventh-day Adventists. The last of these groups celebrates the second advent as part of the religious observance rather than Saturday as the day of rest. Many Christians claim some of the prophecies mentioned in the Bible have already been fulfilled. Others believe they must still come to pass. Undoubtedly, the terminology of these prophecies lends itself to variant interpretations according to denominational preferences.

Because of differences in interpretation, many have claimed messiahship in modern times within Christendom, such as the Rev. Sun Myung Moon, who founded the Unification Church in 1954. There are also differences as to exactly when the end of the world will occur. Joseph Smith, the founder of the Mormon church, anticipated the unfolding of eschatological events around the year 1890, while the Millerites were ready to witness them in 1844 with Christ's awaited second coming.

Islam's prophetic literature has suffered a similar fate. Different scholars interpret prophecy in whatever manner suits their particular religious outlook. The differences arise in the expectation of the Mahdi (Islam's redeemer) and Jesus Christ. Both Shia and Sunni scholars interpret scripture and oral tradition according to their sectarian beliefs.

There is also the view that Islam's prophetic tradition is partly borrowed from Judeo-Christian sources. There may very well be a degree of truth in this claim, given the fact that many of Islam's early adherents were the Jews and Christians of Medina, who, while converting to Islam, passed down their own religious traditions to the new faith. A large portion of Hadith, Islam's secondary source of guidance, is classified as the "Israelite traditions" or *Israiliyat*. These were incorporated into Islamic literature from the Talmud based on the principle that there was no conflict between the *Israiliyat* and the tenets of Islam. The *Israiliyat* were narrations by Jews who had accepted Mohammed's prophetic call. They recounted traditions from Judaism, along with newer ideas from their contact with the prophet Mohammed regarding his character, his conduct, even his daily routine.

Although much doubt has been cast on the authenticity of the narration contained in Hadith including the *Israiliyat*, it is regarded as a diary or record of the twenty-three years of the prophet Mohammed's ministry, and as such is a resource for Muslims second in authenticity only to the Quran. Much of the Islamic eschatological tradition therefore shows signs of considerable similarity between Islam and the Judeo-Christian tradition. For example, the return of a Messiah, apocalyptic events around Jerusalem, and a great tribulation preceding the peaceful era under Christ or the Messiah are all common to the Abrahamic faiths. Differences in interpretation, however, arise as to how these will play out in terms of their impact on Jews, Christians, and Muslims.

Muslims claim that the Quran contains scientific information not known at the time of its revelation. In that sense, it is a book of prophecy as it purports to foreshadow scientific discovery. References in the Quran to apocalyptic events, however, are somewhat oblique and need to be understood in light of other scriptures and sources. The Quran focuses mainly on the absolute certainty of the Day of Judgment, but it does not clearly describe events preceding that day. There is, for example, nothing comparable in the Quran to Ezekiel or the Apocalypse of St. John, both of which focus heavily on apocalyptic events. On the other hand, the hereafter, the day of retribution, the separation of the good from the bad, decisions as to the final abode of an individual be it heaven or hell, and the emphasis on piety and correct belief hold greater significance within the Quranic discourse.

"The Hour," signifying the end of the world, is mentioned on a number of occasions in the Quran. Verse 54:1, for example, states, "The Hour [of Judgment] is nigh, and the moon is cleft asunder." The nature of the Quranic narrative, however, is unique in its referential rather than narrative style, and the Quran only alludes to various events and happenings as they occur and never describes them in a systematic or chronological order. Many Muslim apocalypticists, such as Harun Yahya, have nonetheless ascribed prophetic content to the above verse, suggesting that 54:1 predicts man's conquest of space: When Neil Armstrong and Edwin Aldrin landed on the moon on July 20, 1969, they "cleft it asunder" by digging soil from the lunar terrain. This sort of commentary is common to popular contemporary apocalypticists who attempt to explain the Quranic verses.

Although secondary to the Quran, Hadith is a very important source of knowledge and guidance for Muslims. Its importance lies in the fact that while the Quran posits broad doctrinal, moral and legislative guidelines, Hadith explains, and rather practically demonstrates, how these are to be implemented. The character and conduct of the prophet are the subject matter of Hadith as a practical example for Muslims. How he prayed, how he lived, how he ran his domestic affairs, how he conducted Jihad, all came to be recorded and passed down to successive generations through narrations from his companions, both male and female.

Mohammed's wife Ayesha is credited with narrating much of the corpus of Hadith literature. His pronouncements about the end of times are also recorded in works such as Bukhari, Muslim, Ibn Majah and Daud, which are some of the most authentic compilations of Hadith or oral traditions attributed to the Prophet. Chapters dedicated to a description of apocalyptic events include the Kitab al Fitan or the Book of Tribulations, the Kitab al Iman or Book of Faith, Kitab al Sunnah or the Book of the Practice, and Abwab al Fitan or the Chapters of Tribulation of Muslims. The traditions belong to the era beginning at the time of the Prophet's ministry in the seventh century till about the close of the ninth century when the compilation of the Hadith took place.

Again, entire chapters are devoted to the advent of the Mahdi or redeemer of Islam. Abu Daud contains a chapter entitled *Kitab al Awal an Mahdi* or the First Book of the Mahdi. It is widely held that prior to Jesus' second coming, the Madhi will return as Islam's savior and lay grounds for establishing the faith all over the world, though it must be mentioned here that Hadith pertaining to his arrival are not considered sound by the majority of the scholars. This, however, has not prevented belief in the Mahdi as the prevalent view among the masses.

Apart from the primary sources of Islamic prophecy, numerous commentaries interpreting and describing their impact on current affairs have emerged, both in the medieval era and modern times.

The most authoritative commentary of end-time scenarios is ascribed to the fourteenth-century scholar Ibn Kathir, who wrote voluminous works of history, accounts of apocalyptic events and commentary on religious scriptures. His commentary on the prophesied world order is contained in the book Al Bidayah wal Nihayah, which means "the beginning and the end." It is from this source that accounts of the end of the world have been extrapolated. One section dedicated entirely to end-time scenarios is entitled *The Signs before the Day of Judgment.*

The importance given to prophecy in modern times can best be judged by the enormous amount of literature that has emerged about apocalyptic scenarios both Christian and Islamic. The very fact that such literature continually occupies a prominent place in bookstores suggests a sense of foreboding in the religious public about the end of the world. This surge in apocalyptic literature seeks to explain the information contained in Hadith in light of modern scenarios. The most notable among these is the Egyptian writer Saeed Ayub's *Al Masihad-Dajjal*. Little wonder that many apocalyptic writers are affiliated with radical militant groups such as Palestinian Bassam Jirrar. Modern Islamists in their rhetoric are acting as precursors of the Mahdi, who, apocalyptic literature suggests, is destined to wipe out the Jews, or at least have them convert to Islam.

Among contemporary Muslim commentators on apocalyptic literature is Harun Yahya, a Turkish author whose book *Palestine* describes the Arab-Israeli conflict from a strictly Muslim perspective and proposes acknowledgment of the validity of the Islamic faith by the Jews as perhaps the only solution to the bloodshed. He states in his Preface: "This is our call to the Jews, a People of the Book. As people who believe in God and obey his commands, let us come together in a common formula of 'faith' ... that is where the solution to the Palestinian tragedy and other conflicts in the world lies."

Muslim apocalyptic literature often depicts the world as a dichotomy between Islam and the Infidels — identified largely as Christian and Jewish forces. Armageddon for example will not occur between Islam and Hinduism, or Islam and Secularism, Atheism or Buddhism, although many of these forces may align themselves with either of the two major world contenders. Those contenders are identified by militant Islam's dichotomy as Islam and the "Crusader-Zionist" alliance.

Traditional Muslims, like their Christian counterparts, believe in the literal fulfillment of their prophecies. Perhaps unflinching belief in the imminent destruction of the world has led many to revert to religious precepts and practices because they must soon "meet their Lord." The theology of fear that emerges from the belief that the end of the world is close further fuels the apocalyptic zeal of fundamentalist Christianity and Islam, both seeking to establish their supremacy around the globe.

CHAPTER TWO

An Historical Struggle for Ascendancy

One often wonders how two faiths so different in their understanding of God can both claim to be monotheistic. One believes in God as a trinity, and the other as an indivisible unity, transcendent in every respect. Both Islam's and Christianity's view of God of necessity must consider the nature of Jesus Christ, a subject that has featured in much debate between scholars from both religious traditions. While numerous attempts have been made by Christian priests and academics to explain the Trinity to lay believers and non–Christians, an equal amount of effort has been expended by their Muslim counterparts to dismantle the doctrine, thereby demoting Christ from his divine status as the only begotten son of God to a mere prophet of God, who directly preceded the prophet Mohammed in a long line of prophets.

Quoting profusely from the Quran, Muslims assert Christ was a mere human being, albeit a chosen and elect one of God. According to them he was a prophet and messenger of God, whose message to humanity was no different from the monotheistic beliefs of his forebears. They further state that Jesus himself never claimed to be God's only begotten son, and that his apostles and later followers were guilty of deifying him, based on the belief that he had performed extraordinary miracles and that he had no earthly father. Muslim scholars argue that the deification of human beings comes as a result of human failings, or dependence on physical stimuli as objects of worship and veneration. Although they agree with Christians that Jesus performed many miracles, they assert his power was from God rather than being inherently his own. Muslims also believe in the immaculate conception.

Verses of the Quran describe the annunciation in detail, attesting to the belief in the virgin birth of Jesus. The Quran also accords the highest status to Jesus' virginal mother, Mary or Maryam, announcing she was the most exalted of all women to have ever lived. Although the Quran's references to Jesus' return to earth as the restorer of peace and justice are somewhat oblique, most Muslims believe this will indeed come to pass in the end of days.

Islamic and Christian differences in outlook appear irreconcilable when both sides continue to defend their beliefs with zeal, passion and at times vitriol. Muslims are "worse than Nazis," said Pat Robertson, prominent televangelist and founder of the Christian Coalition, an ultra-fundamentalist Christian organization.[1] He was referring to the anti–Jewish sentiment among fundamentalist Muslims generated by the continuing conflict in the Middle East. Similarly, renowned Muslim historian Dr. Abdur Rauf puts Christians at the top of his list of "dangers" posed to Islam: "Currently Islam faces grave dangers from the following four elements: Christians, Jews, Hindus and Atheists."[2]

Leaving politics aside, the doctrinal differences seem firmly entrenched too, as they are often expressed through periodic public pronouncements and statements of dogma as fact. Tim LaHaye, another well-known Christian evangelist and author of the *Left Behind* series, states: "Our merciful and loving Lord can cleanse us through our faith in Jesus Christ, God's dear Son."[3] Thus Jesus becomes God incarnate, "the Alpha and the Omega, the Beginning and the End, the First and the Last" (Rev. 22:13). Muslims also resort to public declarations about their faith being the ultimate truth and their scripture, the Quran, the "Final Testament superseding" the New Testament of the Christians.

Another source of contention involves the doctrine of the resurrection of Jesus. Much of Christian theology is built around the crucifixion and resurrection of Jesus Christ. It forms the basis of the Christian belief in mankind's salvation. It is only through Jesus' ultimate sacrifice that the sins of humanity could be washed away. Since Islam does not believe in the vicarious atonement of sin or the concept of original sin, it sees no need for such a sacrifice and rejects the doctrine altogether.

Each individual according to Islam is born with a clean slate. The loving and merciful God would not punish each human being for the sins of Adam and Eve, and hence no sacrifice would be needed to redeem humanity. Allah, believed by Muslims to be the author of the Quran, also states that he recalled Jesus to himself alive, and will send him back to earth to restore dignity to Muslims. According to Islam, all prophets were Muslims in a generic sense, because they all surrendered to the will of God (such surrender is the true meaning of "Islam"). Jesus, too, was a Muslim according to this definition. He preached the oneness and unity of God. Muslims assert it was subsequent generations of believers who distorted his message.

Christians and Muslims also doubt the authenticity of each other's scriptures. Christians claim Mohammed copied parts of the Quran from the Bible, or at least drew from the sources known as the Apocrypha, whereas Muslims widely believe that the Bible has undergone drastic change. Muslims claim the Bible's words to be spurious. They insist St. John in his apocalypse probably never declared Jesus "the alpha and the omega" and that the Book of Revelation, like other books of the Old and New testaments, contains interpolations by subsequent authors. The Quran, according to Muslims, encapsulates the messages of all previous prophets including that of Jesus. None of these chosen men of God ever claimed to be his children, either in the literal or metaphorical sense.

Muslims further assert that Jesus' teachings were not being recorded by any scribes when he wandered the hills of Palestine, explaining universal truths to his disciples in parables. This view has been explained in the following excerpt from renowned scholar Maryam Jameelah's book *Islam Versus the West.* In the following passage she disagrees with another Muslim academic, Dr. Taha Hussain:

Dr. Taha Hussain speaks as if Christianity were identical with Islam. He seems to forget that the Gospel the Christians regard as their scripture is not the same Gospel to which the Quran refers. The original message God revealed to Jesus has been lost. All that Christians possess are four of the apocryphal biographies of Jesus which were not canonized until centuries after his so-called death. Although Jesus, like Mohammed, spoke a Semitic language, the Christian scriptures were first recorded in Greek instead. Jesus did not know a word of Greek. The doctrines of the Trinity, the divinity of Christ, original sin, and the vicarious atonement by his alleged death on the cross, originated with Paul — not Jesus. Paul was a thoroughly Hellenized, Greek-speaking Roman citizen who could not but be influenced by his pagan environment. And it was Paul, rather than Jesus, who determined the subsequent history of Christianity.[4]

Indeed Maryam Jameelah, formerly Margaret Marcus, a convert to Islam from Judaism, summarizes the Muslim mindset on Christianity by pinpointing the major areas of disagreement such as the divinity of Jesus, his death on the cross, original sin and vicarious atonement. About the historicity of the Quran, on the other hand, she states:

We have seen how the influence of Greece and Rome permeated the Christian faith from its inception. This was not true of Islam. The Quran is in Arabic, not Greek — and unlike the Christian scriptures, has been preserved in its purity. No Muslim equivalent of Paul ever appeared to corrupt Islam. Aristotelian philosophers like Ibn Rushd had a far greater impact on medieval Europe than the Islamic world. Hellenism was effectively routed by Al-Ghazali and Ibn Taimiyah.[5]

As is evident from the above quotations, Muslims regard most of Christianity as specious, believing wholeheartedly in the pristine authenticity of their own faith which they have defended by quoting from the Bible itself.

Deep in the heart of South Africa emerged a Muslim Bible scholar of the highest repute known to the world as Sheikh Ahmed Deedat. With a thorough knowledge of the Bible, he embarked on a mission to validate Islam's position using not the Quran but the Bible as resource. An entire new era of Bible study was ushered in among Muslim scholars with Ahmed Deedat as its pioneer and champion.

His refutations of Christianity encompassed most of Christian dogma such as the divinity of Christ, the crucifixion and resurrection, as well as the concept of original sin. Although his diligent research enhanced his stature among Muslims immensely, earning him the respect of millions across the various sects of Islam, the Christian world reacted with hostility, spawning a fresh wave of criticism not only on the historicity of the Quran as divine writ, but on the religion of Islam itself as a blasphemy against Jesus.

Abdullah Ibrahim, an Arab Christian, in one of his recent articles entitled "The Trinity Explained to Muslims," suggests Muslims repudiate the doctrine because they do not understand it properly. He argues that Muslims believe Christians worship three gods, whereas in fact "we [Christians] worship one God in Trinity and Trinity in Unity, neither confounding the Persons, nor dividing the Substance" (quoting the Athenasian Creed). He further states that the Trinity is a complicated concept and "the danger one faces when confronted with extreme or complicated ideas is to throw the baby out with the bath water."[6] He concludes this is probably why Muslims reject the doctrine, their own theology being much more simplistic, based on the idea of one indivisible God.

And thus the debate continues over whether it was a god or a mere mortal who roamed the valleys and hills of Judea and Samaria two thousand years ago. There is also disagreement over whether he predicted the advent of another prophet after him. Christians speak about the Comforter or Holy Spirit as part of the divine Trinity, eternally abiding with them till kingdom come. Muslims, on the other hand, convinced the biblical references to the Comforter are allusions to the prophet Mohammed, assert Jesus clearly prophesied the advent of a last messenger of God to humanity.

Of late, the polemics have resurfaced with full gusto on both sides, reviving the historical confrontation over dogma between Islam and Christianity. Western orientalism, already in vogue, surged ahead as a response to Muslim challenges to Christian belief. After the attacks on the United States on September 11, 2001, the scene has intensified even more.

Whether in response to the "white man's burden" or as a symptom of plain mistrust of Islam, the latter half of the twentieth century witnessed the rise of the western orientalist movement after the discovery of oil in the Middle East. The name suggests a sort of general study, but traditional Muslims argue that western orientalism was largely geared towards a study of Islam with the express intent of proving it fallacious. Scholars of the stature of Wilfred Cantwell Smith, Kenneth Cragg and Montgomery Ward spearheaded a subtle and compelling campaign against Islamic doctrine, practice and culture. The perception, true or false, that they created in the minds of Muslim fundamentalists remained one of distrust and apprehension. Lashing out against Wilfred Cantwell Smith's approach, Maryam Jameelah offers the following critique of the renowned Western scholar:

Wilfred Cantwell Smith likes to have himself regarded by Muslims as a sympathetic student of Islam. He claims his observations to be objective, but a careful reading of this book by any sincere, thinking Muslim will clearly reveal the abysmal depths of his hostility. Unfortunately, his thinking represents the views of the majority of orientalists both in my country and abroad. Their basic enmity towards Islam differs from that of the old fashioned Christian missionary only that it is expressed in a much more subtle way."[7]

Maryam Jameelah does not elaborate on who falls under the category of "old-fashioned Christian missionary." She would be inclined to conclude that some of the missionaries have been resurrected in the post–9/11 world. Pat Robertson and Jerry Falwell have often mocked Islam and its founder. They have attacked Islam's core beliefs in the most virulent manner, for which they have had to apologize publicly. Also, soon after 9/11 the 42nd president of the United States referred to the current "war on terror" as a "crusade" and had to retract or explain his pronouncement. Literature circulated among members of the Christian Coalition perpetuates popular Christian belief about Islam being a pagan religion, borrowing aspects of Judeo-Christian monotheism by elevating the moon god Hubal to the rank of Supreme God or Allah. Mohammed, for fundamentalist Christians, remains an impostor who commissioned his companions to copy words of the Bible as they sat in dark inaccessible places, far removed from public gaze. For these Christians therefore, what Mohammed created was a pseudo-religion — far from the ultimate truth and the culmination of all religions, as Muslims regard their faith.

Distrust of Christians and their beliefs is also widespread among Muslims, although somewhat tempered with respect to Jesus. Since they consider him their own prophet, they are deferential in the way they regard him. Their attacks have therefore been confined to proving the Bible and its teachings erroneous. Muslims, by so doing, reject the Triune God of Christianity as the ultimate heresy. *Shirk*, or the associating of partners with Allah, has been designated in the Quran as the biggest sin committed against God. "Allah," translated most accurately as "the Deity," indivisible, transcendent, omnipotent, and omniscient, has no progeny and no need for a son or a consort. For Muslims, he is the opposite of any anthropomorphic notion of deities represented in the traditions of other religions.

This is not to say that Allah does not bestow attributes to His creation such as His Wrath, His Mercy and His Benevolence. His creation nonetheless still remains distinct from Him and is not of the same divine essence. Thus Muslims often accuse Christians of committing the ultimate blasphemy.

Although the doctrinal differences are glaring, there are some points of convergence which often remain sidelined. For example, Mary is revered in Islam, not as *theotokos* or mother of God, but as the saintly mother of Jesus. She is the only woman addressed by name in the Quran. As a child, she was consecrated to God and remained chaste, pious and worshipful throughout her life. She bore one of the five most exalted prophets of God, who according to the Quranic account spoke in his cradle to attest to his mother's virginity. Thus favored by God, Mary remains the symbol of female equality in Islam.

And Muslims never shy away from enumerating the many miracles Jesus performed during his ministry. He raised the dead, he cured the lepers, he gave sight to the blind, and he walked on water.

Nonetheless, while Islam as a daughter religion of Judaism and Christianity absorbed many Judeo-Christian tenets, it continues to be misunderstood in the western world. Needless to say, the distrust is mutual. The doctrinal differences are overwhelming enough for Christians and Muslims to have defended them militarily.

It would be wrong to conclude that the Crusades were wars fought over specific doctrines, yet the mutual suspicion and enmity that the ideological differences generated were compelling enough to spark widespread and prolonged confrontation. Muslim lands had to be freed from "infidel" rule. Western nations had colonized the Muslim world and saw the efforts of Islam as "pernicious." Similarly, the Byzantine Empire, which had fallen to Muslim rulers, had to be "liberated." Spain had to be reclaimed and Jerusalem, where Jesus was crucified, had to be freed from the sinister grip of the "Saracen," a derogatory medieval term used for Muslims.

The Crusaders embarked on military expeditions empowered by a promise of spiritual reward in the hereafter — a promise strongly reminiscent of the contemporary jihadist ideology. Also driven by a sense of duty towards the pope, the Christian warriors resolved to march eastward to free their lands. "Wage a holy war against these disbelievers who have usurped Lord Christ's monastery. Whoever of you participates in this holy war, I shall remit all his past sins. Whoever is killed I shall give him a place in paradise," the pope had assured them.

The Crusades were launched at the beginning of the second millennium, amidst looming prophecies on both sides about the impending destruction of the world. They coincided with the end of the five hundred years of Muslim global dominance, around the year 1106. Both Christians and Muslims were governed by a belief in the Antichrist's imminent appearance. This would be followed by Christ's benign rule. According to Muslims he would "break the cross and kill the swine" and establish Islam on earth permanently.

Christians on the other hand were convinced they were defending God's word on earth. The First Crusade, driven by a newly inspired religious fervor, was a roaring success and Jerusalem fell to the Christians in July of 1099. The Turks, the citizens of Baghdad and the Egyptians all suffered colossal defeat at the hands of the very first crusaders. Their bodies, numbering 200,000, were soon to be displayed in enemy territory under the directive of Pope Urban II, whose primary aim to gain control of the holy city of Jerusalem had been achieved. Jerusalem had remained under Muslim rule since the time of the second caliph of Islam, Omar. Although for the ensuing era, Christian pilgrims had been permitted to visit it every year, the pope was obviously not satisfied with this arrangement for too long.

Christianity had a wider agenda as well. Pope Urban II urged the eastern rulers to reclaim all Christian lands from the Saracens under the "Cross of Christ." Symbolism of a religious bent certainly inspires tremendous zeal in adherents, and many enlisted in this noble effort, proudly wearing and displaying the crucifix on their garments. Such display of religious ardor would continue into the Second Crusade — a decidedly less successful effort for the Christian forces in 1145–1149 — and swelled to its peak around the time of the Third Crusade.

Although Jerusalem had become Christian again, the confrontation between the Crusade and the Jihad had not come to an end. The drama continued to unfold around Jerusalem, where both the crusaders and jihadists were convinced the final conflict would occur. Jerusalem, deferentially known as "Bait-ul-Muqqadus" or holy abode, was fervently revered by Muslims also, foremost for Mohammed's night journey when he arrived there transported by a heavenly white horse. It was never to be conceded to the Christians, but alas it had fallen to the cross.

Nur ud-Din Zangi, crying revenge, now assumed leadership of the Muslims. He led an assault on the Christians under Islam's strident general Sher Koh to recover Jerusalem. Until then he had directed his ire against the "heretic" Fatimid dynasty of Egypt. In January 1167 Sher Koh the Kurd and his nephew Salahuddin Yusuf had led an expedition south. After a continuous campaign in Egypt, the country fell to Salahuddin, known to Christians as Saladin. Sher Koh had died and Saladin was joined by his uncle Ayyub to once again overthrow the Fatimid kingdom. After the conquest of Egypt and Yemen, Saladin assumed leadership of the two territories, now united as a polity. He then allowed Egyptians safe passage to Mecca and Medina. By so doing, Saladin became an instant hero as a liberator of Egyptian Muslims, who had until then lived under an oppressive and "heretical" kingdom. He then went about consolidating his hold on other Muslim lands with an express goal to unite all peoples of Islam under one banner. But his decisive battle would be fought against the Christian armies in the year 1187.

Egypt, Mosul and Damascus all answered Saladin's call for Jihad and the massive army headed towards Jordan on June 26, 1167. The Christian Council of the War had been debating the fate of Jerusalem and how best to repel Muslim onslaught. Divisions soon arose between the Christian Franks, with Raymond of Tripoli being accused of conspiracy with Saladin. He had previously entered into a truce with the Muslim sultan. Consequently, dissension within Christian ranks had become widespread and greatly undermined their resolve. Despite this problem and the lack of a proper strategy, the Christian army launched an offensive on the Muslims. Alas, Christian gallantry would not be sufficient to take on the Muslim forces and the crusading army was soon decimated. On July 4, 1167, it lay besieged by the Muslims. Just a few hundred of the defendants of the cross were left to endure the last blow. And they endured it valiantly. But the true cross had fallen, and Saladin offered a special prayer to thank Allah.

What ensued was sheer horror. Passions ablaze, Saladin ordered the slaughter of the remainder of the Christian army. After this, Tiberias and Acre also fell to the sultan, but this time he offered his enemies clemency.

Christian Jerusalem had refused to surrender to Saladin. The battle for

Date Due <u>DEC 15</u>

Campbellford/Seymour

Public Library

These library materials are
lent to you courtesy of:

<u>KINGSTON</u>

_____

We ask that you return the
materials on time.

Thank You.

the holiest of cities was fought much later, on October 2, 1187, and ended in a decisive victory for Saladin. The Christians were then asked to leave Jerusalem but were allowed forty days to evacuate the city. Under Saladin's express orders, none of them were to be harmed as they left, even though tempers ran high. The deal forged between Saladin and the Christians had to be upheld at all costs.

After the Christian exodus, Saladin went about purging the city of any trinitarian "pollution." All crosses were removed from places of worship including the one atop the Dome of the Rock. Verses of the Quran now replaced the symbols of the Trinity. According to historian Faraj al Sarraf, however, Saladin returned the property, monasteries and churches, including the Church of the Holy Sepulcher, to the Christians. He also writes in his book *Christians in the Holy Land* that Christians were generally happy with the way Saladin had treated them. Among Muslims, of course, Saladin was hailed as the liberator of Islam, and he remains to date the most celebrated of Muslim military heroes.

While there was much jubilation in Muslim lands, history recounts that Pope Urban III died from shock after hearing the news of losing Jerusalem. His successor, Pope Gregory VIII, would hence pronounce the Third Crusade.

The stage was now set for a confrontation between two of the best and bravest military men ever known to history. Richard the Lion Heart, king of England, and Saladin would now come face to face in an ongoing struggle to recapture the holy lands. Again inspired by millenarian belief, many Christians thought the end of the world was close. Christianity had to defeat the ungodly armies of the Antichrist, whom some may have believed to be Saladin. Religious zeal was rife among the Christians, as it was among Muslims.

A crusading army 100,000 strong soon marched to avenge the humiliating defeat of 1187, but Saladin, fortified by his own standing as Islam's great savior and soldier, was yet again able to repel the northern onslaughts. The Christian army, demoralized by defeat after defeat, began to question the religious validity of its cause. Many, it is said, converted to the religion of the Saracens. The Third Crusade also ended in massive Christian casualty and the failure to recapture Jerusalem. Only three thousand from among the soldiers of Christ would escape to safety.

After three years of devastation and carnage, Richard the Lion Heart entered into a truce with Saladin which ensured that "civil liberties will prevail in all territories conquered by the parties. People from both sides will be free to visit each other's territories."[8]

Pope Innocent III, who was elected in 1198, was nevertheless not about to give up the ideal to recover the holy lands. He ordered the Fourth Crusade, appealing to Christian unity with the stated purpose of uniting the eastern and western church. It was widely believed now that the Third Crusade had failed due to the disunity plaguing Christendom.

Given the stated objective of the Fourth Crusade, Richard the Lion Heart first marched towards Constantinople and conquered it on April 13, 1204. Rampant thieving and rape of the beleaguered Byzantine population soon followed that conquest. But although Richard's army had acquired and distributed much, it failed to establish its foothold on the Byzantines, who recovered their rule once again in 1261. Pope Innocent III was unable to unite Christendom. The Fourth Crusade failed in its objectives as well.

After repeated defeats and several failed Crusades, the Christian dream to recover lands from the Muslim infidels came to be slowly abandoned as an achievable goal. Although there were five other Crusades fought after the Byzantine defeat, the era of the Crusades came to a close officially in the year 1270 CE.

Not so in Muslim Spain, where the Christian warriors refused to relent until the "Moors" were ousted, enslaved or forced to accept Christianity. Perhaps the final battle for Christ's rule on earth was to be fought, not in the holy lands, but in a place far away from where he lived, preached, died and rose to heaven.

Spain for Muslims was "Andulus" and "Hispania." They ruled it for approximately eight hundred years, starting with the Visigoth king Roderick's defeat at the hands of General Tariq Bin Ziyad. According to historical accounts, the Spaniards had themselves approached Tariq Bin Ziyad with a request to liberate them from King Roderick's tyrannical rule.

He thus marched north from Morocco and arrived at "Gibraltar," a distortion of the name *Jabal-al-Tariq,* which means the Mountain of Tariq. Indeed the rock where he landed was duly named after the general. Most of Spain came under Muslim rule in 714 CE after the king accepted defeat. Abdul Aziz, son of Governor Musa bin Nusair, who married the widow of then emperor Frederick, was appointed first "amir" or prince of Spain. Frederick's widow became the subjugated Christian population's last hope by inciting hostility between the Shia and Sunni branches of the Muslim conquerors. These warring factions maintained their animosity and mistrust of each other throughout Muslim rule in Spain, which led to the ultimate downfall of Muslims in the Iberian Peninsula.

Tariq Bin Ziyad was a member of the Ummmayyad dynasty, the first Muslim dynasty to rule after the collapse of the "Pious Caliphate."

Ummayyad rule lasted in Spain from 714 CE and ended in 756 CE after Abdur Rahman, another Muslim general, defeated the Ummayyads. With the help of Berber troops from the South, he captured all of Spain, establishing Muslim rule in the entire peninsula. France too was a target of Muslim raids but the soldiers of Allah had to suffer a permanent retreat from the northern borders. Internecine skirmishes continued.

Despite in-house fighting, 756–1036 is remembered as the golden era of Muslim rule in Spain. Abdur Rahman ruled for about thirty-three years and laid the grounds for a flourishing and vibrant Muslim culture. He introduced reforms in the justice system of the country and established seats of learning attracting all citizens of Europe. They were welcomed warmly, irrespective of religious affiliation. Abdur Rahman also constructed magnificent mosques and castles. "Qartaba" or Cordoba was established as the new capital of Muslim Spain with Abdur Rahman not as the "khalifa" or caliph of Islam, but merely its amir or prince. The title "khalifa" would have suggested that all of the peoples of Islam had come to be united under his rule, whereas such was not the case. However, under his rule, and during the remainder of the golden period of Spanish Islam, the Christian armies were kept at bay.

Disintegration nonetheless was soon to set in and the year 1036 marked a new era of discord and disunity which weakened the Muslims considerably, leaving them vulnerable to Christian onslaughts. Internecine warfare had divided Muslim rule into several kingdoms and taifas involved in petty political struggles. Furthermore, accustomed now to a life of luxury, Muslims had become somewhat complacent and apathetic. The earlier objectives of upholding Islam's ascendancy in the world were renounced for more materialistic and selfish concerns.

The Christians united once again to oust the infidels.

The Muslim capital had been moved to Granada during those years of anarchy and confusion. In 1199 CE, Abdullah ez Zagal came to rule the Muslim state of Granada. Although sincere in his mission to once again consolidate Islamic rule in Spain, he was surrounded by traitors who made secret alliances with the Christians.

Such treachery continued for 250 years till the reign of Abu Abdullah Mohammed also known as Boabdil. His nephew colluded with the Christian King Ferdinand III of Seville, enabling Ferdinand to invade the now much weakened Granada. It had functioned as a vassal state for 250 years at the conclusion of which Boabdil would surrender to the Christian troops on January 3, 1492.

Thus began the mass exodus of Muslims from Spain. Boabdil wept as he left the Alhambra Palace forever. The Spanish Inquisition followed. Many

Muslims were burnt at the stake or forced to convert to Catholicism. The cross was permanently established in the peninsula.

Muslim rule in Spain is credited with much of the European renaissance. The great centers of learning established in Granada and Cordoba educated and enlightened many non–Muslim Europeans. They flocked to these cities in the quest for wisdom, knowledge and understanding in both the arts and the sciences. Soon Europe would emerge from the Dark Ages as the leader in the fields of music, literature, art, politics and philosophy. Along with the industrial revolution, which tipped the balance of power in favor of the Christian West forever, a new era of political dominance soon unfolded. Muslim lands plunged into backwardness and degeneration. They also came to be colonized and subjugated by various European powers. Neither the mighty Mughal Empire in India nor the great Ottoman Empire in Turkey would escape the rising tide of western imperialism.

Perhaps the severest blow dealt to Islam's dignity, soul and viability was the disintegration of the Ottoman Empire in 1919. Its territories had extended from Hungary to the Maldives, but now it tottered at the hands of traitors from within and conquerors from without. The Christian European powers capitalized on the Turko-Russian wars, which had weakened the strength of the Ottoman Empire considerably. Barely able to preserve their own independence, the Ottomans lost one territory after another to Christian Russia and Christian Europe.

It was the year 1908 which marked the beginning of the end. Dissent, division and treachery from within were undoubtedly factors leading to the change in fortune of the *Uthmani* or Ottoman caliphate. Betrayal of the Sultan was a commonplace occurrence, and many from within the military ranks of the empire now colluded with the enemy, forming secret alliances and forging political deals.

In 1908, the military commander of Salonika led a revolt against sultan Abdul Hamid, which ended in the siege of the sultan's government. They demanded he hold elections and create a proper legislative body or parliament. The sultan was deposed, to be replaced by his own brother, sultan Mohammed Khamis. Promoting secularism, the rebels replaced Islamic law with Secular law and the Arabic language with Turkish as the main language of religious instruction. Even the *Adhan*, or call to prayer, would be conducted in Turkish henceforth.

What further weakened the sultanate or caliphate was the Russian invasion of Turkey in the year 1912. Massacre and plunder followed the invasion, but circumstances eventually proved detrimental for Russia rather than Turkey, for there emerged a rift between the Christian nations over the division of territories. Exploiting this rift, Mustafa Kemal Pasha, a Turkish military officer, liberated his nation from foreign rule in 1916. This was the beginning of Mustafa Kemal Pasha's rise to political power in Turkey, but the task of rebuilding his beleaguered nation proved to be a long and arduous one.

He therefore decided to collaborate wholeheartedly with national reconstruction movements. Governed more by a nationalistic and patriotic zeal than by a religious one, Kemal — who would later be known as Kemal Ataturk or "father of the Turks" — increasingly distanced himself from the notion of a pan–Islamic Muslim nation. He outlawed the wearing of the *hijab*, banned Arabic from prayer services and eventually abolished the caliphate. He was elected Turkey's first president in March 1924, declaring Turkey a republic and officially replacing the caliphate, which as an institution had thus far served as a symbol of Muslim political unity.

Muslims still express nostalgia for that fabled Muslim unity under the Ottoman caliphate. They have never recovered from the disintegration of the Muslim empire that weakened the strength of the Muslims as a global force. Many movements to revive the caliphate germinated in the aftermath of the dissolution of the Ottoman Empire, such as the Khilafat Movement of India.

Yet dissent is both natural and endemic to Muslims. Numbering some 1.6 billion, they come with a diverse understanding of their faith, over and above the fact that they belong to different ethnic and racial groups speaking several distinct languages. There have been numerous political rifts among Muslims over territorial disputes, ideological issues and sectarian differences. Internal mistrust and hostility is rife among Islam's adherents, and the forces of disintegration appear to be as yet insurmountable. Nonetheless, many among them have been nurturing the hope of once again unifying these warring groups under the single ideology of Islam. Their much awaited redeemer, the Mahdi, will restore them their dignity, once he emerges out of the depths of abysmal despair.

The current political, economic and social plight of Muslims is a vestige of the blow dealt to Muslim civilization at the beginning of the 20th century. Ever ready to blame the West for their misery, Muslims continue to harbor resentment against Christendom, exacerbated recently by conflicts sparked by the brutal attack on the World Trade Center and the Pentagon on September 11, 2001. The wars in Afghanistan and Iraq continue to fuel these sentiments, resulting in ever-increasing mutual suspicion, distrust and animosity.

CHAPTER THREE

What the Prophets
of Old Foretold

Both fundamentalist Muslims and their Christian counterparts believe the end of the world is nigh. This common perception is based on the remarkable similarity between the apocalyptic literatures of both faith traditions. Followers of both Islam and Christianity also see striking parallels between the prophesied world events and the current political climate. Both traditions predict wars or "rumors of wars." They also forecast great disparity in wealth and resources between not only individuals but nations. The rich will become richer and the poor will become ever more impoverished due to the exploitative strategies of global markets and economies. Debauchery, fraud, brutality and countless other human vices will increase manifold. Both religious traditions therefore feel the stage is now set for a final showdown between good and evil, and in both traditions it is Jesus who will return one day and set things right.

Differences nonetheless appear in the apocalyptic accounts of the Bible, the Quran and Hadith, largely involving details and the actual sequence of the unfolding of end-time world events. The narrative is similar in terms of factual data but vastly different in its purported impact on Jews, Christians and Muslims, due to differences in interpretation and understanding of religious precepts and aspirations that often surface in the popular commentaries of the prophesied events.

It is often claimed, for example, that biblical references to political alliances, governments, wars and foreign policies of nations revolve around the formation of the state of Israel in 1948. Isaiah 11:11–12 is commonly cited:

And it shall come to pass in that day, that the LORD shall set his hand again the second time to recover the remnant of his people, which shall be left, from Assyria, and from Egypt, and from Pathros, and from Cush, and from Elam, and from Shinar, and from Hamath, and from the islands of the sea. And he shall set up an ensign for the nations, and shall assemble the outcasts of Israel, and gather together the dispersed of Judah from the four corners of the earth.

Amos 9:14–15 confirms the prophecy:

And I will bring again the captivity of my people of Israel, and they shall build the waste cities, and inhabit them; and they shall plant vineyards, and drink the wine thereof; they shall also make gardens, and eat the fruit of them. I will plant them upon their land, and they shall no more be pulled up out of their land which I have given them, saith the LORD thy God.

Many religious people therefore believe that the creation of Israel must be viewed as the starting point from which all dramatic apocalyptic occurrences will unfold, involving the realignment of nations, the birth of new conflicts and the resultant destruction. In the midst of twenty-two hostile Arab states, the stage would now be set for the final conflict between the sons of Abraham: Ishmael and Isaac. The creation of Israel will also signal the end of the "age of the gentiles," the term gentile referring to all non–Jews. The western Christian nations will hence no longer dominate the political and economic scene of the world, as the prophet Jeremiah is said to have predicted in the following verses, although it is Muslim nations specifically who are currently at war with Israel.

Therefore all they that devour thee shall be devoured, and all thine adversaries, every one of them, shall go into captivity; and they that spoil thee shall be a spoil, and all that prey upon thee will I give for a prey [Jer. 30:16].

The creation of Israel in 1948 brought in an influx of Jews from over a hundred different nations of the world, where "God's chosen" had been scattered due to his "wrath" over the repeated violation of the covenant: "Behold, I will gather them out of all countries, whither I have driven them in mine anger, and in my fury, and in great wrath; and I will bring them again unto this place, and I will cause them to dwell safely," said the LORD through the prophet Jeremiah (Jeremiah 32:37). Perhaps as a fulfillment of this prophecy, even Ethiopian Jews, who bear little cultural or ethnic similarity to Jews in general, were rescued by Israeli airplanes in 1979 and brought to Israel, although these African Jews, previously known as "Falashas," remain a marginalized community within the country.

The restoration of Palestine to the Jews remains, from a Judeo-Christian perspective, God's fulfillment of a promise to Abram, or Abraham, as he later came to be known in the Bible. Story has it that he left his city of Ur in ancient Mesopotamia following God's commands and came to live in the land of Canaan, which would have included modern Israel, the Palestinian territories and neighboring areas of Syria and Lebanon. There, God rewarded him for his sacrifice and abject devotion by promising Abraham that the land would forever belong to his progeny and that all nations of the world would come to be blessed through him:

> Now the LORD had said unto Abram, Get thee out of thy country, and from thy kindred, and from thy father's house, unto a land that I will shew thee; And I will make of thee a great nation, and I will bless thee, and make thy name great; and thou shalt be a blessing: And I will bless them that bless thee, and curse him that curseth thee: and in thee shall all families of the earth be blessed [Gen, 12 : 3].

According to biblical narrative, Abraham fathered many nations. including the desert dwellers from the progeny of his eldest son, Ishmael. Ishmael was born not of Abraham's wife, Sarah, but of Sarah's handmaid, Hagar. He also fathered six other sons from his wife Keturah, whom he married after Sarah died. But according to Jewish belief, God chose the progeny of Isaac, Abraham's son through Sarah, as his covenanted people, who would eventually come to inherit the holy land. It is only the "children of Israel"—Israel being Jacob's title — who according to the Bible would return to Israel in the latter days "and seek the LORD their God, and David their king; and shall fear the LORD and his goodness in the latter days" (Hosea 3:5). Exclusive Jewish claims to the land are also rooted in Genesis, when Sarah demands of Abraham, "Cast out this bondswoman and her son: for the son of this bondswoman shall not be heir with my son, even with Isaac" (Gen. 21:10).

Whether such claims are legitimate or not, the latter half of the prophecy by Hosea indicates the Jews would still be searching for their Messiah when they return to Israel after their centuries old exile. According to evangelical Christians, in "seeking the Lord their God," the children of Israel will convert to Christianity by accepting Jesus as the Messiah whom they had rejected during his first advent. Once the Jews are established in Israel, they will never again be ousted because Israel will have acquired a "new heart" and a "new spirit" (Ezekiel 36: 26). Israel, the land, will also be a reward for fearing "the LORD and his goodness" (Hosea 3:5). It is a scenario in which fundamentalist Christians, who traditionally opposed the Jews for their purported murder of Christ, find themselves supporting extremist Jews. Although the conflict is territorial and political, controversy also springs from disagreement over which of the sons of Abraham is entitled to inherit the land, and hence the whole issue assumes a religious tenor. The modern conflict between Israelis and Palestinians and the enmity it has generated between fundamentalist Christians and Muslims often finds basis in verses such as the above.

Muslims vehemently argue that Ishmael was part of God's covenant with Abraham. They point out that God made his covenant with Abraham, not Isaac, and such a covenant would have to include his eldest son Ishmael (Gen. 17:4). They insist that history as portrayed in the Bible was deliberately distorted in order to marginalize Ishmael's role as Abraham's firstborn son. All of Abraham's progeny was to inherit the promised land without exception. They quote the Bible as well as their own scripture to support this claim in the following verses, by stressing God's covenant to include all of Abraham's progeny:

> And as for Ishmael, I have heard thee: Behold, I have blessed him and will make him fruitful, and will multiply him exceedingly; twelve princes shall he beget, and I will make him a great nation [Gen. 17:20].

A verse of the Quran gives further assurance to Muslims that ascendancy in the world is determined through faith and righteous action rather than by ethnic affiliation. Since Muslims are the final bearers of God's message, it is they who will "inherit the earth." The verse reads:

> We wrote down in the psalms, after the Reminder came, "It is my righteous servants who will inherit the earth" [Quran, 21:105].

Faith and righteous actions, not lineage, were also conditions for the sons of Isaac, again expressed below in the Quranic verse according to Islamic exegesis:

> Musa [Moses] said to his people, "Seek help in Allah and be steadfast. The earth belongs to Allah. He bequeaths it to any of His servants He wills. The successful outcomes for those who do their duty." They said, "We suffered harm before you came to us and after you came to us." He said, "It may well be that your Lord is gong to destroy the enemy and make you the successors in the land so that he can see how you behave" [Quran, 7: 128–129].

The Quran continues to address the Jews and predicts that Jews will become influential twice in the world and twice will be punished by God for their "iniquity." Jews being thus influential could also be interpreted to mean they will come to establish a country of their own and God may yet reinstate the children of Israel in the holy land as the following verses suggest:

> In the book [Torah] we solemnly declared to the Israelites: Twice you shall do evil in the land. You shall become great transgressors.

> And when the prophecy of your first transgression came to be fulfilled, we
> sent against you a formidable army which ravaged your land and carried out
> the punishment you had been promised [Quran, 17:4].

The above is possibly a reference to the destruction of the First Temple by the Assyrian forces.

The Quran further states:

> Then we granted you victory over them and multiplied your riches and your
> descendants, so that once again you became more numerous than they. We
> said: "If you do good, it shall be to your advantage, but if you do evil, you
> shall sin against your own souls."
>
> And when the prophecy of your next transgression came to be fulfilled, we
> sent another army to afflict you and to enter the Temple as the former entered
> it before, utterly destroying all that they laid their hands on [Quran, 17: 5–6].

In 70 CE, the Roman army, in an attempt to quell the Jewish rebellion,
completely destroyed the Temple in Jerusalem. It was never again to come
under Jewish control, although the Bible is replete with references to the
Temple being built before Christ's second advent. Perhaps the biblical verse
pertaining to the Temple and the return of the Jewish people to Israel finds
corroboration in the following statement of the Quran:

> We said: "Your Lord may yet be merciful to you. If you again transgress, you
> shall again be scourged. We have made hell a prison house for the unbelievers"
> [Quran, 17: 8].

Taking the Quran seriously, Muslims believe Jews will come to be established once again in the holy land. However, they are swift to point out that
Jewish "iniquity," now particularly evidenced in the ongoing conflict with
the Palestinians and most recently with Lebanon's Hezbollah, will eventually cause their downfall, as the Quran states: "If you again transgress, you
shall again be scourged."

Closely associated with the establishment of Israel in the holy land is
the rebuilding of the Third Temple. It is an important event in a series of
apocalyptic events that will herald the second advent of Christ.

But whether the Temple will be rebuilt is a question that must be
explored more through biblical references, as neither the Quran not Hadith
elaborate the issue in depth. This is not to suggest that Muslims refrain from
interpreting biblical prophecy in a manner that will further their own political agenda for the region. Many regard the construction of the Al-Aqsa
Mosque on the site of the Temple of Solomon as a fulfillment of the biblical prophecies pertaining to the Third Temple. They find support for this
contention in the belief that the God who spoke to Jews, Christians and

Muslims is one and the same. Since Muslims believe in the continuity of revelation and God's message to humanity, there is a belief among Muslim apocalypticists that the frequent biblical references to "my people," interpreted in the Judeo-Christian tradition as the Jews, actually refer to Muslims or any other community who upholds pure monotheism. According to this interpretation, God sees no distinction between believers of old to whom promises were made and contemporary Muslims who are believers of today. As David Cook points out in his article entitled *The Beginnings of Islam as an Apocalyptic Movement*:

> Part and parcel of the messianic kingdom was the construction of the Dome of the Rock in Jerusalem on the site of the Second Temple, which was destroyed in 70 CE. These inscriptions are largely citations from the Qur'an and consist in their entirety of statements about Jesus, frequently to deny the doctrine of the Trinity and to accord Jesus the position of a prophet. Once again, this focus upon Jesus is striking. Though Trinitarian Christians in the final analysis see these inscriptions as an attack on Christianity, it may very well be that original intent was instead to focus upon purification of Christianity from the principal offensive element in the eyes of the early Muslims — the divinity of Jesus — and at the same time turning the focus upon Jesus the man who would establish the messianic kingdom for both Christians and Muslims in the immediate future.
>
> Nor were Jewish expectations ignored in this building. It is clear that Jews served in the Dome of the Rock for some 50 years after its construction as part of those venerating the site. From a very early tradition, the Ummayyad builder of the Dome, 'Abd al-Malik, is actually compared to King David:
>
> > Ka'b found written in one of the books: "Jerusalem — which is *Bayt al-maqdis*— and the Rock is called the Temple: I will send to you My servant 'Abd al-Malik who will build you and decorate you. I will return to Bayt al-maqdis its earlier dominion, and I will crown you with gold, silver and coral, and I will send My people to you, and I will place My Throne upon the Rock. I am the Lord God, and David is the king of the *Banu Isra'il*."
>
> It is clear that in this early Muslim tradition, the position of 'Abd al-Malik is that of a renewer. What is he renewing? Most probably a type of the Third Temple, remembering that the Jews during the Byzantine-Sasanian war of 602–28 had made an effort to rebuild this structure after Jerusalem fell to the Sasanians in 614.[1]

Yet, in order to unravel the claims of the Al-Aqsa being a contemporary fulfillment of the Third Temple, one must look at biblical references. It is widely held among Christian interpreters of prophecy that the reconstruction of the Temple must predate Christ's second coming. For this reason, many fundamentalist Christians support Israel's right not only to exist, but also to expand by extending its boundaries to Jerusalem as the capital of Israel, for it will facilitate the construction of the Temple, paving the way for Christ's return. The Antichrist's reign will also predate Christ's return. The Antichrist will commit his abominations in the rebuilt Temple, desecrating the precincts by declaring himself God, as evident from the following prophecy:

> [He] opposeth and exalteth himself above all that is called God, or that is worshipped; so that he as God sitteth in the temple of God, shewing himself that he is God [2Thessalonians 4].

While the New Testament merely alludes to the Third Temple, it is in Ezekiel that we find details of the actual construction, the timeline and the structure and locations of the Temple. The Al-Aqsa mosque would probably not fit the profile of the Third Temple when subjected to a comparison with the following:

> Afterward he brought me to the temple, and measured the posts, six cubits broad on the one side, and six cubits broad on the other side, which was the breadth of the tabernacle. And the breadth of the door was ten cubits; and the sides of the door were five cubits on the one side, and five cubits on the other side: and he measured the length thereof, forty cubits: and the breadth, twenty cubits. Then went he inward, and measured the post of the door, two cubits; and the door, six cubits; and the breadth of the door, seven cubits. So he measured the length thereof, twenty cubits; and the breadth, twenty cubits, before the temple: and he said unto me, This is the most holy place [Ezekiel 41: 1–4].

All this will be made possible only after Israel recaptures Jerusalem from the Muslims before the second coming of Christ. Luke 21:24 says:

> And they shall fall by the edge of the sword, and shall be led away captive into all nations: and Jerusalem will be trodden down of the Gentiles, until the times of the Gentiles be fulfilled [Luke 21:24].

The 1967 war between Arabs and Israelis resulted in the capture of Jerusalem by the Israeli forces. A clear prophecy of the Bible had already come to pass as marking the end of the "times of the Gentiles." The Jews, on the other hand, would regain their strength and influence on the global scene as well as in their ancient land.

Political alliances in the end times will also determine the course of the conflicts. Here the role of Russia in relation to Israel needs to be discussed in light of prophecy. Both Ezekiel and the book of Daniel suggest an uncomfortable relationship between the two countries. Ezekiel states:

> And say unto them: Thus saith the LORD God; Behold, I will take the children of Israel from among the heathen, whither they be gone, and will gather them on every side, and bring them into their own land [Ezekiel 37: 21].

And further:

> I will make them one nation in the land upon the mountains of Israel [Ezekiel 37: 22].

This will be followed by a confrontational relationship, described in Ezekiel 38–39, with "Gog of the land of Magog." According to Flavius Josephus, the well-known first century Jewish historian, "Magog" is a distorted form of "magogites," the name given to the Scythians by the Greeks. They lived in the caucuses now inhabited by Muslim nations such as Azerbaijan, Uzbekistan, and Turkmenistan. They are said to be the progenitors of the Russians who migrated to the North. Hence the political climate of the end times will be characterized by tension between Israel and the land of Magog or modern Russia. Could this mean that the Muslim nations of the North or the land of Magog will unite with their southern co-religionists to lead a war against Israel?

Israel's presence right in the heart of Arab lands will also lay the seeds of a bloody conflict in the region. The book of Daniel declares that "the King of the North" will descend — upon Israel, some interpretations hold — "like a whirlwind ... with many ships" (Daniel 11:40). The many ships may be interpreted as the twenty-two hostile Arab nations surrounding Israel who have constantly been at war with the Jewish state, aided in part by Russia. In 1971, for example, Iraq had signed a new treaty with the Soviet Union which expressly stated its purpose as empowering Arabs against Israel. Perhaps the USSR was motivated not because of an inveterate animosity towards Israel, but because of its own expansionist agenda in establishing an imperial force in the Middle East to gain access to the region's many resources.

Prior to the breakup of the Soviet Union, many Arab nations had come together to form a military and political alliance with the great superpower as well as among themselves. Egypt, Sudan and Syria all provided the necessary bases for Soviet expansionism, which in the present time has come to be greatly undermined due to the dismemberment of the Soviet Union. Nonetheless, even in recent times, Russia resisted the idea of the present war in Iraq and offered to negotiate a truce between Saddam Hussein and U.S. president George W. Bush.

Daniel 11 also refers to another political alliance that will emerge from the East. This alliance will amass an army of 200 million people as combatants in the final battle of Armageddon. Interpreters of Bible prophecy understand this to mean Communist China, given the fact that it is the only country with a capability of producing an army of 200 million, making it likely that China will be a major player in the final conflict between good and evil.

Rev. 9:16 states:

> And the number of the army of the horsemen were two hundred thousand
> thousand; and I heard the number of them [Rev. 9:16].

All this, while the world will be leaning towards a diabolical world government under the Antichrist's global influence. Ten rulers in particular from
the Mediterranean nations will come under his political control:

> And the ten horns which thou sawest are ten kings, which have received no
> kingdom as yet; but receive power as kings one hour with the beast. These
> have one mind, and shall give their power and strength unto the beast [Rev.
> 17:12–13].

In recent times many alliances have been formed on the pretext of
advancing economic progress and political consolidation, but so far none fits
the description contained in the prophecy cited above. The Arab nations
formed the League of Arab Nations, and the western European nations have
recently united in a common goal to further the cause of economic advancement by establishing the European Union. South Asian nations have formed
regional treaties amongst them such as SAARC, but a political union of the
nature described in Daniel 11:2–3 is as yet unseen.

Nonetheless, when the Antichrist assumes power over the major part of
the world (Rev. 13:3: "and all the world wondered after the beast"), he will convert the currencies of the world into one currency. If the Eurodollar can be interpreted as a fulfillment of this prophecy, then the empire of the Antichrist would
perhaps emerge from Europe. The Antichrist will be so powerful that he will
be performing "great wonders, so that he maketh fire to come down from heaven
on the earth in the sight of men" (Rev. 13:13). This indicates the Antichrist
will be a warrior inflicting death and destruction on humanity through his
militaristic goals. The Antichrist's diabolical rule will last seven years.

His tight control over his subjects will be achieved through an enor-
mously efficient tracking system. The Antichrist will mark each individual
living during his rule:

> And he causeth all, both small and great, rich and poor, free and bond, to
> receive a mark in their right hand, or in their foreheads; and that no man
> might buy or sell, save that he had that mark, or the name of the beast, or the
> number of his name. [Rev. 13:16–17].

Therefore, with the absolute authority he will come to enjoy, the
Antichrist will rule the world ruthlessly through his militaristic agenda. The
abomination of desolation referred to in Daniel and Matthew will be as follows under his rule:

When ye therefore shall see the abomination of desolation, spoken of by David the prophet, stand ... then let them which be in Judea flee into the mountains: Let him which is on the housetop not come down to take anything but of his house: Neither let him which is in the field return back to take his clothes. And woe unto them that are with child, and to them that give suck in those days! But pray ye that your flight be not in the winter, neither on the Sabbath day: For then shall be great tribulation, such as was not seen since the beginning of the world to this time, no, nor ever shall be [Matthew 24:15–21].

The Antichrist will also be a key player during the battle of Armageddon, which will forever determine the fate of history. The battle will begin just prior to Jesus' second coming. Revelation 16:16 states, "And he gathered them together into a place called in the Hebrew tongue, Armageddon"; this has been interpreted to mean that Megiddo, in northern Israel, which is approximately a twenty-mile land strip, will be the battle scene for the final conflict. All the alliances will converge at Megiddo to advance the Antichrist's nefarious agenda.

The battle will be fierce:

the spirits of devils, working miracles ... which go forth unto the kings of the earth and of the whole world, to gather them to the battle of that great day of God Almighty [Rev. 16:14].

The Antichrist will achieve widespread popularity among the peoples of the world as a messenger of peace. He will sign a peace treaty with Israel (Dan. 9:27), which he will break at the midpoint through the tribulation. According to Matthew, wars and conflicts will have become commonplace, causing massive loss of human life:

And except those days should be shortened, there should no flesh be saved; but for the elect's sake those days shall be shortened [Matthew 24:22].

Several wars will have preceded the Antichrist's rise to power, and a conflict-ridden world will readily believe his false promises of bringing security to it. Many will follow him based on his false promise of establishing everlasting peace. They will also be duped by those proclaiming themselves the Christ or the Messiah. Wars will continue during the Antichrist's hypocritical reign, causing even more damage to life and collateral. The following verses from Luke paint a gory picture of the many faces of death, destruction and treachery that will come to pass in the latter days:

And he said, Take heed that ye be not deceived: for many shall come in my name, saying, I am Christ; and the time draweth near: go ye not therefore after them. But when ye shall hear of wars and commotions, be not terrified: for these things must first come to pass; but the end is not by and by. Then said he unto them, Nation shall rise against nation, and kingdom against kingdom: And great earthquakes shall be in divers places, and famines, and pestilences; and fearful sights and great signs shall there be from heaven [Luke 21: 8–11].

Ironically, the Antichrist will also persecute the Jewish people, subsequent to his signing a false peace treaty with them. He will come to overpower them as the following passage suggests:

I beheld, and the same horn made war with the saints, and prevailed against them [Dan 7:21].

This does not mean, however, that humanity will become extinct. Before complete annihilation sets in, Jesus will return as the true prince of peace. (Circumstances surrounding his return form the subject matter of another chapter of this book.)

Once Jesus returns, of course, the final battle of Armageddon — which will have begun already — will be brought to a close with the triumph of good over evil. The Antichrist will be killed in a violent manner and thrown into the lake of fire (Dan. 7:11). The thousand-year peaceful rule will then ensue, as detailed in the following verses from Micah:

In the last days it shall come to pass, that the mountain of the house of the LORD shall be established in the top of the mountains, and it shall be exalted above the hills; and people shall flow unto it. And many nations shall come and say, Come, and let us go up to the mountain of the LORD, and to the house of the God of Jacob; and he will teach us of his ways, and we will walk in his paths: for the law shall go forth of Zion, and the word of the LORD from Jerusalem. And he shall judge among many people, and rebuke strong nations afar off; and they shall beat their swords into plowshares, and the spears into pruning hooks; nation shall not lift up a sword against nation, neither shall they learn war any more [Micah 4;1–4].

The Bible mentions a certain tribulation that will precede the second advent of Jesus. However, those who are true believers will be rescued from the abomination of desolation. Nonetheless Christians, towards the end of times, will be persecuted for their beliefs. They will be harassed simply for believing in Christ as their savior. Again Luke contains the warning of great suffering for the followers of Christ:

But before all these, they shall lay their hands on you, and persecute you, delivering you up to the synagogues, and into prisons, being brought before kings and rulers for my name's sake [Luke 21: 12].

The scenario for the Muslims will be no different, as they believe they too will be persecuted for their beliefs. Tim LaHaye states in his book *The*

Merciful God of Prophecy that 66 million Christians have thus far been persecuted for their beliefs since the beginnings of their faith; however, Muslims again suggest the biblical references to those suffering in Jesus' name most likely apply to them rather than to Christians, who, according to Islamic belief, have distorted the original message of Jesus. The following Hadith describes conditions for Muslims living in the end times:

> Narrated Zainab bint Jahsh: The prophet got up from his sleep with a flushed red face and said: None has the right to be worshipped but Allah. Woe to the Arabs, from the Great evil which is nearly approaching them. Today a gap has been made in the wall of Gog and Magog like this (Sufyan illustrated this by forming the number 90 or 100 with his fingers). It was asked: Shall we be destroyed though there are righteous people among us? The prophet said, Yes, if evil increases [Bukhari: Muhammad Muhsin Khan, Vol. 9, no. 181].

In another Hadith Mohammed is reported to have said, "I see afflictions falling upon your houses as raindrops fall" (Bukhari: Muhammad Muhsin Khan, Vol. 9, no 182).

Many have interpreted this Hadith to mean the current bombing of Iraq and Afghanistan. The allusion to "afflictions falling upon houses like raindrops" is understood as bombs falling from the sky.

The one who will lead the reign of terror against Muslims of course is the Antichrist, known to Muslims as the Masih-ud-Dajjal. It is interesting to note that adherents of both Islam and Christianity believe it is their religious community that will be targeted for persecution from the Antichrist. According to Hadith literature, which tends to be more anti–Semitic than the Quran, the Masih-ud-Dajjal will be Jewish in origin, and will come to dominate the entire world through his machinations. In Hadith literature he is known as the Masih-ud-Dajjal, or false Messiah, because he will be a leader of the Jews with whom Muslims will experience much enmity towards the end of times. The Jews will have accepted him as their promised Messiah. According to Muhammad Yasin-Owadally, "The Jews will definitely give the monster [Dajjal] the name of al–Massih because they will mistake him for the Messiah, whom they will glorify to restore the kingdom of Israel to them."[2]

According to Owadally, the Dajjal will also declare himself prophet and then Allah. He will lead many astray with his false claims. They will obey him without questioning. Owadally states in his book *Emergence of Dajjal: The Jewish King:* "He will pretend that he is the Mighty Allah, but Allah is not one-eyed and no one of us will be able to see Allah until we die."[3]

Through his diabolical powers the Dajjal will be able to achieve the impossible. Before his appearance, for example, the world will have suffered famine for two years. Upon his arrival he will order rain to fall, thereby alleviating hunger from the famine-stricken communities. The rain will produce food in abundance. Because of this amazing feat, people will begin to follow him in throngs.

Muslims, however, will not believe in him. Consequently they will continue to suffer famine and hardship under his rule and he will persecute them even more by stripping them of their wealth and resources. Their refusal to believe in the Dajjal as Allah will invite more hostility against them in the form of wars, subjugation and imprisonment.

By proclaiming himself Allah, the Dajjal will also create a false paradise and hell. By depriving Muslims of their wealth and resources he will have cast them into "hell." On the other hand, his followers will enjoy material wealth as an illusion of a false paradise. His followers will support and defend every single move of the Dajjal. Needless to say, Muslims view the prosperity of the West and Jewish influence on the one hand, and their own sorry plight on the other, as a fulfillment of this prophecy.

The Dajjal according to Hadith will also perform some of the same miracles attributed to Jesus. He will heal the sick, give sight to the blind and cure the leper. He will also be able to give life to the dead. Here, one may simply attribute the Dajjal's modern "miracles" to the many advances in science and technology rather than a belief in miraculous occurrences.

Once the Dajjal's evil empire is firmly established in the world, he will begin to preach a hedonistic philosophy based on materialism. He will therefore justify all sinful activity as an inescapable reality intrinsic to human nature. Many will embrace his message because of the license it will provide them. Nothing will ever be deemed sinful or reprehensible. Hence the world will drown in a state of anarchy, moral laxity and degradation. Yet while his followers will be basking in carnal and material pleasure, Muslims will suffer all sorts of tragedies because of their continued refusal to accommodate the Dajjal and his false claims.

Even the holy city of Medina will be attacked by the Jews because, according to Owadally's commentary of Hadith quoted above, they will be among the followers of Dajjal. They will have conquered Jerusalem already and proceed to conquer Medina as well:

> The prophet sent us on our foot so that we may acquire booty. We returned but acquired nothing of a booty. When he recognized a great fatigue on our faces, he stood amongst us and said, "O Allah entrust them not to me lest they may be weak on their account, and entrust them not to themselves lest they may become weak on their account, and entrust them not to the people lest they may place their needs over theirs." Afterwards he placed his hand on my

head and said, "O Ibn Hawalah, when you will see the rule coming down to the Holy land [Jerusalem], earthquakes, troubles and major events shall be near and the Hour shall come nearer to men than this hand of mine to your head."[4]

It is inferred from the above Hadith that Jerusalem will be temporarily under non–Muslim control before it is reconquered by them prior to "the Hour."

The Dajjal will make his appearance during the period marking Jewish control over Jerusalem. As stated in the Hadith quoted above, he will also lead an attack on Medina. He will then attempt to conquer Mecca, but divine plan will forbid him from entering the holy precincts of the city of Mecca, as God will have commissioned several angels to guard its outer boundaries. The Dajjal and his army of Jews will also be prevented from entering Medina according to the following authentic Hadith:

> Narrated Anas bin Malik: The Prophet said: "Al Dajjal will come and encamp at a place close to Medina and then Medina will shake thrice whereupon every Kafir [disbeliever] and hypocrite will go out [of Medina] towards him" [Bukhari: Muhammad Muhsin Khan, Vol. 9, no. 239].

Of course, this will not be possible for the Dajjal without the collusion of some Muslims who will abandon their own faith and follow the ways of the Jews and Christians, according to the following Hadith:

> Narrated Abu Said Al-Khudri : The Prophet said: "You will follow the ways of those nations who were before you, span by span and cubit by cubit, so much so that even if they entered a hole of a mastigure, you would follow them." We said: "O Allah's Apostle! [Do you mean] the Jews and the Christians?" He said, "Whom else?" [Bukhari: Muhammad Muhsin Khan, Vol. 9, no. 422].

Consistent with the belief that Muslims will mimic the Christians and Jews is the following Hadith which suggests Islam will disappear from among Muslims, except from Medina:

> The prophet said, "Verily belief returns and goes back to Medina as a snake returns and goes back to its hole [when in danger]" [Bukhari: Muhammad Muhsin Khan, Vol. 3, no. 100].

Since Islam will no longer be a uniting force among the different Muslim countries, a devastating war will be fought between two groups of Muslims. Some have concluded that this war was the Iran-Iraq war of 1988. The following Hadith, produced partially, predicts such a war:

> Narrated Abu Huraira: Allah's Apostle said: "The Hour will not be established till two big groups fight each other whereupon there will be a great number of casualties on both sides and they will be following one and the same religious doctrine" [Bukhari: Muhammad Muhsin Khan, Vol. 9, no. 237].

In its broader application, the conflict can also include the current debates and discourse over the true spirit and intent of Islam — for example, whether it is a secular religion, whether it is misogynist, or whether it allows for any flexibility in interpretation. Indeed there is an intra-religious debate taking place in the Muslim world over precept and practice, which often assumes a belligerent and confrontational tenor.

With wars are associated fires, destruction and mass casualty. According to Hadith, a massive fire from the East will also signal the end of times. After the first gulf war, Iraqi president Saddam Hussein, in an act of defiance against the Americans, ordered the burning of the oil wells in Kuwait. The blaze took several months to quell. The relevant Hadith on the authority of Abu Huraira states:

> Narrated Abu Huraira: Allah's Apostle said, "The Hour will not be established till a fire will come out of the land of Hijaz, and it will throw light on the necks of the camels at Busra" [Bukhari: Muhammad Muhsin Khan, Vol. 9, no. 234].

Obviously the fire will extend throughout a vast land mass, if its light is to be seen from as far as Syria. The Hijaz spoken of in Hadith covers the entire area that now forms Yemen, Iraq, Kuwait and modern Saudi Arabia.

"Gog of the land of Magog" also play a sinister role in their dealings with Muslims. While the Quran only alludes to the "Yajuj and Majooj" — the Arabic for Gog and Magog — Hadith are replete with legends of these mysterious people who are doomed to live a life of isolation till the end of times. Many Muslims believe they reside behind a mountain range in the northern regions of the earth, as yet undiscovered by the rest of the world. Each day the Gog and Magog dig a tunnel through the mountain in an attempt to free themselves from their confinement. Each day they are prevented though divine intervention. However, their destructive forces will be unleashed towards the end of times causing great devastation on earth:

> They said: O Zulqarnain [presumably Alexander the Great], surely Gog and Magog make mischief in the land. Shall we then pay you a tribute on condition that you should raise a barrier between us and them? He said: That in which my Lord has established me is better, therefore you only help me with workers, I will make a fortified barrier between you and them [Quran, 18:95].

The Quran further suggests the Gog and Magog could not penetrate the barrier against Zulqarnain. Although Zulqarnain thanked God, he warned of the impending danger that will befall people living in the end of days in the following verse of the Quran:

> He said: This is a mercy from my Lord, but when the promise of my Lord

comes to pass, He will make it level with the ground, and the promise of my Lord is ever true [Quran, 18: 9].

This verse of the Quran has been explained in detail by Mohammed Yasin-Owadally. In his book *Emergence of Dajja: the Jewish King*, he states:

They will first pass by the waters of Tiriya which they will drink up to the last drop.... They will then reach up to the Khamar hill near Jerusalem and being puffed up by their power they will shoot their arrows toward the heaven to destroy the inhabitants of heaven after they have finished with the inhabitants of earth. Allah will return their arrows besmeared in blood."[5]

If, however, Josephus' explanation of the identity of Gog and Magog is accepted as true, Muslims may interpret the Soviet invasion of Afghanistan as the prophesied invasion by the Gog and Magog, prophesied in Hadith (Bukhari: Muhammad Muhsin Khan, Vol. 9, no. 181, quoted above).

The Muslim community living in the end of days will also experience much disunity and discord. This will lead to political skirmishes and wars among the Muslims as well. Moreover they will be in a state of ignorance over the basic tenets of their faith. Those with little or no faith will become the defenders of the beliefs and principles of Islam. The following Hadith describes these political events and the dearth of scholarship among Muslims:

Narrated Abdullah: The Prophet said, "Near the establishment of the Hour, there will be the days of Al-Harj, and the religious knowledge will be taken away [vanish, i.e. by the death of Religious scholars] and general ignorance will spread." Abu Musa said "Al Harj" in Ethiopian language means "killing." Ibn Masud added: I heard Allah's apostle saying: "[it will be] from among the most wicked people who will be living at the time when the Hour will be established" [Bukhari: Muhammad Muhsin Khan, Vol. 9, no. 187].

Towards the end of times, the Muslims will be embroiled in a battle with the "Romans." Scholars and commentators of Hadith suggest Romans stands for Christians, the Roman Catholic Church being the symbol of the largest division within Christianity. If the recent wars in Afghanistan and Iraq can at all be characterized as wars between Christians and Muslims, the prophecy can be deemed fulfilled. Some of the details of the battle between the Muslims and the "Romans" are described in the following Hadith on the authority of Abu Huraira:

The prophet said, "The Hour will not come until the Romans camp at al-A'amsn or Dabiq. An army composed of the best people on earth at that time will come out from Medina to meet them. When they have arranged themselves in ranks, the Romans will say, do not stand between us and those who took prisoners from amongst us. Let us fight with them. The Muslims will say,

No, Allah, we never stand aside from you and our brothers. Then they will fight. One third will run away and Allah will never forgive them. One third will be killed, and they will be the best of martyrs in Allah's sight. One third who will never be subjected to trials and tribulations will win, and will conquer Constantinople. Whilst they are sharing out booty, after hanging their swords on the olive trees, Satan will shout to them that the Dajjal has taken their place among their families. They will rush out, but will find that it is not true. When they come to Syria, the Dajjal will appear, while they are preparing for battle and drawing up the ranks. When the time for prayer comes, Jesus son of Mary will descend and lead them in prayer. When the enemy of Allah like the Dajjal sees him, he will start to dissolve like salt in water, but Allah will kill him.[6]

The above Hadith also points to dissension among Muslims. Three broad categories of Muslims are described here: those who will avoid fighting the infidel armies, those who will be martyred and those who will emerge triumphant against the Christian forces. The Muslim army will be led by the Mahdi carrying seventy banners and 1200 persons under each banner. The battle scene will be Syria where the Christian army will have amassed. The group that will surrender to the Christian army as predicted by Hadith will never be forgiven by Allah. The remaining victorious Muslims will proceed to fight other infidel forces and most of them will be martyred. Although few in strength, they will demoralize the Christian armies to the extent that the latter will no longer wish to fight and will flee from the battlefield. After the victory in Syria, the Muslim army led by the Mahdi will proceed to conquer Constantinople by the sheer strength of the "Takbir," the declaration of the greatness of God as "Allah o Akbar." The groups are equally divided as constituting one third of the entire Muslim population for each category. According to another Hadith, however, the destruction to life will be so massive that only one out of every hundred will survive. (Muslim: Kitab ul Fitan 8,177,178)

While Bible prophecy speaks of alliances between the ten Mediterranean nations, Hadith suggests that the Christian world will also be divided in its mission either for or against the Muslims. When U.S. president George W. Bush sent troops into Iraq, many in Europe opposed it. The streets of Europe and America were crowded with people protesting the planned U.S. attack on Iraq, carrying slogans such as "no blood for oil." Those familiar with apocalyptic literature among Muslims cited the divisions in the Western world as a fulfillment of this prophecy. The Hadith allowing for this interpretation reads as follows:

Awf ibn Malik reported that the Prophets said: the Jews split into seventy-one sects: one will enter Paradise and seventy will enter Hell. The Christians split into seventy-two sects; seventy-one will enter Hell. By Him in Whose hand is my soul, my Ummah will split into seventy-three sects: one will enter Paradise and seventy-two will enter Hell." Someone asked, "O Messenger of Allah, who will they be?" He replied, "The main body of the Muslims" [Abu Daud: Book of Sunnah, no. 4572, 4573].

Perhaps the most compelling prophecy contained in Hadith alludes to a war fought near the River Euphrates over "mountains of gold":

Narrated Abu Huraira: Allah's Apostle said, "Soon the river 'Euphrates' will disclose the treasure [the mountain of gold], so whoever will be present at that time should not take anything of it." Al-A'ra'j narrated from Abu Huraira that the Prophet said, "It [Euphrates] will uncover a mountain of gold" [Bukhari: Muhammad Muhsin Khan, Vol. 9, no. 235].

The River Euphrates, rendered into Arabic as the Furaat, was home to the ancient Mesopotamian civilization which flourished in the northern regions of what is now Iraq around 4000 BCE. It runs through three Muslim countries, Iraq, Syria and Turkey, giving rise to political tensions between the neighbors over the supply of its waters. This only increases the tensions caused by Iraq's oil wealth (the country's oil reserves rank second largest in the world).

Babylon is another ancient name for modern Iraq. Bible prophecy along with Hadith indicates that Babylon will also be the stage for every decisive apocalyptic war. Revelation 9:14–16 describes how Babylon, established around the Euphrates, will be completely destroyed in the war along with one third of humanity wiped out:

Saying to the sixth angel which had the trumpet, Loose the four angels which are bound in the great river Euphrates. And the four angels were loosed, which were prepared for an hour, and a day, and a month, and a year, for to slay the third part of men.

Much of popular religion finds concordances between prophetic literature and recent world history. The belief that we are living in the end times is gaining popularity among the laity, particularly from among the three faiths claiming origin from the patriarch Abraham. Added to this belief is also a conviction in the ultimate triumph of each respective worldview. Popular websites and internet discussion forums are testimony to the influence apocalyptic belief has come to wield on the masses. The following quote from one Muslim website confirms this finding, as it comments on the emergence of a tyrannical world leader, who will proclaim himself the Messiah:

And then in the third, final and briefest stage of the master-plan, a Pax Judaica world-order is about to replace Pax Americana.... Israel would replace USA as the ruling State in the world and when that occurs, a Jew would eventually rule the world from Jerusalem and claim to be the true Messiah! But he would not be Jesus the true Messiah. Rather, Prophet Muhammad explained that he would be Dajjal the false Messiah (Anti-Christ).

We are now very close indeed to culmination of that devilish master-plan that has been ominously unfolding ever since the island Britain startled the world a few centuries ago by becoming the first ruling State in post-biblical history.[7]

CHAPTER FOUR

Mahdi, Islam's Archetypal Redeemer, and Other Muslim Messiahs

After the lesser signs of the hour appear and increase, mankind will have reached a stage of great suffering. Then the awaited Mahdi will appear. He is the first of the greater and clear signs of the hour. There will be no doubt about his existence, but this will only be clear to the knowledgeable people. The Mahdi will rule until the false Messiah (Masih-ud-Dajjal) appears, who will spread oppression and corruption. The only ones who will know him well and avoid his evil will be those who have great knowledge and Iman (faith). The false Messiah will remain for a while, destroying mankind completely, and the earth will witness the greatest tribulation in history. Then the Messiah Jesus will descend, bringing justice from heaven. He will kill the Dajjal and there will be years of safety and security.[1]

Ibn Kathir, famous Muslim historian and exegete of the Quran, sums up the role of the Mahdi, Islam's awaited redeemer, in the above quotation taken from his book *The Signs before the Day of Judgement.*

Millenarianism, often understood as the belief in apocalyptic occurrences at the close of each thousand years, is common to the three monotheistic faiths rooted in the Abrahamic tradition. Associated with millenarianism is the belief in a redeemer who will appear in the end times to restore justice and peace to a much troubled world. Often within Islam, the concept has been politicized to form the basis of numerous messianic movements, particularly in times of crises for Muslims. Many religious and political leaders therefore emerged throughout Islam's history to declare themselves the

Mahdi or Messiah, proclaiming they were sent by Allah to rescue the Muslim community from oppression or annihilation.

While the concept of the Mahdi arose largely from Shia Islam, the minority sect of Islam, belief in the Mahdi came to be firmly lodged among Sunni masses as well. Many Sunni scholars, however, insist there is no solid basis for the doctrine of the Mahdi, either in the Quran or Hadith. They assert that many of the Hadith alluding to the Mahdi are *zaeef*, or of doubtful authenticity. Yet this did not prevent Shia and Sunni clerics from constructing an ideological framework around the awaited Mahdi.

Ibn Kathir, of Sunni background, regards the awaited Mahdi as one of the "Rightly guided caliphs and imams." (The title "Mahdi" also means "one who is rightly guided.") He quotes the following Hadith in *The Signs before the Day of Judgement*:

> Abu Said al-Khudri reported God's messenger as saying, "The Mahdi would be of my stock, and will have a broad forehead and a prominent nose. He will fill the world with equity and justice, as it was filled with oppression and tyranny and will rule for seven years" [Abu Daud: Kitab-ul-Mahdi, no. 4272].

Another Hadith predicts the advent of the Mahdi in the following words. On the authority of Abdullah Ibn Masud, the prophet Mohammed is reported to have said:

> If there were only one day left for the world, that day would be lengthened until a man from among my descendants or from among people of my household was sent; his name will be the same as my name, and his father's name will be the same as my father's name. He will fill the earth with justice and fairness, just as it will have been filled with injustice and oppression. The world will not end until a man of my household, whose name is the same as mine, holds sway" [Abu: Kitab-ul-Mahdi, no. 4269].

The two Hadith quoted above provide the reader with some clues about the characteristics of the awaited Mahdi. What is quite clear is that he will be a descendent of Mohammed and his own name will be Mohammed. Also, his father's name will be Abdullah — the same as Mohammed's father's name. He will be a just ruler. As described in Hadith, he will have a broad forehead and a pronounced nose.

Also according to Hadith, he will appear at a time of great misfortune for Muslims. Some of these conditions have been described in the Hadith quoted below:

> Abduallh ibn Umar said: The prophet came to us and said, O Muhajirrun [immigrants from Mecca to Medina], you may be afflicted by five things. God forbid that you should live to see them. If fornication should become widespread, you should realize that this has never happened without new diseases

befalling the people which their forebears never suffered. If people should begin to cheat in weighing out goods, you should realize that this has never happened without drought and famine befalling the people, and their rulers oppressing them. If people should withhold zakat [poor-due], you should realize that this has never happened without the rain being stopped from falling, and were it not for the animal's sake, it would never rain again. If people would break the covenant with Allah and his messenger, you should realize that this has never happened without Allah sending an enemy against them to take some of their possessions by force. If the leaders do not govern according to the Book of Allah, you should realize that this has never happened without Allah making them into groups and making them fight one another [Ibn Majah: Kitab-ul-Fitan, no. 4019, 2/1332].

Thus, according to the above account, Muslims will have become utterly destitute. A subjugated people, they will be governed ruthlessly by dictators who will miss no opportunity to torture and oppress them. The conduct of the Muslims in general will reflect a sharp deviation from Quranic norms and edicts. This will often be cited as the cause of their downfall. Since they will have abandoned their covenant with Allah, they will remain vulnerable to attacks by non–Muslim forces.

Many contemporary Muslims see similarities between the events predicted in the Hadith above and the political conditions of the modern era. Consequently, they believe the current generation may very well witness the advent of the Mahdi. Events today signal the beginning of the end times, they assert. Muslims are convinced that their rulers oppress them. Saddam Hussein of Iraq, Hafez Assad of Syria, and the dictatorial Islamist regimes of North Africa are often cited as glaring examples of such tyrannical rule. They also feel Western forces are out to obliterate Islam and Muslims as prophesied above: "Allah sending an enemy against them to take some of their possessions." They are equally distraught because of internal dissension and discord. Moreover, they are convinced that corruption and dishonesty now plague the Muslim world because of endemic poverty. Drought and famine afflict many African Muslim nations such as the Darfur region in the Sudan. In short, some Muslims are convinced all the prophecies regarding the end times and the arrival of the Mahdi have been fulfilled in recent history.

This does not belie the fact that Mahdism has existed throughout Islam's history from the very beginning. Each generation interpreted conflict in their time to spell the end of days. The first Muslim to be declared Mahdi was Ibn al-Hanafiya, the son of Ali, the fourth caliph of Islam. He died without achieving much, and many years later, Mohammed Nafs-al-Zakiyah (the pure soul) was declared the Mahdi. He was a descendent of Imam Hassan, the prophet Mohammed's grandson through his only surviving daughter, Fatima.

Imam Jaffer Sadiq, the founder of Shia jurisprudence, also fathered many such Mahdis. Both he and his sons were declared Mahdi by their followers. However, the Shia doctrine of the Mahdi evolved around the year 869 with the purported disappearance of the twelfth imam, known to Shia Islam as Mohammed al-Mahdi, son of imam Hassan al-Askari. The occultation of this imam has been described in detail in Shia creed. Since the Shia have remained a persecuted sect throughout history because of their small numbers in Sunni majority countries, they have continually based their hope for deliverance on the reappearance of the Mahdi who went into occultation.

According to historical accounts, Imam Askari died without issue, but the Shia believe he had secretly fathered a son called Mohammed. The child's birth had been kept a guarded secret because of imminent danger to his life. He went into occultation when he was five years old by disappearing into a tunnel but would reappear at the end of days. Ibn Babuya al-Suduq, a famous Shia scholar of the tenth century, explains the occultation and the Shia doctrine of the Mahdi as follows:

> We believe that the proof of Allah in this earth and his vicegerent [khalifa] among his slaves in this age of ours is the Upholder [Qaim: of the laws of God], the Expected One, Mohammed Ibn al Hassan al Askari [i.e. the twelfth imam]. He it is whom God will make victorious over the whole world until from every place the call to prayer is heard and every religion will belong entirely to God exalted be He. He is the rightly guided Mahdi about whom the prophet gave information that when he appears, Jesus son of Mary will descend upon earth and pray behind him. We believe there can be no other Qaim than him. He may live in the state of occultation for as long as he likes.[2]

The Shia doctrine of the Mahdi confers semi-divine qualities to the awaited redeemer. He abides eternally and may do so indefinitely. The Sunni view is slightly different.

When Sunni scholars of the repute of Maulana Maududi elaborated the concept of the Mahdi, they gave further credence to the belief in the "Expected One" among Sunni masses. Contrary to the opinion of other scholars, Maududi held that some of the references to an end time deliverer of the Muslims may indeed be authentic. He rejected the belief, however, that the Mahdi's appearance would be a millenarian occurrence. According to him it could happen at any point in time when conditions for Muslims would become unbearable politically, economically and socially. A leader, he said, will arise, who will resuscitate Islam's true beliefs and practices, which in his opinion should always be regarded as the panacea for the woes experienced by Muslims. With a far more pragmatic approach to Mahdism, Maududi also discarded the belief in the occultation of the Mahdi, as that would imply a miraculous occurrence. Although Islam's millenarianism is imbued with miraculous occurrences, Maududi refuted all these claims. The Mahdi in his opinion will simply be a political leader whose rise to power will be a propitious event for Muslims, for he will be able to rescue them from the depths of despair. The Mahdi will do so not only through his political strength, but also his sagacity, wisdom and the vast knowledge that he will have acquired in various disciplines. According to Maududi's understanding, the Mahdi will not declare himself the Promised One. Muslims will be able to recognize him on their own.

Maududi as a scholar of Islam has exercised tremendous influence on Sunni Muslims. His interpretations of Quranic verses and Hadith are readily embraced by Sunnis all across the world. It is therefore commonly held that the Sunni view of the Mahdi, which points to a universal redeemer of Islam as a political leader, has gained preeminence among Muslims. The leader's confrontation with the Masih-ud-Dajjal also signifies that he will be instrumental in establishing a political order that would free the world from tyranny, injustice, persecution and economic imbalances. He will wage a righteous Jihad against the forces of evil represented by the Dajjal.

Ibn Kathir, presenting another Sunni view, also refutes the Shia claims by stating outright that the awaited Mahdi

> is not the Mahdi who is expected by the Shia, who they claim will appear from the tunnel in Sammarra.... The truth of the matter is that the Mahdi whose coming is promised at the end of time will appear from the East, and people will swear allegiance to him at the Kaaba as some Hadith indicate.[3]

Ibn Kathir quotes the following Hadith to support his assertion:

> Umm Salamah reported that the Prophet said, "People will begin to differ after the death of a Khalifa [caliph]. A man from the people of Medina will flee to Mecca. Some of the people of Mecca will come to him and drag him out against his will. They will swear allegiance to him between rukn and al mazam, an army will be sent against him from Syria, it will be swallowed up in the desert between Mecca and Medina. When the people see this, a group of people from Syria and Iraq will come and swear allegiance to him. Then, a man from Qureish whose mother is from Kalb will appear and send an army against them and will defeat them. This will be known as the battle of Kalb. Whoever does not witness the spoils of this battle will miss much. The Mahdi will distribute the wealth, and will rule the people according to the Sunnah of the prophet. Then he will die, and the Muslims will pray for him" [Abu Daud: Kitab-ul-Mahdi, no. 4273].

It is evident from the above Hadith that the Mahdi will attempt to evade the responsibility of battling the forces of evil. As described in the Hadith, the Muslims will have to drag him out of oblivion, much against his will. When, however, he agrees to accept the monumental task, he will lead them into battle and victory. Initially he will eradicate oppression from Muslim lands. To achieve this end he will launch an attack on the ruling dictator of Syria and defeat him. He will then proceed to unite the Muslims and assume their leadership. As a just ruler, he will also restore to Muslims their dignity, wealth and resources. However, as seen earlier, his mission will not be confined to ameliorating conditions for Muslims alone.

The Mahdi will also engage in confrontation with the Masid-ud-Dajjal or the Antichrist who will appear towards the end of the Mahdi's rule. By this time the Mahdi will have prepared ground for Jesus' return. He will reorganize the resources, wealth and military strength of the Muslims, thus paving the way for the final struggle between good and evil. But it is Jesus who will lead the final battle.

Preparing the ground for Jesus will also entail a struggle with many smaller Dajjals. Perhaps an explanation of the word "Dajjal" is forthcoming here. Before the appearance of the Masih-ud-Dajjal or Antichrist, there will have appeared thirty other "Dajjals" or "liars." Each one of them will claim to be a messenger of God, which is why each one of them will be called "Dajjal" or liar. There are many reports contained in Hadith describing the thirty Dajjals.

In the hadith produced partially on the authority of Abu Huraira, Mohammed is reported to have said:

> Narrated Abu Huraira: Allah's Apostle said, "The Hour will not be established (1) till two big groups fight each other whereupon there will be great number of casualties on both sides and they will be following one and the same religious doctrine, (2) till about thirty Dajjals [liars] appear, and each one of them will claim that he is Allah's Apostle, (3) till the religious knowledge is taken away [by the death of religious scholars]" [Bukhari, Muhammad Muhsin Khan, Vol. 9, no. 237].

The chief Dajjal, known as the Masih-ud-Dajjal, has been described as blind in one eye which looks like a "floating grape." He will be of stocky build with the words "*ka fa ra*" (disbeliever) imprinted on his forehead. Only Muslims will be able to read the words. (*Bukhari: Muhammad Muhsin Khan, Vol. 9, no. 242.*) His rule will be marked with

> years of confusion. People will believe a liar, and disbelieve one who tells the truth. People will distrust one who is trustworthy, and trust one who is treacherous, and the Ruwaibidah will have a say. Someone asked, who are the

Ruwaibidah? He said: those who rebel against Allah and will have a say in general affairs [Ahmad: 3/220].

The Dajjal will therefore encourage disbelief, treachery, deceit and corruption, as will his subordinates. Under such circumstances, the Mahdi will serve as the beacon of hope for Muslims who will choose to remain loyal to the message of Islam.

Although different roles have been assigned to the Mahdi in Shia and Sunni belief, they both agree that conditions for the arrival of the Mahdi are now ripe. Muslims are down-trodden, they are being attacked by Western powers, they are fighting among themselves, and they are economically unstable. Social conditions are also hostile to growth or change.

As seen previously, this view has surfaced many times toward the end of each century or millennium. For Sunni Muslims, the beginning of each century of the Hegirah calendar (the Islamic calendar) would spell hopeful anticipation for a new Mahdi. To address this need, many religious leaders over time have declared themselves the promised redeemer. While many of them only claimed to be reformers, some claimed Mahdihood or Messiahship. A number of them were applauded, while others were declared heretics. A few were able to start new trends and movements within Islam. Of the several Mahdis and Messiahs of Islam, three deserve special mention, as their legacy survives to the present date.

Most modern messianic movements within Islam began in the nineteenth century. The political climate for Muslims at the time was such that the Ottoman Empire, which had remained the symbol of Muslim unity for centuries, was showing signs of disintegration. Also, late in the eighteenth century, Napoleon had invaded Egypt. Western colonialism was given free rein allowing the rapid influx of Christian missionaries in Muslim lands, the invasion of Western economic interests on their territory, and the exercise of political control over their resources.

All this created an atmosphere of hostility towards Western nations among the Muslim masses. Feeling utterly helpless, they looked for solace many times in their apocalyptic beliefs. In this climate of anxiety and hostility, three men in three different parts of the Muslim world arose to declare themselves Islam's redeemer. Mirza Ali Mohammed Bab in Iran, Mirza Ghulam Ahmad in India, and Mohammed Ahmad, who came to be known popularly as the "Mahdi of Sudan," all declared themselves to be the "Expected One."

Shiraz, Iran, was home to Mirza Ali Mohammed, the son of a local cloth merchant, whose books are regarded as some of the earliest revelations of the Baha'í faith. Born in 1819, he received his religious education in Kerbala and Najaf, Iraq, becoming quite well versed in the Shia *Asna Ashari* tradition of belief in twelve imams or spiritual leaders. His first treatise, *Ziyarat Nama*, which is an exposition of the Shia philosophy, embodied basic Shia beliefs centered on the hopeful expectation of the promised Mahdi. It was not long before Mirza Ali Mohammed would declare that he was in direct communication with the imam who was now in occultation. His declaration coincided with the year 1844 CE, which holds special significance in Shia belief as described by one renowned Shia scholar, Moojan Momen, who states:

> The approach of the year 1260 [Islamic; 1844 AD] was accompanied by a general rise in expectancy of the return of the Hidden imam. This was the year that marked the one thousandth anniversary of the disappearance of the Twelfth imam and the beginning of the period of Occultation. There were several indications in the Quran and in the traditions that the dispensation of Mohammed would be one thousand years long and thus the year 1260 was greatly anticipated throughout the Shia world.[4]

Mirza Ali Mohammed, fully aware of this hopeful anticipation, took the opportunity to declare himself the Promised One or the Bab (Gate), as he later came to be known. Surrounded by a group of disciples, he dispatched letters to Shia clergy announcing the arrival of the awaited Mahdi while he made preparations to embark on a pilgrimage to Mecca and Medina. Disillusioned with the general condition of Muslims, he wrote an exposition of his impressions of the pilgrimage, commenting on the general plight of Muslims. He called this work *Book Written between Two Holy Places*.

However, it was not until later that he proclaimed a break from Shia Islam. Having declared himself the twelfth imam, he insisted he had been commissioned by God to revoke Islam and introduce a new universal faith in its place. The boldness of his assertions brought him much ignominy from the Shia clerics who promptly declared him a *kafir* or apostate. The Iranian government followed suit.

The involvement of the government meant imprisonment for the Bab. This, however, by no means quelled the Babi movement. In fact, the Bab continued to gain support due to the persecution that he suffered. One of his ardent supporters was the Iranian poetess Quratul-Ain, who once appeared without a veil in public, when such temerity would be unheard of. Perhaps she drew strength from the conviction that she was highly respected for her poetic gifts all across Iran. Although she never met the Bab, she remained his earnest supporter. She was able to inspire others to believe in the Bab as well, and the movement showed no sign of abating. The government hence decided to suppress the movement by force. Riots ensued, and Babis and non–Babis continued to spill each other's blood.

Since Shia clerics had declared the Bab and his followers apostates, there were calls to kill them according to the punishment for apostasy in Islamic law. Government officials consequently went on a rampage, killing Babis. They also came to the conclusion that the movement would be suppressed only if their leader was executed publicly. Bab, the Iranian Mahdi, was hence executed by a firing squad before thousands of followers on July 9, 1850. He was only thirty-one years old at the time of his execution.

Although his execution earned sympathy for the Babis in some quarters, the movement nonetheless suffered a setback in terms of propagation. Further animosity was generated against the Babis when two Babi youth made an assassination attempt on the ruling king or shah of Iran. Another series of pogroms ensued with Quratul-Ain, the Babi poetess, as its most prominent victim. It is said that before her death she proclaimed, "You can kill me as soon as you like, but you cannot stop the emancipation of women."[5]

It was the Bab who had initiated social change. He had advocated equal rights for women passionately in his book entitled *Bayan* (Narration). His other religious ideals included world peace, freedom from superstition and heralding the arrival of "He whom God would make Manifest." He firmly believed that "He whom God would make Manifest" was clearly prophesied by Moses, Jesus and Mohammed. He would serve as a beacon of hope for troubled humanity, said the Bab, because he would deliver all from such ills as wars, poverty and strife. With a new universal religion, he would deliver much-needed peace to mankind.

"He whom God would make Manifest" turned out to be one of the followers of the Bab. As a Babi, Mirza Husain Ali had escaped persecution and imprisonment mainly due to his family's wealth and influence. He came to inherit an entire estate from his father. With such wealth at his disposal, Mirza Husain Ali was able to wield considerable influence on the masses, providing much-needed impetus to the Babi movement. During the mass execution of the Babis following the assassination attempt on the shah, Mirza Husain Ali, too, had suffered imprisonment but was released because of political connections. While incarcerated, he started receiving "revelations" and declared himself to be "He whom God would make Manifest." As one would expect, Mirza Husain Ali, now known as the Bahaullah, or the "Glory of God," was exiled from Iran because of his claims to prophethood.

Bahaullah and his followers left Iran and settled in Baghdad, Iraq. While in Iraq, Bahaullah wrote *Kitab-e-Iqan* (The Book of Certainty), which elaborates his religious doctrines. Both the Bab and Bahaullah's writings represent a clean break from Islam. They declared that God destroyed the world in a spiritual sense with the arrival of each new prophet. The appearance of the Bab and Bahuallah therefore ushered in a new era through new prophetic witnesses. This was the beginnings of the Baha'i faith, as Babis now came to be known as Baha'is. Although Baha'i was rooted initially in Shia Islam and its doctrine of the hidden imam Mahdi, Bab and Bahaullah founded a religion which appears to be growing in popularity because of its message of peace and universalism, as well as its feminist ideology.

While Iran had been dealing with its Mahdis and Messiahs, Qadian, a Punjabi village in India, witnessed the birth of Mirza Ghulam Ahmad. He grew up to be a devotee of Islam in the Sunni tradition and spent his time in the study of Islamic theology and world religions. Soon he would pen his research in the form of a book entitled *Barahin-e-Ahmadiyah* (The Proofs of Mohammed). He is also the founder of the Ahmadiyah movement in Islam, which started with Mirza Ghulam Ahmad's declaration that he had been commissioned by God to bring much-needed reform to Muslims.

It is widely believed among orthodox Sunnis that Mirza Ghulam Ahmad was aided in his mission by the British government, whose stated policy of "divide and rule" was expressed in their approval of Mirza Ghulam Ahmad's introducing a dissident faction within Islam. Therefore, although Mirza Ghulam Ahmad had come under attack from Sunni clerics for his declarations, he continued to enjoy the protection of the British government.

His views were widely publicized in 1882, when he went a step further by announcing that he had received a direct revelation from God. He said he had been commissioned by God to be the savior of the world, about whom prophecies had been made in all the scriptures including the Quran. Due to the continued support and protection of the British, Mirza Ghulam Ahmad was also able to establish a school of theology, where he trained missionaries to propagate his version of Islam.

At the outset, he had claimed only to be a Muslim reformer, but he was now also asserting he was "Masih Maud," or the Messiah Jesus incarnated in the person of Mirza Ghulam Ahmad. He arrived at this conclusion through a unique interpretation of Hadith literature and Quranic injunctions pertaining to Jesus. Whereas the majority of Muslims believe Christ ascended to heaven alive, Mirza Ghulam Ahmad asserted that Jesus escaped the treachery of the Romans and Jews by fleeing to India, where he completed his ministry. He preached there for many years, married and then died a natural death, according to Ghulam Ahmad's view. In his book *Jesus in India* he claims there is a tombstone of a prophet named "Yeshua" in the

Indian state of Kashmir. He explains that this prophet "Yeshua" had traveled from Palestine around the time of Jesus' crucifixion. Other artifacts
found in Kashmir, he asserts, fully corroborate his theory. The entire discourse in the book *Jesus in India* is geared towards establishing the view that
it is not Jesus himself who will return to earth. Someone in his stead,
embodying his spirit, will actually perform the role of the redeemer or savior of the world. He used the terms Mahdi, Messiah and Savior interchange-
ably for himself, as the situation demanded.

Another distinctive feature about Mirza Ghulam Ahmad's philosophy
was his unique interpretation of the concept of Jihad. He preached that Jihad
was not a militaristic tool available to Muslims. He sanctioned it only as a
war in self-defense and only as a last resort. He further went on to suggest
that the world would have to be convinced about the "truth of Islam" only
through religious argument, not through force. Many attribute his pacifist
philosophy to his alleged collusion with the British government.

Although he continued to enjoy the protection of the British, trouble
nonetheless arose for the Ahmadiyah movement when Mirza Ghulam Ahmad
issued yet another pronouncement, this time declaring himself a prophet.
The finality of the prophet Mohammed being one of the cardinal tenets of
the Islamic faith according to the orthodox view, this declaration won him
much infamy. Anyone claiming to be a prophet after the prophet Mohammed
would have to be declared an impostor. Since his followers also associated
supernatural powers with Mirza Ghulam Ahmad, opponents of the movement began to declare Mirza Ghulam Ahmad and his followers heretics. His
followers tried to assuage tension by suggesting that Mirza Ghulam Ahmad
was not a challenge to the Prophet Mohammed, as he was only a *Zilli* or
shadow prophet, not introducing a new faith. This did not convince the
orthodoxy, who remained adamant about excommunicating the Ahmadis.
The movement continued to suffer censure. Perhaps this is why there were
a mere 50,000 adherents of Ahmadiyah Islam when its founder died.

After his death he was succeeded by Khalifa Nurudin, who led the
movement forward as it began to gather momentum after Ghulam Ahmad's
death. His successors and followers continued to elevate Mirza Ghulam
Ahmad's status from reformer, to redeemer, to messiah and then to prophet.
His son and successor described his father's mission in a letter to the Prince
of Hyderabad, India, saying:

> I shall now try to disprove the notion that since the Dajjal has not yet made
> his appearance, it is not still time for the Messiah to appear. I would say in
> reply that the Dajjal has already appeared, but people have failed to recognize
> him. The meaning of the word Dajjal is, according to the Arabic lexicons, a

counterfeiter. It may now be clear to your Highness, that by the peril of the Dajjal it meant nothing but the menace of these societies whose ministers are just endeavoring in a thousand ways to win the world to their preposterous doctrines. That the Dajjal would be blind. Such figurative meanings are not farfetched, rather they are supported by the Hadith. The same view is also corroborated by the hadtih that "he will break the cross," that is, the Promised Messiah will refute the Christian creed with arguments and signs so that at last the cross will be broken, meaning that most people will accept Islam and Christianity will lose its influence. Our belief that all these things are to be found in the Holy Founder of the Ahmediyah movement, Hazrat Mirza Ghulam Ahmed (on whom be peace and blessings of God) whom God raised for the reformation of the present age. He claimed to be the Messiah for the Christians, the Mahdi for the Muslims, Krishna or the Neha Kalnak Avatar for the Hindus, a Mesio Darbahm for the Zoroastrians. In short he was the promised prophet of every nation and was appointed to collect all mankind under the banner of one faith. In him were centered the hopes and expectations of all nations. He is the Dome of Peace under which every nation may worship its Maker. He is the opening through which all nations may obtain a vision of their Lord and his is the center at which meet all the "radii" of the circle. It is ordained there, that the world shall find peace and rest only through him.[6]

Mirza Bashiruddin was obviously addressing objections to Mirza Ghulam Ahmed's vacillation between sometimes declaring himself Mahdi and other times Messiah and prophet. There were other objections to his ideology as well, particularly his disdain for the concept of Jihad, since the Mahdi among traditional Muslims would have been a warrior for the cause of Islam. Mirza Ghulam Ahmad had expounded a far more pacifist view of the concept. He was also chided for declaring that Muslims who did not believe in his message were non–Muslim. Ironically, the government of Pakistan under the prime ministership of Zulfiqar Ali Bhutto declared Ahmadis, as the followers of Mirza Ghulam Ahmad came to be known, a non–Muslim religious minority in Pakistan after anti–Ahmadiyah riots broke out in the country in 1974.

The Ahmadiyah community continues to be ostracized as a religious group in various parts of the Indian subcontinent. After the partition of India and Pakistan in 1947, the headquarters of the Ahmadiyah community were moved from Qadian to a small town in Pakistani West Punjab, called Rabwa.

Both Mirza Ghulam Ahmad and Mirza Ali Mohammed Bab based their claims on the doctrine of the Mahdi. While the Bab declared his movement to be a different religion from Islam, Mirza Ghulam Ahmad insisted he was not bringing a new religion and that he was actually restoring Islam's pristine message for the modern generation. They both preached a philosophy of non-violence.

The political turmoil in Iran and India had witnessed two Mahdi movements there. Many miles away, a similar state of affairs was to give rise to Mohammed Ahmed's popularity as the "Mahdi of Sudan." Capitalizing on the political unrest, the degenerate social conditions and the general state of decay in his country, in the late 1800s he announced to the Sudanese people that he had been commissioned by God to restore dignity not only to them, but also to Muslim nations throughout the world.

Muhammed Ahmed's onslaught on imperialism included a country-wide rebellion against foreign rule. However, his animosity was also directed against the established clergy of his country. He believed their practices to be retrogressive and therefore not in the true spirit of Islam. He consequently set about to purge Islam of all its foreign and alien elements. Acting on the "authority of the prophet of Islam" he said he would receive instruction directly from the prophet Mohammed.

Another contestant at that time for the position of Mahdi was a Libyan called Mahdi Al-Sanyusi. The Mahdi of Sudan wrote to him saying he should relinquish his title because Mohammed Ahmed was the true Mahdi:

> In the name of God, the Compassionate, the Merciful from the poor servant of his Lord Al Mahdi Ibn al Syyid Abdullah to his beloved in God the Khalifa Mohammed Al Mahdi Al-Sanyusi may God keep him, amen.
>
> Most beloved and true believer in the law of the Prophet and honorable guide of God's worshippers, know beloved that I and my helpers were expecting you to revive true religion before Mahdihood was inspired in me. Who am I but a humble servant? I wrote to you but you did not answer me, therefore I conclude my letter did not reach you.
>
> I was told by the Lord of existence, Mohammed that I am the expected Mahdi, and he placed me on his throne several times in the presence of the four caliphs and the poles [saints]. He also girded me with his sword in the presence of the saints, the angels and Al-Khidr. I was told that none could gain the victory over me having received the sword of victory from him.[7]

The Mahdi of Sudan was clearly more militaristic than the Bab or Mirza Ghulam Ahmad. It was evident he would not tolerate any rival claimants to his title. He later went on to award the Mahdi Al-Sanyusi a secondary status by suggesting he was one of his own ministers because the prophet of Islam had said so. His subsequent military expeditions enabled him to conquer Khartoum, the capital of Sudan, where he declared a "Mahdiyah" state. Within six months of this conquest, the Mahdi of Sudan died. His successors displayed no interest in carrying the movement forward.

The three Mahdis discussed above left a lasting impact on nineteenth century politics in Muslim communities. The twentieth century witnessed the birth of several new Muslim nations as they gained independence from colonial rule. Millenarianism was giving way to nationalism, as Muslims began to experiment with the idea of nation-states and the new perils of self-rule that it entailed.

It was only recently that Mahdism and millenarianism resurfaced in the politics of the Muslim world. As seen earlier, both the Shia and Sunni factions of Islam had produced Mahdis and Messiahs throughout Islam's history. The most recent leader to be declared Mahdi belonged to the most orthodox tradition of Islam, known as Wahabi Islam. With loyalties to the *Ikhwanul Muslimin*, a fundamentalist and militaristic movement within Islam, Juhaiman al Utaibi led an attack on the Grand Mosque at Mecca on November 20, 1979.

He was accompanied by four hundred followers who were quickly able to occupy the mosque. Once that was accomplished, the Mahdis declared a Jihad on the Saudi government for supporting American interests.

Their main demand, however, was to consolidate strict Wahabi Islam in all of Saudi Arabia. During the siege, a Mahdi was elected. Although Juhainman al Utaibi had led the attack, he was not chosen as the Mahdi. Instead, a man by the name of Shaikh Abdul Aziz Baz, the head of "the Higher Council of Iftah and Research," was bestowed that honor.

The Saudi government had been taken by surprise. Under strict Islamic law they could not shed blood around the holy precincts of the mosque. However, the clergy in this case ruled in the government's favor, allowing its forces to kill the insurgents in order to repossess the mosque. Almost all of the insurgents were either killed or captured as a result.

Most recently, the insurgency in Iraq has also witnessed messianism and Mahdism at work. Muqtada al-Sadr, the rebel Shia leader, calls his army the "Mahdi Army" to resist American occupation. Driven by a religious zeal and presentiments of future glory, the warriors of the Mahdi army launch daily attacks on American interests.

In neighboring Iran, President Mahmoud Ahmadinejad is certainly inspired by a messianic philosophy rooted in the Shia tradition awaiting the imam Mahdi who went into occultation. He fervently believes, as many other Muslims do, that the Messiah is coming because the world of Islam is in a state of utter turmoil. He is also driven by the conviction that he himself must somehow prepare the way for the Messiah's or Mahdi's arrival by establishing a government in Iran that would honor him and facilitate his mission to defeat the "infidel" armies. In this mission he feels divinely inspired, and he declared at a U.N. gathering in September 2005 that he felt the presence of God around him as he prayed, "Hasten the emergency of your last repository, the Promised One, that perfect and pure human being, the one that will fill this world with justice and peace."[8] He stated his claim for feeling divine presence was "not an exaggeration" and that the audience listening to his speech was "astonished, as if a hand held them there and made them sit. It had opened their eyes and ears for the message of the Islamic Republic."[9]

Mahdism therefore continues to emerge in Muslim societies when conditions become hostile. In the current political climate, Muslims feel continually threatened by their enemies. They are fighting wars of independence; they are resisting occupation; they are challenged by poverty and general anarchy in their own lands. The expectation of the archetypal Mahdi is growing stronger by the day. Each year Muslims wait for the Mahdi to appear during the Hajj season, for based on Hadith he will be spotted around the Kaaba in Mecca. Thus far they have been disappointed, but they continue to nurture the hope that someday soon, their deliverer will appear to salvage them from their current state of anarchy and despair.

CHAPTER FIVE

Jesus: Son of God or Muslim Prophet?

Two thousand years ago, a messiah ascended to heaven alive, according to both Islam and Christianity. Both traditions wait in hopeful anticipation of his return to earth. Both assign a pivotal role to him in the shaping of apocalyptic events.

Muslims insist, though, that he never died on the cross. Someone in the likeness of Jesus was put on the cross while Jesus ascended to heaven unharmed. "They slew him not, nor crucified him, but it was made dubious to them," says Islam's holy book, the Quran (Quran, 4:157).

The circumstances around Jesus' ascension have been further described in the Quran as follows:

> Those that disagreed about him were in doubt concerning him; they knew nothing about him that was not sheer conjecture; they did not slay him for certain. God lifted him up to Him [Quran, 4:158].

Throughout its discourse, the Quran refers to the creation of seven heavens — the number seven signifying infinity. It is widely held among Muslims, according to their Hadith literature, that Jesus is alive and resides in the second highest heaven. Based on the anecdotal account of the prophet Mohammed's night journey across the heavens known as the Miraaj, Mohammed met Jesus on the second heaven, conversed with him about future occurrences and joined him in the worship of Allah. The prophet Mohammed is even credited with describing Jesus' physical characteristics, saying he was of "moderate height and was red-faced as if he had just come out of a bathroom" (Bukhari: Muhammad Muhsin Khan, Vol. 4, no. 647).

Christianity, formulating its theology on the salvation of man through the sacrifice of "the lamb," asserts the crucifixion of Jesus is historically documented fact. He died a brutal death on the cross under the most treacherous of circumstances, but was resurrected on the third day and ascended to heaven after meeting some of his disciples. He will return to earth in full glory in order to defeat the forces of evil. When he returns, he will also establish the kingdom of God and everlasting peace on earth.

While Islam is also hopeful about a similar turn of events, it claims Jesus will establish Islam as God's kingdom on earth. Curiously, Jesus is mentioned thirty-five times in the Quran, compared to the scant five times the messenger of Islam, Mohammed, is named in the scripture. The prominence that Jesus enjoys in the Quran points to the pivotal role he is prophesied to play in the shaping of the world order under the banner of Islam.

Both Christianity and Islam therefore claim Jesus as their own. Many adherents of both religions who wish to pursue a policy of appeasement believe that Jesus will unite all peoples of the earth under one belief. When Jesus returns, according to Islam, he will bring Christians and Muslims together by eliminating doctrinal differences between them. According to Hadith, he will "break the cross and kill the swine," the cross of course being a symbol of Christianity. The whole world will begin to believe in the worship of the One True God — a statement implying that the doctrine of the divinity of Jesus will come to be repudiated by Christians themselves. Those who accept Jesus' call will end up being one community of believers.

The Christian view of world unity is similar, though obviously in conformity with Christian precepts. The peoples of the world will accept Christ as their savior. Even the Jews, who rejected him as the promised messiah two thousand years ago, will one day be converted to Christianity.

Both the Bible and Hadith detail circumstances about his second coming, including his actual descent from heaven. Whereas the biblical accounts suggest a majestic descent on earth, Hadith keeps Jesus' second coming somewhat low profile. Before his advent, the Masih-ud-Dajjal or Antichrist will have already wreaked tremendous havoc on earth. He will have gained control over the earth, aided by supernatural powers, coupled with his own treachery and conniving. Oppression will be widespread all across the world because of the Dajjal's political and economic influence. The righteous will be outnumbered. Just before the return of Jesus, there will be a community of eight hundred Muslim men and four hundred Muslim women who will be preparing to wage a war to fight the widespread tyranny of the Masih-ud-Dajjal, or simply Dajjal, as he is often called. It is these twelve hundred Muslims who will receive Christ when he returns to earth a second time.

The Mahdi, Islam's redeemer, will also be present when the propitious circumstances unfold. He will be preparing to lead the community of believers into the dawn prayer known to Muslims as Fajr. At that moment, Jesus will descend on earth carried on a cloud suspended by two angels — perhaps the only similarity between the biblical and Islamic accounts.

The Hadith also include indications as to the geographic location where the descent will occur. Some accounts suggest it will be Damascus, Syria. Others indicate the descent will occur in the Al-Aqsa Mosque in Jerusalem — the mosque built on the site of the ancient Jewish Temple of Solomon. Hadith recount that Jerusalem will be under Muslim control at that time.

The community of twelve hundred believers will insist on knowing the identity of the newcomer. Jesus will then introduce himself, while asking them about their war or "Jihad" against the Dajjal. Their leader, the imam Mahdi, upon discovering the identity of Jesus, will want to forgo his position of leadership. He will request that Jesus lead the morning prayer, but Jesus will decline. The prayer will hence proceed as planned. Upon its completion, Jesus will predict victory for the forces of righteousness over the tyranny of the Dajjal. He will confront the Dajjal at the "Gate of Ludd." The Dajjal will begin to "melt" upon seeing Jesus. This will immediately put an end to war and treachery that will have plagued the nations of the world until then. An era of peace and harmony will ensue on earth after the death of the Dajjal.

Once the kingdom of God under Islam is established, Jesus will rule the world in a just and equitable manner for forty years. He will establish the law of the Quran, lead people in worship, and restore dignity to Muslims such as they once enjoyed in the pristine era of Islam (Tirmidhi: Abwab-ul-Fitan, no. 2345).

These events, including the description of Jesus and the circumstances of his return, are summarized in the following Hadith as narrated on the authority of Abu Hurrairah, one of the most prolific narrators of Hadith. He quoted the prophet Mohammed as saying:

> The prophets are like brothers. They have different mothers but their religion is one. I am the closest of all the people to Jesus son of Mary, because there is no other prophet between him and myself. He will come again, and when you see him, you will recognize him. He is of medium height and his coloring is reddish-white. He will be wearing two garments and his hair will look wet. He will break the cross, kill the pigs, abolish the Jizya [tax collected from non–Muslims] and call the people to Islam. During his time, Allah will end

every religion and sect other than Islam, and will destroy the Dajjal. Then peace and security will prevail on earth, so that lions will graze with camels, tigers with cattle, and wolves with sheep; children will be able to play with snakes without coming to any harm. Jesus will remain for forty years, then die, and the Muslims will pray for him [Ahmad: 2/406].

As an aside, the Hadith quoted above is somewhat reminiscent of Isaiah and Old Testament prophecies of the end times in their references to animals living peacefully with humans (see, for example, Isaiah 11:6–8). They give credence to the view that a significant portion of Islam's eschatological literature is derived from what is known as the "Israelite traditions" within Hadith literature.

Islam's kingdom of God will not only have wealth in abundance, but that wealth will be distributed equitably among peoples throughout the four corners of the earth. The world will also become a more spiritual place as materialism will decline in appeal. No one will care about amassing wealth. Humanity will prefer to bow to the one true God rather than indulge in luxury. Since greed will be eradicated from human societies and religion will become supreme, there will be no reason left for animosity or strife in the world.

But whereas Jesus makes a quiet, unobtrusive reentry into the Muslim realm, to his Christian faithful he arrives on earth a second time in splendor and glory. The fact that many believe the Bible contains some three hundred prophecies referring to Jesus' return is telling in how much the prophet, savior and "Son of God" is awaited among Christians. Numerous books have been written on the second coming. Many commentaries containing interpretations of scriptural prophecy comprise modern Christian apocalyptic literature. Islam, perhaps may never be able to catch up with Christian enthusiasm about the second advent of Christ.

Rescuing his true followers from an imminent tribulation, Jesus will first meet the select group in the air in what is known as the Rapture. Thus many of his followers, both dead and living at the time, will receive spiritual bodies enabling them to meet Him in the clouds. St. John described this event in the book of Revelation as follows:

> After this I looked, and, behold, a door was opened in heaven: and the first voice which I heard was as it were of a trumpet talking, with me; which said, Come up hither, and I will shew thee things which must be hereafter. And immediately I was in the spirit: and, behold, a throne was set in heaven, and one sat on the throne [Revelation 4: 1–2].

But whereas the Rapture will occur only between Jesus and his elect, his actual descent will be witnessed by all on earth as he will descend "with a shout, with the voice of the archangel, and with the trump of God" (1 Thessalonians 4–16).

To his apostles, Jesus announced the circumstances and purpose of his return just prior to his capture by the Romans when he said: "I will come again, and receive you to Myself; that where I am, there ye may be also" (John 14: 3).

Again, Acts 1:11 states: "This same Jesus, which is taken up from you into heaven, shall so come in like manner as ye have seen him go into heaven." As a commentary to this verse, Stephun Guakroger, author of the "Baker Bible Guides" series *The Book of Acts: Free to Live,* states that the resurrection of Jesus is a "major emphasis in the book of Acts." He further goes on to say that "Acts does not present arguments in order to prove the resurrection, it simply accepts it as fact. For those who had seen, touched and spoken with Jesus, the issue was beyond doubt!"[1]

1 Peter 5:4 also describes his descent on earth and how glorious an event it will be: "And when the Chief shepherd shall appear, ye shall receive a crown of glory that fadeth not away."

Matthew 24: 29–30 describes Jesus return in greater detail:

> Immediately after the tribulation of those days shall the sun be darkened, and the moon shall not give her light, and the stars shall fall from heaven, and the powers of the heavens shall be shaken: And then shall appear the sign of the Son of man in heaven: and then shall all the tribes of the earth mourn, and they shall see the Son of man coming in the clouds of heaven with power and great glory.

Daniel, often interpreted as prophetic literature, describes the descent of "One like the Son of Man" from heaven in the following words:

> I saw in the night visions, and, behold, one like the Son of man came with the clouds of heaven, and came to the Ancient of days, and they brought him near before him. And there was given him dominion, and glory, and a kingdom, that all people, nations, and languages, should serve him: his dominion is an everlasting dominion, which shall not pass away, and His kingdom that which shall not be destroyed [Daniel 7: 13–14].

Christ will be followed by a heavenly procession. He will land on the Mount of Olives, on the outskirts of Jerusalem, causing the mountain to collapse. Other geological changes will also take place upon Christ's descent on earth. Politically, Jerusalem will become the capital of Christ's earthly kingdom. The following prophecy describes some of these events in detail:

> And the seventh angel poured out his vial into the air; and there came a great voice out of the temple of heaven, from the throne, saying, It is done. And there were voices, and thunders, and lightnings; and there was a great earth-

quake, such as was not since men were upon the earth, so mighty an earthquake, and so great. And the great city was divided into three parts, and the cities of the nations fell: and great Babylon came in remembrance before God, to give unto her the cup of the wine of the fierceness of his wrath. And every island fled away, and the mountains were not found. And there fell upon men a great hail out of heaven, every stone about the weight of a talent: and men blasphemed God because of the plague of the hail; for the plague thereof was exceeding great [Revelation 16:17–20].

As seen earlier in one of the Hadith quoted above, Jerusalem will play a central role in the unfolding of apocalyptic occurrences for Muslims as well. Jerusalem will now be under Islamic rule. The recapture of Jerusalem by Muslims will provoke an attack on Medina, as the following Hadith suggests on the authority of Muadh Ibn Jabl:

The prophet said: "The building of Bait-ul-Muqqadus [Al-Aqsa, Jerusalem] will be followed by the destruction of Yathrib [Medina], which will be followed by a fierce battle, which will be followed by the conquest of Constantinople, which will be followed by the appearance of the Dajjal" [Abu Daud: Kitab al Malahim, no. 4273].

Although the Christian and Muslim narratives differ as to the circumstances surrounding Christ's reentry, they agree that his primary mission will be to establish true faith and belief. He will accomplish this by uniting people under one belief, whether it is Islam or Christianity. They also agree that Jesus' return heralds the kingdom of God where justice, equity, egalitarianism, peace and harmony will prevail. Jesus will also eradicate all social evils from human societies, such as rampant adultery, corruption and deceit. Yet it remains to be seen whose version of justice, peace and harmony will be implemented by the awaited Messiah.

Verse 55 of the Quranic chapter entitled "House of Imran" states:

And remember when Allah said: O Jesus! Lo I'm gathering thee and causing thee to ascend unto Me and am cleaning thee of those who disbelieve and am setting those who follow thee above those who disbelieve until the day of resurrection. Then unto Me ye will all return, and I shall judge between you as in that wherein ye used to differ [Quran, 3: 55].

The verse above predicts world domination for the community who believes in Christ over "those who disbelieve" in him until the Day of Judgment or end times. In its most obvious and literal reading, it validates the Christian position that it is Christianity's beliefs and value system that will become the dominant ideology of the world, for the Gospel will be preached everywhere (Matthew 24:14).

Muslims, however, look at things a little differently. Keeping in view the Quran's insistence on the continuity of divine revelation through time, Jesus and those who accepted his message two thousand years ago were Muslim, because they had "surrendered to the will of God." A Muslim, according to this generic definition, is simply one who surrenders to the will of God. As this verse lends itself to various interpretations, a controversy arises as to which community the verse may have been referring to when it spoke of the followers of Jesus.

A contemporary commentary of the Quran by renowned Islamic scholar Ahmed Ali suggests the references to disbelievers and followers in the above Quranic verse may refer to dissenting views among the Jewish people. He points out that the ascetic group called the Essenes was at odds with other Jews and may have been the intended subject of the cited reference in the Quran. His explanation, however, does not shed light on which of the communities living in the end times will have world domination. Yet, according to the following verse of the Quran, this will not be an issue because:

> There is not one among the People of the Book [Jews and Christians] who will not believe in it before his death and he [Jesus] will be a witness over them on the day of resurrection [Quran, 4: 158].

The above verse, read in conjunction with the following verse of the Quran, clears the picture for Muslims as to what is meant by "the followers of Christ":

> They make of their clerics and their monks, and of the Messiah, the son of Mary, Lords besides God, though they were ordered to serve one God only. There is no God but Him. Exalted be He above those they deify besides Him. They would extinguish the light of God with their mouths; but God seeks only to perfect His light, though the infidels abhor it. It is He who has sent forth His apostle with guidance and the True Faith, that he may exalt it above all religions, though the idolaters abhor it [Quran, 9: 31–33].

The verse above clearly indicates that Islam will become the dominant religion of the world, as it will be exalted "above all religions." As the "true faith," it upholds belief in one God alone, not the deification of Christ or any other human personality. Islam was also the religion of Jesus, Muslims insist. Those who uphold his religion are his true followers — namely, the Muslims. Those who deify Christ, on the other hand, cannot be his true followers because Christ never claimed divine sonship, according to the recognized tenets of Islam. Its followers, hence, shall gain ascendancy, as believed widely by Muslims according to this interpretation. Harun Yahya, a prolific Turkish writer, makes the following comment on this controversy in his explanation of what is meant by the verses above:

In the 55th verse of Surah [Chapter] Al Imran, we learn that Allah will place the people who follow Isa [Jesus] above those who disbelieve until the Day of Rising. It is an historical fact that, 2000 years ago, Isa's disciples had no political power. Christians who lived in that period and our own have believed a number of false doctrines, the chief of which is the doctrine of the Trinity. Therefore as is evident, that they will not be able to be referred to as followers of Isa, because it says in several places in the Quran, those who believe in the Trinity have slipped into denial. In such a case, in the time before the hour, the true followers of Isa will overcome the deniers and become the manifestation of the divine promises contained in Surah Al Imran. Surely, this blessed group will be made known when Isa returns to earth.[2]

Such assertions by Harun Yahya may not preclude the possibility that Jews and Christians, indeed all people who accept true belief, will be provided the opportunity to attain God's mercy. The verse also predicts that all peoples of the world, or at least the "People of the Book" (understood as Jews and Christians), will come to accept Islam's position that Jesus Christ did not die on the cross. They will also acknowledge that he will die a natural death at some future date. Upon Jesus' return, they will accept Islam's view that he was a mere prophet of God. In short, they will all convert to Islam (Quran, 4: 158).

Perhaps the most telling verse of the Quran about Jesus' second coming is the one stating, "He will be a sign of the hour," signifying the Day of Judgment (Quran, 43:61). According to this verse, Jesus will certainly play a pivotal role in shaping world events around the end of days, whether in physical or spiritual form.

Another verse of the Quran which makes something of an oblique reference to Jesus' second coming is the one which suggests he will be taught the "book." Since Jesus already knew the Torah, the book can only mean a reference to the Quran, according to popular commentators of prophecy. Thus he will come to earth a Muslim and will be taught the philosophy and teachings of the Quran: "He will teach him [Jesus] the Book and Wisdom, the Torah and the Gospel" (Quran, 3: 48).

The reference to the Torah and the Gospel also carries the promise of salvation for all monotheistic believers, provided, according to Muslims, their faith is purified from false dogma. According to Muslims, it must be consistent with Islam's generic concept of undiluted monotheism which they consider to be the essence of most major faith traditions.

Hadith, however, often regarded as a commentary on the Quran, elaborate circumstances around Jesus' second coming in greater detail and with much greater frequency. In prophesying the Messiah's return, the prophet of Islam is said to have uttered the following:

By Him in Whose Hands my soul is, the son of Mary will shortly descend amongst you people [Muslims] as a just ruler and will break the cross and kill the swine and abolish the Jizya [tax collected from non–Muslims]. Then there will be abundance of money and nobody will accept charitable gifts [Bukhari: Muhammad Muhsin Khan, Vol. 4, no. 657].

Muslims often wonder why the prophet Mohammed prophesied that the Jizya will be removed. Happily they conclude that Islam's supremacy will have been established everywhere and there will be no non–Muslims left to take the Jizya from. Many non–Muslims have commented on the concept of *Dhimmitude* in Islam. This tax, called the Jizya, was obligatory on non–Muslims residing in a Muslim majority state, as they were not under obligation to fight Jihad. The tax would be imposed in lieu of the duty to undertake Jihad. Since, according to the above, there will be no non–Muslims left, there would be no reason to impose Jizya.

In another authentic compilation of Hadith known to Muslims, the prophet Mohammed is again reported to have said:

How happy will you be when the Son of Mary will come down among you and your imam will be from amongst you [Muslim: 1 / 290].

Further analysis about the significance of Jesus' second coming for Islam and Muslims is warranted here. It is widely believed among Muslims that Jesus will not introduce a new faith but will merely restore Islam to its pristine form and establish it all across the world. He will neither add anything to its beliefs, nor subtract anything from its original message. However, since Muslims regard Islam as the perfected faith, the culmination of all previous divine messages, Jesus will come to free it from any foreign doctrines. By so doing he will establish correct belief among all nations of the world.

For Muslims, he will also return as judge between people, although not in the Christian sense of commanding the right to dispense divine judgment between good and evil. Divine judgment, Muslims say, is reserved for Allah the Almighty alone. Jesus will only judge as a fair ruler over the worldly affairs and temporal laws of human beings.

On the political scene, Jesus will engage in battle as well. Muslims share the belief with Christians that he will also kill the Antichrist, known to Islam as the Masih-ud-Dajjal, in a bloody confrontation.

The Judeo-Christian view is similar to the above conclusions in some aspects and different in others. The prophet Isaiah declared that a Messiah will "gather all nations" (Isaiah 66:11). It would be safe to conclude that the Hebrew prophet meant that the Messiah will gather them under one belief, one government and one law.

Matthew sheds some further light on the role of the Messiah, now believed to be Jesus, upon his return:

> When the Son of Man shall come in his glory, and all the holy angels with him, then shall he sit upon the throne of glory: And before him shall be gathered all nations: and he shall separate them one from another, as a shepherd divideth his sheep from the goats: And he shall set the sheep on his right hand, but the goats on the left.... And [the unworthy] shall go away into everlasting punishment: but the righteous into life eternal [Matthew 25:31–33, 46].

Matthew of course is alluding to a heavenly judgment between good and evil. The earth according to Matthew will be purged of its evildoers, who will be doomed to eternal damnation. Clearly Jesus' role is much more amplified in Christianity, for he will mete out not only temporal, but also heavenly judgment with regard to sin and retribution. He will also engage in battle to remove all traces of evil from the earth — a daunting task, as the abomination and desolation, as well as the tribulation, will precede his second coming.

The Islamic and biblical accounts also differ as to the length of Jesus' reign on earth. According to Hadith he will tarry only forty years, will get married and then die a natural death. According to the Bible, on the other hand, as indicated in Revelation 19, he will rule for an entire millennium, ushering in a thousand years of peace on earth.

Alas, the peaceful era of the millennium will come about only after the final battle between good and evil, popularly known as Armageddon, is fought. Peace will be achieved after the bloodiest house-to-house war in the cities of the world, including Jerusalem. As described below, the forces of evil will be wiped out completely:

> And I saw an angel standing in the sun; and he cried with a loud voice, saying to all the fowls that fly in the midst of heaven, Come and gather yourselves together unto the supper of the great God; That ye may eat the flesh of kings, and the flesh of captains, and the flesh of mighty men, and the flesh of horses, and of them that sit on them, and the flesh of all men, both free and bond, both small and great. And I saw the beast, and the kings of the earth, and their armies, gathered together to make war against him that sat on the horse, and against his army. And the beast was taken, and with him the false prophet that wrought miracles before him, with which he deceived them that had received the mark of the beast, and them that worshipped his image. These both were cast alive into a lake of fire burning with brimstone. And the remnant were slain with the sword of him that sat upon the horse, which sword proceeded out of his mouth: and all the fowls were filled with their flesh [Revelation 19:17–21].

Thus the annihilation in terms of human cost will be massive, almost wiping out the human population. A similar scenario spelling disaster of global proportions appears in Hadith when they describe the tribulations, the battles and the conflicts around the end of days.

On the authority of Abu Huraira, Mohammed is again reported to have said:

> Time will pass rapidly, good deeds will decrease, miserliness will be thrown [in the hearts of the people], afflictions will appear and there will be much al-Harj." They said, "O Allah's Apostle! What is al-Harj?" He said, "Killing! Killing" [Bukhari: Muhammad Muhsin Khan, Vol. 9, no. 183].

The actual unfolding of the battle of Armageddon will be a little different when Jesus leads Muslims through it. One description comes from Ibn Kathir in the following words based on Hadith:

> Abduallah Ibn Amr said, "The prophet said, 'The Dajjal will appear in my Ummah [community] and will remain for forty —' I cannot say whether he meant forty days, forty months, or forty years —'Then Allah will send Jesus son of Mary, who will resemble Urwah Ibn Masud [a companion of the prophet]. He will chase the Dajjal and kill him. Then the people will live for seven years, during which there will be no enmity between two persons. Then Allah will send a cold wind from the direction of Syria, which will take the soul of everyone who has the slightest speck of good or faith in his heart. Even if one of you were to enter the heart of the mountain, the wind would reach him there and take his soul. Only the most wicked people will be left, they will be as careless as birds, with the characteristics of beasts and will have no concern for right and wrong. Satan will come to them in the form of man and will say, "Don't you respond?" They will say, "What do you order us to do?" He would order them to worship idols, and in spite of that they will have sustenance in abundance, and lead comfortable lives. Then the trumpet will be blown, and everyone will tilt their heads to hear it. The first one to hear it will be a man busy repairing a trough for his camels, he and everyone else will be struck down. Then Allah will send [or send down] rain like dew, and the bodies of the people [the dead] will grow out of it. Then the trumpet will be sounded again, and the people will get up and look around. Then it will be said, "O people, go to your Lord and account for yourselves." It will be said, "Bring out the people of Hell," and it will be asked "How many are there?" The answer will come: "Nine hundred and ninety-nine out of every thousand." On that day a child will grow old and the shin will be laid bare'" [Muslim: 41 / 7023].

Jesus will be able to kill the Dajjal with divine aid. The miscreant will simply melt upon seeing Jesus. Although much destruction will have preceded the final conflict between the Christ and the Antichrist, the ultimate battle will be a symbolic triumph of good over evil with no actual combat between the two.

Another Hadith describes events that will precede and follow the final triumph in greater depth:

Ibn Masud reported that the prophet said, "On the night of the Isra [the prophet Mohammed's journey through the heavens], I met my father Abraham, Moses and Jesus, and they discussed the Hour. The matter was first referred to Abraham, then to Moses and both said, I have no knowledge of it. Then it was referred to Jesus who said no one knows about it except Allah. What my Lord told me was that the Dajjal will appear, and when he sees me he will begin to melt like lead. Allah will destroy him when he sees me. The Muslims will fight the kafirs [infidels] and even the trees and rocks will say, 'O Muslim there is a kafir hiding beneath me, come and kill him.' Allah will destroy the kafirs, and the people will return to their own lands. Then Gog and Magog will appear from all directions, eating and drinking everything they find. The people will complain to me so I will pray to Allah and He will destroy them, so that the earth will be filled with their stench. Allah will send rain which will wash their bodies into the sea. My Lord has told me that when that happens, the Hour will be very close, like a pregnant woman whose time is due, but her family do not know exactly when she will deliver" [Ibn Majah:1/375].

While there are remarkable similarities in both accounts as to how Armageddon will unfold, it is obvious that Christians and Muslims remain divided over whose behalf Jesus will be fighting. The above references from Hadith indicate there will be a clear distinction between Muslims and non–Muslims, described above as *kafirs* or those who reject true belief. With Jesus on their side, aided by divine intervention, the Muslims will be victorious and Jesus will reign among them for forty years. Peace will prevail, but things will slowly begin to deteriorate again. The deadly Gog and Magog will be unleashed from their confinement, wreaking havoc on human societies. Whereas the Christian kingdom of God will be an everlasting one, Islam's encounter with peace will be far more ephemeral, suggesting the final retribution will be in another realm. Paradise will not be of this earth but elsewhere, according to Islam. These differences may surface because of the differing status awarded to Jesus in Christianity and Islam. Only a divine son of God could rule the earth eternally, whereas a prophet, being a mere mortal and subject to all the vicissitudes of human existence, will return to earth for only forty more years.

The Hadith ust quoted, read in conjunction with other Hadith quoted previously, suggest that the Muslims will experience something akin to the rapture. They will be saved from the final tribulation that will unfold just before the unleashing of the Gog and Magog. A wind from Syria will bring gentle death to the Muslims and "the Hour" will fall only on the most wicked people on earth.

With Jesus' rule firmly established, true religion will unite the peoples of the earth. As mentioned earlier, Christians claim the world will become one under Christianity, and Muslims firmly believe the entire world will convert to Islam. Those who rejected Islam will have already perished during the final battles between Muslims and *kafirs*. Christianity, too, will have triumphed over non–Christian forces.

In spite of the opposing viewpoints over whose ideology will prevail, one sees a curious concordance of meanings upon examining the etymology of the word "Gospel" and the Quranic word "Basharah."

Matthew 24:14 states that the "gospel of the kingdom shall be preached in all the world for a witness unto all nations." This will occur after Christ defeats the forces of evil. According to Douglas Harper's *Online Etymology Dictionary*, the word "Gospel" or "Godspel" is an old Anglo-Saxon word meaning "good message" or "good news."[3] According to introductory material in an edition of the Bible known as Today's English Version, the Gospel is the "good news that Jesus is the promised Savior, the one through whom God fulfilled the promises he made to his people in the Old Testament. This good news is not only for the Jewish people, among whom Jesus was born and lived, but for the whole world."[4] Thus as a universal deliverer of mankind, Jesus in his second advent will bring peace and security to all nations of the world. The Christian Gospel is also the·"good news" for the salvation of man, premised on the belief in Christ as lord and savior.

The Arabic word "Basharah," occurring numerous times in the Quran, also means "good news" for believers. The prophet of Islam is referred to in the Quran as *Mubashir un wa Nazira*, or the bearer of glad tidings and a warner. Also, ten from among the chosen companions of the prophet of Islam, who during their lifetime had been given the "good news" of attaining salvation, are referred to by Muslims as the *Ashara Mubasharah*. They are the "ten given the good news," derived from the root word Basharah.

According to Quranic belief, both the Gospel, known as *Injeel*, and the Basharah of the Quran refer to God's divine revelations and the promise of salvation that they carry. For more liberal segments within religious communities, the concordance in meanings points to a basic underlying unity in the messages and tenets of all faiths.

Thus the question still remains: whose version of the kingdom of God will be established on earth?

Although Christians and Muslims both assert Jesus will be fighting the final war on their behalf, universalists among religious people may resolve the polemics on either side by suggesting the final conflict will be a war between the general forces of good and evil, transcending religious barriers. Clear-cut demarcations along religious lines perhaps belie the true purport of the final conflict, according to the forces of liberalism. Whether Jesus is Son of God or Muslim prophet, his second coming will end strife, treachery and discord on earth, replacing it with tolerance, humanity and love. This alone, for many, is comforting enough.

CHAPTER SIX

Christian Fundamentalism: Then and Now

According to a popular dictionary definition, fundamentalism is a "religious movement or point of view characterized by a return to fundamental principles, by rigid adherence to those principles and often by intolerance of other views and opposition to secularism."[1]

It is in the nature of things that fundamentalism will reassert itself with greater vigor when opposed by forces both external and internal, as did Christianity in the late 19th and early 20th century. A need was felt within American Protestant Christianity to redefine the basic tenets of the faith in order to preserve them from the onslaughts of Darwinism, scholarly criticism of the Bible, and the secularism and liberalism espoused by some Protestant churches (which went so far as to doubt the immaculate conception of Jesus).

Mormonism and "Romanism" were also ideologies that had to be countered through a fundamentalist definition of the core doctrines of Protestant Christianity. The Mormons had evolved into a sect quite distinct from mainstream Christianity, with their polygamous lifestyle and a separate religious text called the Book of Mormon. "Romanism" was used by Protestants to denote Roman Catholicism as a heresy in Christianity.

The core beliefs of Christianity, centered on the inerrancy of the Bible, the immaculate conception, vicarious atonement, the resurrection of Jesus and the authenticity of his miracles, came to be clearly outlined and defended with tenacity in response to the aforementioned forces. At the Niagara Bible Conference (1878–1879) organized by conservative evangelical Protestants, these five essential "fundamentals" were enumerated (laying the groundwork for the later development of the word fundamentalism). Expounding on these were series of twelve volumes of essays and articles entitled *the Fundamentals: A Testimony to the Truth*." Between the years 1910 and 1915 Christian Fundamentalism therefore came to be defined as "strict adherence to Christian doctrines based on a literal interpretation of the Bible"[2]

While fundamentalism can be linked primarily to Protestant Christianity as the originator of the ideological base of the movement, it has emerged as a revivalist movement throughout the religious landscape of the world. Catholicism, arguably, has not deviated much from the "fundamental" tenets of Christian belief, as the task of interpreting and applying religious dogma has remained more or less centralized in the Vatican. And although voices of dissent within Catholicism have challenged traditional interpretations, asking for the right to abortion, the legalization of divorce and the ordination of women priests, Catholicism has by and large retained its historical character. Since the Reformation involved a break from Catholicism and the authority of the Pope initially, Protestantism branched off into many different denominations, bringing scripture within the reach of the laity, hence subjecting it to several different interpretations and understandings. Perhaps this is why a greater need was felt within Protestantism, rather than within Catholicism, to reclaim the fundamentals of the faith.

Nonetheless, fundamentalism among Catholics was also seen in the 2003 opening of Ave Maria University in Florida. The project of billionaire Tom Monaghan, the university is building a permanent campus about a hundred miles north of Miami. The campus is intended to be the center of an entirely new town, also named Ave Maria, expected to occupy some 5,000 acres and support a population of about 30,000. Monaghan, the founder of Domino's Pizza (and now nicknamed the "Pizza Pope"), believes he is carrying out God's will on earth, finding support from very close quarters to seats of power such as Florida governor Jeb Bush, who converted to Catholicism and was present at the February 2006 groundbreaking ceremony of the new campus. Jeb Bush stated that Ave Maria (Hail Mary), the new town, would be a place where the melding of faith and practice will take place freely. Whether this will indeed happen remains to be seen. At a Catholic conference, Monaghan states that pharmacies in Ave Maria would not be allowed to sell contraceptives and that cable TV stations would not be allowed to show pornography. Monoghan later said he misspoke, but the American Civil Liberties Union is concerned and has promised to keep an eye on the town.[3]

But it is not only within the major divisions of Christianity that one witnesses a reversion to fundamental beliefs. There seems to be a worldwide movement back to the essential beliefs and religious identities across the world. In practically all religions, a segment of adherents shows a proclivity towards reinstating the core beliefs of the faith as lived doctrines. Fundamentalists also believe in interpreting religious doctrines in the most literal sense, because they do not believe in subjecting them to interpretation at all, or acknowledging hermeneutics, which take into consideration the social, political or economic context of revelation. The doctrines are to be accepted *prima facie*.

Many among Hindus, Buddhists and Jews have reverted to interpreting their various scriptures literally, and sometimes militantly. While the Hindu Mahasaba movement of the early twentieth century had declared India sacred ground and Hindu blood sacred, Theravada Buddhism, historically supporting a peaceful ideology, has also recently shown pockets of violence in countries like Thailand, Burma, Cambodia and Sri Lanka. Militant extremist Jews also resort to violence to further their agenda in Palestinian territories. But with the exception of Islam and Christianity, the fundamentalist movements of other faiths do not envision worldwide conversion or demonstrate ambition to transcend national boundaries, although Buddhism has on occasion been classified as a missionary faith. Hinduism is largely confined to India, and militant Judaism confines its goals to the restoration of ancient Israelite lands to contemporary Jews, which involves the unearthing of biblical claims mainly on the territories of ancient Judea and Samaria. Islam and Christianity are the only two faiths with an ideology that seeks to establish its set of beliefs all over the world. The philosophies of both religions envisage a world order under the benign rule of the coming messiah, who will establish peace and justice in the world. They therefore proselytize to other faiths. Militancy, too, is an option that is available to both the Christian and Islamic missions. In fact, the militant strain of both faiths believes that justice will come about only as a result of large-scale warfare and destruction. Both faiths predict global wars as the cataclysmic events that will usher in a new era. However, it is Protestant Christian fundamentalism alone that concerns us in this chapter.

The fundamentalist movement did not start with a militaristic world view. Its main focus was the preservation of what were perceived as the pristine tenets of the faith for wayward Christian souls. After the initial brainstorming of the basic tenets of the Christian faith in the Niagara Falls Bible Conference of 1878–79 and the General Assembly of the Presbyterian Church, the fundamentalists proceeded to write extensively in support of their rediscovered doctrines in various articles and journals in the early twentieth century.

Their discourses on reestablishing their faith also rested on their deprecations of the industrial revolution, which, they said, had bred greed, leading to what they deemed an erosion of moral values. Darwin's theory of evolution was considered the main culprit in causing the moral and spiritual downfall of nations. Futher, the Evangelicals feared that the then-popular Social Gospel would come to supplant the Gospel of Christ as a source of moral rectitude, although the message propagated in the Social Gospel was similar to Jesus' teachings contained in the canonical Gospels. This in itself was anathema to the religious right, as the left absorbed within its philosophy the willingness to secularize Christianity, reconcile Darwinism with religion, and advance the cause of social reform. Protestantism faced a challenge from within through the Social Gospel movement. The influx of new immigrants with their own unique and sometimes heretical understanding of Christian precepts also required a response from the defenders of the true faith.

Liberalism in religious theology, which had sought to reconcile Darwin with scripture, was increasingly seen as a threat to the core beliefs of the faith. Henry Ward Beecher, as the chief exponent of the new theology, chose to give the concepts of heaven and hell a metaphorical rather than literal reading. He also acknowledged the right of people to disagree in their understanding of religious precepts. Deviation would not be regarded as heresy. His loose interpretations afforded him the opportunity to publish a work entitled *Evolution and Religion*, where he attempted to explain the commonalties between the two points of view. His ideas were widely embraced by the general public.

Against these social tides and conflicting ideologies, orthodox Christianity asserted itself once more as a viable, living force. Dwight L. Moody is perhaps regarded as the main architect of this school of thought as he reasserted the inerrancy of the Bible and established a link between prophecy and the advent of Christ centered around the notion of premillennialism. Although he maintained a cordial relationship with the liberals, he began to expound his philosophy, which became the cornerstone of fundamentalist thought. His approach in dealing with heretics was to follow the example of Christ, as stated in his own words:

> Christ's teaching was always constructive.... His method of dealing with error was largely to ignore it, letting it melt away in the warm glow of the full intensity of truth expressed in love.... Let us hold truth but by all means let us hold it in love, and not with a theological club.[4]

The fundamentalists were strongly influenced by the prophetic content of the Bible, which led to the organizing of several conferences to study prophecy. These are known as the Niagara Bible conferences and the International Prophecy conferences. Their assiduous study yielded what came to be known as "premillennialism" and "dispensationalism." These intellectual movements came to be associated with fundamentalist Christianity as they were accepted, to varying degrees, within the churches.

One of the leading exponents of this movement was William Bell Riley, the Baptist founder of the World Christian Fundamentals Association in 1919, along with James M. Gray. The early part of the century also included the rise of the Pentecostal movements, with the Pentecostal Holiness churches, the Church of God and the Church of God in Christ. They were supported in their efforts by organizations such as the Bible League of North America, the Bible Crusaders of America, Anti-Evolution, Defenders of Christian Faith and the Flying Fundamentalists.

Postmillennialism relies on the verse "And these shall go away into everlasting punishment: but the righteous into life eternal" (Matthew 25:46) and therefore optimistically focuses on the defeat of evil. In contrast, premillennialism rests on the belief that the Antichrist has corrupted the world already with the rampant spread of moral anarchy and licentiousness. Interpreting Bible prophecy literally, the premillennialists believe Jesus will return on earth before the inauguration of the peaceful millennium to eradicate the corruption caused by the Antichrist. In contrast to millennialism, which sees the kingdom of God as a spiritual rather than an actual physical one, premillennialists argue that all the prophecies contained in the Book of Revelation, Daniel, Ezekiel and Jeremiah, to mention only a few, will come to pass exactly as predicted.

Dispensationalism elaborates the view that God will establish seven covenants with his people. These will be expressed as various polities, empires and economies in the different stages of human history. Six have already come to pass. The seventh dispensation, too, is coming to a close, which will mark the arrival of the kingdom of God on earth. The founder of this particular school of thought was the Englishman John Nelson Darby, leading spokesperson of the Plymouth Brethren movement, which flourished during the first half of the 1800s. His main thrust was the eschatology of the Bible, focusing mainly on the second coming of Christ. His views were widely embraced in America and became the topic of discussion at various religious institutes such as the Moody Bible Institute and the Philadelphia Biblical University.

The fundamentalists published voluminous expositions in the form of ninety-four essays which refuted scholarly criticism of the Bible. These essays, written by 64 American and British Protestant evangelists, expounded the basic tenets of Christianity in the essays as follows: Foremost, the inerrancy of the Bible was upheld. The German higher criticism of the Bible pointing out inconsistencies in the text was discounted based on the rationale that the Bible itself was perfect, but that copying errors were responsible for the apparent contradictions in the text. The scripture had to be perfect because it was divinely inspired. There were hence several attempts made to reconcile the conflicts and inconsistencies in the text.

Belief in the virgin birth of Christ was again revived in order to reestablish the divinity of Jesus, which was now being vigorously challenged. Christ had to be accepted as the savior through whom all would attain salvation. "I am the light of the world" (John 8:12) was to be understood literally along with all other tenets of the faith. Related to this was the belief in vicarious atonement of sins, for Christ had died on the cross for the sins of humanity. The least his followers could do was to acknowledge his sacrifice.

Since Evangelicals asserted Christ's divinity, they firmly believed in his many miracles, which were "authenticated" once again by them. They maintained that the powers to perform those miracles were inherent in Christ, for he was divine.

Christ would return and establish a millennial kingdom. It was crucial to believe in this, especially to counter the rising tide of secularism, or the secularizing of Christianity as evidenced in the Social Gospel movements.

These details add up to a clear picture of the salient features of early Christian fundamentalism as a reactionary force against the general tide of liberalism and reformist ideologies. The early fundamentalist Christians were literalists. However, they upheld the sanctity of the American state and insisted on the separation of church and state, something that would distinguish Christian fundamentalism from Islamic fundamentalism, which recognizes no dichotomy between religion and state. Nevertheless, as political activists, they were instrumental in banning Darwinism from being taught in schools in the Southern states. At that level the activism was led by groups such as the Bible League of North America and Anti-Evolution. One of their most publicized victories was the "Scopes Trial" held in Tennessee in 1925. The fundamentalists sued John Scopes, a high school science teacher, for contradicting the state's Butler Act, which expressly prohibited the teaching of any "theory that denies the story of the Divine Creation of man as taught in the Bible." He was accused of teaching the students that man had evolved from a lower species.

Apart from reclaiming their theological base as demonstrated in the above trial, the fundamentalists preached a philosophy primarily of self-effacement and reclaiming their spiritual past which had dissipated. George

Marsden sums up the characteristics of American Christian fundamentalism:

> American Protestant Fundamentalists are not only more or less traditional Protestants, they are also Americans. So they are committed to important dimensions of the modern eighteenth- and nineteenth-century American outlook, including professedly high regard for the scientific method and modern nationalism, and for separation of church and state. Although some of their theocratic rhetoric may be at odds with these traditions, their philosophy is nonetheless enough a product of the American heritage to be a long way from most other militant religious traditionalists.[5]

After the initial ambitious crusades to reclaim their faith from liberal forces, American Christian fundamentalism dwindled for the period between the two world wars, although work continued in various Baptist and Presbyterian churches such as the Orthodox Presbyterian Church and Regular Baptist Churches. This was partly due to the fact that other Orthodox Christians who did not consider themselves fundamentalists also began to repel the onslaughts of liberalism through their writings such as those of Karl Barth. However, the forces of moral anarchy and change reasserted themselves after the close of World War Two, again providing reason for the fundamentalists to counter them. This time the problems confronting them were the increase in the crime rate in the burgeoning metropolises and the erosion of family values. Pornography had also become widespread. The 1960s spawned the sexual revolution. Bikinis, "free love" and Bohemianism expressed as the hippie culture became the order of the day.

Once society had become so morally degenerate from the Christian fundamentalist standpoint, new initiatives has to be launched to stem the disturbing tide. New fundamentalist organizations therefore sprang up. These included the New Christian Right, Christian Voice, and the Moral Majority. In a 1970 Gallup poll 75 percent of Americans interviewed said religion had become irrelevant in their lives. But with the efforts of the religious right, 87 percent of Americans would indicate that religion was indeed important in their lives exactly a decade later. This was made possible partly through the efforts of extremely high profile evangelists such as Jerry Falwell and Pat Robertson.

By that time the fundamentalists, too, had divided into two camps. Some discarded the usage of the term, concluding it had assumed negative connotations, and began to use the term "Evangelicals" instead. The very name indicated that the Evangelicals sought to gain acceptance by converting large masses of people to their cause, both Christians and non–Christians. The Evangelicals were trans-denominational, with membership including Episcopalians, Presbyterians, Baptists and Methodists.

These newest fundamentalist movements have now become powerful political forces as interest groups affecting political, moral and social change. Sharing characteristics with the old Christian Right, the contemporary Christian Right movements also show abhorrence for liberalism. They uphold the distinction between church and state although they do not advocate Christian apathy towards politics as a means for social change. Again they are literalist in their interpretations of the Bible, contending that the scripture must not be subjected to any interpretation by liberal religious scholars. It is perfect because it is revealed. Some of the leading figures in this movement are Jerry Falwell, Pat Robertson, Billy and Franklin Graham, Tim LaHaye, and Hal Lindsey, with their common ideological enemy identified as secular humanism, and most recently radical Islam.

The new fundamentalists were driven by the same religious zeal that inspired their predecessors to "oppose Satan," to continue the work of the Lord, and to fight against anyone who was now deemed the enemy of God or Christianity. They therefore faced challenges that their predecessors had not faced. There was the enemy from within, which attacked the very foundations of Christianity, in the form of liberalism. The enemy from without was communism and its professed atheism. The latest enemy would manifest itself as Islamic militancy, belief and practice. Socially, homosexuality and its gradual acceptance into American society also posed new threats and challenges, and promiscuity was now more widespread than before. It too had to be opposed.

As mentioned earlier, Jerry Falwell was foremost in representing the New Christian Right. As a devout Baptist, he sensed an erosion of moral values from the very fiber of American society. Falwell died in 2007, but his campaign continues, run from the Liberty Baptist Church and the Liberty Baptist University in Lynchburg, Virginia, established in 1971. The university is open to all Evangelical hopefuls, but it also has a diverse secular curriculum. According to its mission statement, the university

> continues the philosophy of education which first gave rise to the university, summarized in the following propositions.
>
> God, the infinite source of all things, has shown us truth through Scripture, nature, history, and, above all, in Christ.
>
> Persons are spiritual, rational, moral, social and physical, created in the image of God. They are, therefore, able to know and to value themselves and other persons, the universe and God.
>
> Education as the process of teaching and learning involves the whole person, developing the knowledge, values and skills that enable the individual to change freely. Thus it occurs most effectively when both instructor and student are properly related to God and each other through Christ.[6]

Again as the main focus of its objectives, the university states that it will strive to "develop Christ-centered men and women with the values, knowledge, and skills essential to impact tomorrow's world." One of its stated aims is to "encourage a commitment to the Christian life, one of active communication of the Christian faith, personal integrity, and social responsibility, which, as it is lived out, points people to Jesus Christ as the Lord of the universe and their own personal Savior."[7] As part of the messianic outlook, Falwell's institution is governed by Christ's instruction in Matthew 28: 19–20, that the Gospel must be preached throughout the world. Characterized more appropriately as "open fundamentalists," Jerry Falwell's followers are also known as creationists, dispensationalists, and inerrantists.

The Christian Right has since become politically very active. According to a recent article entitled "Jerry Falwell in the 21st century" published on the website RenewAmerica.us, writer Adam Graham states that Jerry Falwell was instrumental in having Ronald Reagan elected in 1980. Falwell also started the Moral Majority, a movement that would rally Christians to exercise their right to vote in order to play an active part in the political decision-making process. The Christian Right therefore, has been successful in mobilizing Christian vote as evidenced by electing Republicans such as Reagan, George Bush, and George W. Bush.

In addition to the above, Jerry Falwell's organization publishes a monthly newspaper called *The National Liberty Journal* which demonstrates an avowedly political agenda against civil rights for homosexuals, discourses on the extent of religious freedom a society must allow, and discusses other current political issues. The paper also includes articles on Bible prophecy centered around the second coming of Christ, consistent with the fundamentalist Christian predilection towards millenarian scenarios.

The focus of the Christian fundamentalists has recently widened to include international issues. The stance has now changed from merely gathering the Christian flock to propagating the faith so as to provide an opportunity for non–Christians "to attain salvation." If Christ is to be the Lord of the world and if the Gospel, as the scriptures say, is to be preached in all four corners of the world, then Christians must lead this movement to its rightful conclusion in the realization of the eschatological goal. And consistent with biblical eschatology, Falwell's organization has a strong pro–Israel outlook, now often referred to as Christian Zionism. Because of his pro–Israel stance, Falwell was known to have made demeaning comments against the religion of Islam, stating, "I think Mohammed was a terrorist.... I read enough by both Muslim and ... non–Muslims [to decide] that he was a violent man, a man of war."[8] Jerry

Falwell's remarks sparked riots in the Muslim world. He later apologized for these remarks.

Christian fundamentalists have taken the Bible to the grassroots through televangelism. The pioneer in this field is the legendary evangelist Billy Graham. Preaching through the television sets, he has brought Bible study right to the homes of millions of followers both within and outside of the United States. He also heads the Billy Graham Evangelistic Association. While early Evangelism was geared towards reclaiming the American public from the perils of disbelief, the Evangelistic Association decided to extend its missionary work among non–Christians. It therefore met in Amsterdam in 1983, 1986 and 2000 to discuss strategies to bring the message of the Gospels to non–Christians. Christian missionaries from Third World countries were invited to attend these conferences so they would return home and preach the Gospel in their home countries to the grassroots. Billy Graham's mission received a wide audience; the 1996 Broadcast of the Global World Mission was viewed by an estimated 2.5 billion people around the globe.

. Franklin Graham, Billy Graham's son, has inherited his father's gift of propagating the Gospels to the masses. He runs an organization called Samaritan's Purse which distributes charities to the poorest of the poor of the world. His recent Christmas shoebox campaigns have invited some censure, for among the gifts it provides for poor children worldwide it has included Bibles. Many who objected stated this was a form of exploiting the poverty of Africa and Asia by offering their citizens bribes as an enticement to receive the Christian message.

Samaritan's Purse has also been busy in Iraq. Along with providing social services to the war-torn country, Samaritan's Purse has distributed Bibles that have been translated into Arabic. Its shoebox campaign extends to the impoverished masses in Romania, Ukraine and Mozambique. Recently, it extended a helping hand in Pakistan, where an earthquake rendered over three million people homeless and disabled in the country's northern regions. Tim Holmes, heading the Samaritan's Purse team from the UK, provided the affected population with tents, blankets, soaps, heaters and sleeping bags. The team provided the same material help to six schools in the region. Although their work in Pakistan was driven only by altruistic reasons, Samaritan's Purse has come under fire for proselytizing there as well.

Both Billy and Franklin Graham have written extensively on theological issues and propagate their views to the Christian and non–Christian world through their writings as well. Some well-known titles include *The Name, Rebel with a Cause, Angels* and *What the Bible is All About,* which have been translated into thirty-eight different languages of the world.

Pat Robertson has become one of the most controversial leaders of the Christian ultra-right because of his recent statements against Islam and its adherents, particularly after the attacks of September 11, 2001. He founded the Christian Coalition and chaired it until recently. Its mission, he says, is "to mobilize Christians — one precinct at a time ... — until once again we are the head and not the tail, and the top rather than the bottom of our political system." He further states that "the Christian Coalition will be the most powerful political force in America.... We have enough votes to run this country ... and when the people say we've had enough, we're going to take over."[9]

Pat Robertson obviously considers political activism imperative to further his agenda. His vision of America will exclude people who are neither Christian or Jewish:

> When I said during my Presidential bid that I would only bring Christians and Jews into the government, I hit a firestorm. What do you mean? The media challenged me. You're not going to bring atheists into the government? How dare you maintain that those who believe in the Judeo-Christian values are better qualified to govern Americans than Hindus and Muslims? My simple answer is, Yes, they are.[10]

According to some of the rhetoric quoted above, Pat Robertson seems to be forgetting the distinction between church and state characteristic of Christian fundamentalism. What he proposes is a virtual theocracy run only by Jews and Christians, thus going counter to many of the values the United States of America embodies in its constitution. It is also common knowledge that Pat Robertson and the Christian Coalition keep close ties with the Republican party, supporting them through funds and letters of appreciation.

Pat Robertson's television show *The 700 Club*, sponsored by the Christian Broadcasting Network, is also inspired by a strongly apocalyptic agenda. In a 2005 article published on CBN.com, Chris Mitchell, CBN's Middle East bureau chief, writes: "This Christmas season it's exciting to realize that the scene of the second coming is just a few miles away from the scene of the first. The Mount of Olives where Jesus will one day come back to is just down the road from Bethlehem where Luke tells us he was born in a manger."[11]

Pat Robertson again drew fire from the media when, basing his comments on biblical references to Israel, he said that the stroke that disabled Israeli prime minister Ariel Sharon in January 2006 was Sharon's punishment from God for "dividing God's land" by pulling Israel out of Gaza. On *The 700 Club*, he proclaimed, "Woe unto any prime minister of Israel who takes a similar course to appease the [European Union], the United Nations or the United States of America." Says a CNN.com article of January 6, 2006, Daniel Ayalon, Israel's ambassador to the United States, compared Robertson's remarks to the overheated rhetoric of Iranian President Mahmoud Ahmadinejad."[12] Ahmadinejad's opposite but equally fanatical millenarian view calls for the destruction of Israel based on his interpretation of Islamic scripture and prophecy.

Controversy appears to follow Pat Robertson wherever he goes with his pronouncements. In 2005 he called for the assassination of Venezuelan president Hugo Chavez because "he has destroyed the Venezuelan economy, and he's going to make that a launching pad for communist infiltration and Muslim extremism all over the continent."[13]

Needless to say, Pat Robertson has assumed a militaristic stance which does not preclude violence to achieve its stated agenda. His program is watched by about a million viewers and is broadcast through an ABC family cable network. The funds for the network are donated by the Christian Broadcasting Network donors. Not only does Robertson draw criticism through his statements, he was also accused of using tax-exempt cargo planes from one of his charities to provide services to his diamond mining operation in Zaire.[14]

Bob Jones III, grandson of the founder of Bob Jones University, perhaps presents a comparatively tolerant face of ultra-right Christian fundamentalism compared to his colleague Pat Robertson. Initially a "whites only" college, Bob Jones University now admits students of all races and boasts 70,000 alumni and five thousand students from all over the United States and thirty different countries. The university offers a wide secular curriculum in addition to an emphasis on Bible study. Part of its mission statement reads:

> Bob Jones University seeks to maintain high academic standards, an emphasis on culture, and a practical Christian philosophy that is both orthodox and fervent in its evangelistic spirit. Relying upon the strength of God, Bob Jones university continuously strives to be the best school it can be, to the honor and glory of Christ.

The creed of the university also embodies the five fundamentals as enunciated by the early fundamentalists:

> I believe in the inspiration of the Bible (both the Old and the New Testaments); the creation of man by the direct act of God; the incarnation and virgin birth of our Lord and Savior, Jesus Christ; His identification as the son of God; His vicarious atonement for the sins of mankind by the shedding of His blood on the cross; the resurrection of his body from the tomb; His power to

save men from sin; the new birth through the regeneration by the Holy Spirit, and the gift of eternal life by the grace of God.[15]

Bob Jones III clearly views his mission as pacifist in nature as opposed to Pat Robertson's rather militaristic outlook, and he prefers to disassociate his work with the term fundamentalism. However, he leads an unrelenting campaign against abortion, homosexual unions, euthanasia, embryonic stem cell research and security for homosexuals against hate crimes. Bob Jones University, which, as mentioned earlier, initially started out as a "whites only" college, has not been able to shed its image as a racist institute. Bob Jones University has in the past implemented a ban on interracial dating. The justification provided for such an overt act of racism was the following rationale:

> We stand against the one-world government, against the coming world of anti–Christ, which is a one world system of blending, of all differences, of blending of national differences, economic differences, church differences, into a big one ecumenical world. The Bible is very clear about this.[16]

However, after an uproar over the policy sparked by media attention, Bob Jones University lifted the bans. Interesting to note however, in the above statement is the apocalyptic tone which shows the university attempting to repel conditions that would make possible the one-world diabolical kingdom of the antichrist.

While Bob Jones and his university were forced by public opinion to soften their rhetoric, self-proclaimed oracles like Hal Lindsey continue to demonize Muslims. Lindsey paints a vivid apocalyptic scenario. He does not apologize for stating plainly that Jews and Christians are pitted against Islam and in this regard he believes in the literal fulfillment of prophecy. The preservation of the true Christian faith is also crucial to him because Islam, according to him, denies all the fundamental beliefs of Christianity and he would lead a personal crusade against such an onslaught.

Hal Lindsey of course has exercised tremendous influence on the masses through his bestseller *The Late Great Planet Earth* (first published in 1970). In this book Hal Lindsey establishes a clear link between the prophetic material of the Bible and recent world history such as the Cold War, the creation of the state of Israel and the Communist threat, but he leaves out Islamic radicalism, as that movement had not surfaced fully when the book was first published.

Nonetheless, relying once again on a very literalist approach to Bible prophecy, Hal Lindsey now equates the world of Islam with the Prince of Persia. If the current posture of Iran's new president Mahmoud Ahmadinajed is to be taken at face value, he may very well spearhead the conflict between the Judeo-Christian world and the world of Islam with his nuclear agenda as well as his own distinctly apocalyptic vision.

Tim LaHaye and Jerry B. Jenkins are two other very popular apocalyptic writers whose books sell by the millions among the Christian Right. Novels in the "Left Behind" series speak of the rapture, the tribulation and the diabolical rule of the Antichrist all in fictional form.

What the writers hope to achieve by propagating the apocalyptic scenario is greater religiosity, an uncompromising stand against forces deemed hostile to Christianity, widespread acceptance of Christ as savior and an inspiration to amass many good deeds because the world is coming to an end. Books in the Left Behind series have also been turned into movies.

From the above account of evangelical work in North America as a continuation of the Christian fundamentalist movement, it is obvious that the focus has shifted from "gathering the flock" to wanting to counter the spread of Islam or at least the spread of the influence of Islam through evangelizing. Islam is not just seen as a physical threat; it is also perceived as a cultural invasion of Judeo-Christian values. An effort therefore is also now under way to befriend Muslims in order to entice them towards accepting Christianity's message. Some of the criticism that Hal Lindsey has received from other Christians is that he is alienating Muslims unnecessarily through his unrelenting rhetoric against them. They feel it will endanger their chances of evangelizing to Muslims.

Christian fundamentalism now sees as its priority the conquest of Islam as a world power. This must be done through persuasion and, if need be, force. The 2004 elections in the United States once again saw George W. Bush in the White House. Many Christian fundamentalists see him as the vehicle through which radical Islam can be defeated. Many of them campaigned indefatigably for his victory. Buses ran across the American South to garner support for Bush in the elections of 2004 and his war with Iraq as a fight against terror.

According to Michael Northcott in his book entitled *An Angel Directs the Storm*, the official position of Christendom was opposition to the war in Iraq, but that belied "the extent to which millions of American Christians, including not only Southern Baptists, but the fast growing conservative churches and suburban 'megachurches' supported the war." The Democratic congressional victory of 2006, however, is an indicator that the support for the war soon eroded considerably.

Nonetheless, according to recent surveys and sample polls, about 40 percent of Americans now consider themselves Evangelical Christians. The

Christian fundamentalist message has indeed been embraced by the grassroots who come out in throngs to promote conservative Christian values, usually laced with strong religious and apocalyptic undertones.

America sees itself as the only superpower with a mission to rectify the wrongs in the rest of the world. It must bring democracy to the authoritarian politics of Asia and Africa. It must lead the world in defeating all the forces of evil, be them communism or Islamism. These were some ideals cited as the reasons to go to war with Iraq along with the perceived threat of the presence of weapons of mass destruction in the hands of the Saddam Hussein regime. In his inaugural address of 2001 George W. Bush expressed his mission as the restorer of justice in the world and the American vision as the champion towards this end:

> We have a place, all of us, in a long story — a story we continue, but whose end we will not see. It is the story of a new world that became a friend and liberator of the old, a story of a slave-holding society that became a servant of freedom, the story of power that went into the world to protect but not possess, to defend but not to conquer.[18]

When the United States went to war with Iraq it went as a defender and champion of liberty and democracy for all the oppressed peoples of the world. It was alleged that Saddam Hussein had run torture camps in the Kurdish regions of the country. He had led pogroms against the Shia insurgency after the first Gulf War. He had executed all political opponents in the most ruthless manner; anecdotal accounts suggested his sons Uday and Qusay fed many of the country's political dissidents to hungry lions.

George W. Bush, who converted to fundamentalist Christianity under the guidance of Billy Graham, has enjoyed a close relationship with the Evangelicals. Billy's son Franklin was invited to bless the inaugural event in 2001 after the much disputed election of 2000 with Al Gore as Bush's opponent. Stephen Mansfield quotes George Bush in his book entitled *Faith of George Bush* as saying, "I feel like God wants me to run for President. I can't explain it but I sense my country is going to need me." Mansfield concludes that the forty-third president is among a small number of American presidents to have undergone a profound religious transformation as an adult. He further states, "He came to the Presidency, then, with the zeal of the newly converted."[19]

Thus many Evangelicals see Bush as their hope for bringing the American apocalyptic agenda to fruition. Much of it has to do with supporting former Israeli prime minister Ariel Sharon's plan for a pullout from the occupied Palestinian territories and supporting Sharon's version of a two-state solution to the Arab-Israeli conflict. Many from among the political pundity surmise that the only Palestinian state envisioned by Sharon would be confined to the Gaza strip and a few fragmented territories in the West Bank. This was confirmed after Sharon's plan was revealed in the April 2004 meeting in the Rose Garden of the White House where he refused to relinquish claims on over 40 percent of the West Bank territories. Bush applauded Sharon's decision unconditionally, some think in perfect solidarity with the Evangelical agenda of fortifying Israel's position in the Middle East.

Recently televangelist John Hagee also announced his solidarity with Israel and stated unequivocally that 40 million American Evangelicals supported Israel. His announcement also marked the launching of a pro-Israel Christian lobby called Christians United for Israel. Through sheer strength of the numbers supporting the cause, the group is poised to surpass the influence of AIPAC, the American Israel Public Affairs Committee. Israel's consul general in New York, Arye Mekel, also met with Hagee and endorsed the group, stating that he welcomed the American Evangelical support of Israel. Hagee's aforementioned support is apparently rooted in the Bible, though he didn't elaborate it as such. The connection is definitely one of apocalyptic significance, the relevant Bible verse being "And say unto them, Thus saith the LORD God; Behold, I will take the children of Israel from among the heathen, whither they be gone, and will gather them on every side, and bring them into their own land" (Ezekiel 37: 21).

Others also see the war in Iraq as an attempt to establish Israel's hegemony in the region by destroying any of its avowed enemies. Saddam Hussein had made open threats to Israel. It is also alleged that he funded many of the suicide bombings in Israel, by offering incentives to beleaguered Palestinian families who would offer their sons — in some cases even daughters — for Jihad by accepting a donation of twenty-five thousand dollars. It is said that the current intifada suffered a blow after Saddam's defeat and capture.

Although George W. Bush may be their only hope towards reestablishing Christian values domestically, the president appears to be conflicted in his role as president and heir to a billion dollar oil industry. His family's relationship with the Bin Ladens has come into question as has his connection with UAE control of seaports in the United States. Dubai also supports the boycott of Israel. A conflict of interest therefore often emerges between Bush the Evangelical President and Bush the business tycoon.

That the Evangelicals' focus has shifted, though not entirely, from influencing domestic policy to foreign policy after the election of George W. Bush is evident in many of their statements supporting Israel and denouncing Islam. Gary Bauer, a longstanding Evangelical who also runs a website called "American Values" to propagate his views about family life, American values, and freedom of religion, does not mince words when he states that Islamic terrorists are the biggest threat to the security of American civilization. Also a longtime Republican who held many offices during the Reagan administration, Gary Bauer, through his many discourses, argues that America's hegemony is legitimate because America will champion Christian values in the world, a view that is perfectly aligned with any end-time scenarios of the Gospel being preached across the world. He is therefore openly pro-Israel. Through his perceptions of a clearly Christians-versus-"other" dichotomy, he appears to be confirming Samuel Huntington's thesis about the clash of civilizations with Islam and the West pitted against each other over values and aspirations. Huntington states in his book *The Clash of Civilizations and the Remaking of World Order*, "For forty five years the Iron Curtain was the central dividing line in Europe. That line has moved several hundred miles east. It is now the line separating the peoples of Western Christianity on the one hand, from Muslim and Orthodox peoples on the other."[20]

Many have argued that such a dichotomy is too simplistic, as orthodoxy exists within Christianity and certain factions within Islam are clamoring for Western-style modernization. This, however, coupled with the fact that Islam is categorized as a Western religion, reinforces Hal Lindsey's view pitting the extremists from both faiths against each other. There is a desire among both to convert each other to their own way of thinking as well as to propagate their own religiosity in uncharted territories such as the communist countries of Southeast Asia. It is noted that Christianity is slowly gaining ground in South Korea. Islam too appears to be appealing to African Americans and Hispanics as it is perceived as less racist than Christianity, which often depicts Jesus as blond and blue-eyed. Islam, according to the *World Christian Encyclopedia*, is growing at a phenomenal rate because of both conversion and the higher birth rate among its adherents. It is expected to be the world's largest religion in the year 2025 with a following of 30 percent of the world population. This phenomenon is a direct threat to Christian Evangelism and its apocalyptic mission.

CHAPTER SEVEN

Jihad: A Theoretical and Historical Framework

Injunctions on Jihad "in the cause of Allah" number over one hundred and fifty in the Quran. They belong mostly to the Medinan period of early Islamic history where the nascent Muslim community was able, for the very first time, to establish a society and polity with the prophet Mohammed as both its spiritual and political leader. During the first thirteen years of the advent of Islam, Muslims had come under continual attack from the pagan Meccans, who saw in the new ideology a threat to their age-old beliefs and customs, as well as their economic and political dominance.

Mecca, housing the Kaaba — a cubical structure that Muslims believe to be the first shrine dedicated to the worship of the one true God — was in the sixth century of the Christian era the center of a flourishing trade. Each year merchants from Abyssinia and neighboring countries traveled towards it to buy and sell idols to be placed in the Kaaba, which now stands in the heart of the grand mosque in Mecca. The Kaaba had been truly defiled by the presence of these idols. The symbol of ancient monotheism had to be purged of the polytheistic heresy of the Meccan pagans.

The Qureish, a prominent Meccan clan, were the longstanding custodians of the Kaaba and ironically the tribe to which the Prophet of Islam belonged. They were the progeny of those who settled in the valley of Paran ever since Hagar and her infant son Ishmael had been left there by Abraham, the patriarch of the three monotheistic faiths. The Bible had prophesied that Ishmael too would multiply and become a great nation. When "Zam-Zam" erupted from the ground in the valley of Paran to quench the abandoned baby Ishmael's thirst, a new community would soon be established in the valley that would come to be known as modern Mecca. The tribe called Jurhum soon passed by the destitute mother and son and, seeing a fountain whence the two drank, offered them safety and sustenance in exchange for the use of the spring water.

Ishmael bore twelve sons, one of whom was purportedly the progenitor of the Prophet Mohammed. He is known in the Bible as Kedar, though the view that Mohammed descended from Ishmael and Kedar is also the subject of modern controversy. Alternative theories about Mohammed's lineage suggest his family may have been Yemeni, practicing the ancient Sabian monotheistic faith. Muslims nonetheless see references in the Bible to Kedar as the fulfillment of God's promise to Ishmael. The Bible holds Kedar as being synonymous with the Arab nations of the desert.

Isaiah states:

> Let the wilderness and the cities thereof lift up their voice, the villages that Kedar doth inhabit: let the inhabitants of the rock sing, let them shout from the top of the mountains. Let them give glory unto the LORD, and declare his praise in the islands [Isaiah: 42:11–12].

Islamic sources tell us that the Arab religions sprang from the same monotheistic tradition that their brethren, the Israelites, were given — the one handed down to them by their father Abraham. But this great monotheistic legacy inherited by the descendants of the monotheists Ishmael and Kedar was lost to rampant idolatry in time. In the year 610 CE, a forty-year-old merchant by the name of Mohammed Bin Abdullah, who was also widely known as "Sadiq" (the truthful) and "Ameen" (the trustworthy), quietly and almost plaintively confided to his wife Khadijah about a revelation he had received from God most high through his angel Gabriel. The angel had asked the Prophet to "recite" or "read" but the Prophet was unlettered and expressed his inability thrice before he could comply with the angel's wishes by reciting the word of God after him:

> Recite in the name of thy Lord
> Who created man from a blood clot
> Recite for thy Lord is most Beneficent,
> Who taught man by the pen,
> Taught man what he knew not [Quran, 96: 1–5].

And thus began the revelations that came to be known as the Quran, or "the reading." Mohammed was then assigned the task of restoring monotheism to the Arabian peninsula and eventually to the rest of the world.

Distraught at the prospects of assuming such an onerous burden, the

Prophet had hurried home to Khadijah who was fifteen years his senior. She reassured him that he was indeed a messenger of God, and by readily accepting the new message, she became the very first convert to Islam. Later, Mohammed's closest friend, Abu Bakr, and his young cousin Ali, the son of the Prophet's uncle Abu Talib, accepted the new message without any resistance. The message also found sympathy among the weak and oppressed like Bilal the slave, who is credited with originating the *Adhan* or call to prayer.

These modest gains would not be enough to repel the onslaughts of the powerful Meccans. Therefore, Islam was first preached in stealth. Three years after the first revelation, God decreed in the Quran that it was now time to proclaim Islam to everyone. At that point the persecution of the Muslims at the hands of the pagans began in earnest. Muslims were tortured, they were assaulted, they were murdered and they were ostracized. Heavy sanctions were imposed on them, but their faith sustained them, providing them with the necessary courage and resilience to survive the most extreme forms of persecution.

Two years after the declarations of the new faith, a small party of Muslims attempted migration to Abyssinia to escape the humiliation they were suffering at the hands of their own kith and kin. Nagasshi, then Christian king of Abyssinia, offered them refuge, stating that only a fine line divided the beliefs of his faith and the new faith of Islam. Those who were left behind continued to suffer persecution without retaliating even in the slightest. No permission to fight or resist the onslaughts of the Meccans had been issued from Allah, therefore Muslims quietly accepted their fate as the will of God, for the word Islam meant "submission to his will."

Three hundred miles north of Mecca was a group of settlements called Yathrib which had been embroiled in tribal warfare with neighboring tribes and towns for quite some time. Hearing of the new prophet and his reputation as a peacemaker and trustworthy merchant, they sent a mission to request him to migrate to Yathrib, known now as Medina, to mediate in their ongoing disputes. The Prophet readily accepted but before he could proceed with the migrations, he sent many of the early Muslims before him so that they could now live in relative safety.

His own journey was fraught with dangers. Accompanied only by his companion and friend Abu Bakr, the Prophet took the longer route to Medina so as not to be followed by those who wished to kill him, for the would-be assassins had been promised one hundred female camels as reward for the deed. The night before his intended journey to Medina they had besieged his house, but through miraculous occurrences the Prophet left the house without the pagans even noticing, sources say.

They followed his trail up to the cave known as Saur where he was hiding with his companion, but again miraculously, a spider had woven a web at the entrance of the cave, giving the impression to the pagans that no one could have entered it without destroying the web. He arrived safely in Medina and the children welcomed him by singing the following lyrics, beating their hands on the daff, an older version of the drum used for rhythmic accompaniment:

> O the white moon rose over us
> From the valley of Wada
> And we owe it to show gratefulness
> When the call is to Allah
> O you who were raised amongst us
> Coming with the Word to be obeyed
> You have brought to this city nobleness
> Welcome, best caller, to God's way.

Soon the Prophet and his companions were settled in their new surroundings. They were hosted by the Medinans, who had now been declared the "ansars" or the helpers of the Muslims, as well as their brethren in faith. This was not, however, the end to the troubles of the fledgling Muslim community. Pagan animosity was still rife. According to a well-known Hadith the head of the city-state of Medina was sent a letter by the pagan Meccans demanding he not give refuge to the Muslims there. They swore that if he did not comply with their wishes they would "kill their fighting men and capture their women" (Sunan Abu Dawood, Vol. 2, pg. 495).

Word went around in the newly emerging Muslim community at Medina that the pagans were preparing a large army of a thousand soldiers to annihilate the "curse" of Islam once and for all. Their caravan had traveled to Syria and was planning to stop at the wells of Badr after which an attack on the Muslims would be launched.

It is here that the Muslims would intercept them without giving them any warning, based on the newly emergent philosophy of Jihad expressed in the very first Quranic verse permitting it: "Fight in the way of Allah against those who fight you, but begin not hostilities. Lo Allah does not love transgressors" (Quran, 2:190).

The first of over one hundred and fifty verses of the Quran exhorting Muslims to defend themselves, their faith and their honor would continue throughout the narrative of the Quran. The word used for the fighting would come to be known as Jihad.

Although the word Jihad, derived from the Arabic *jahada* meaning to struggle, has a much wider meaning, it is popularly understood only as a struggle in battle. An entire ideology of Jihad has emerged from the verses of the Quran which has meant different things to different people, but has never before acquired as virulent a form as it has in modern times. According to the most benign definition, often regarded as an apologetic rendering of the term, Jihad is an inner struggle to fight one's evil propensities. The human being is vulnerable to many temptations that lead him to wrong actions and beliefs. Jihad therefore becomes a daily struggle to combat these internal forces rather than a battle to repel an external enemy. Dr. Amir Ali, in his article entitled *Jihad Explained*, notes that "the Arabic words for 'war' are "harb" or "qital," which are found in the Quran and Sunnah."[1] He further goes on to argue that the term Jihad has been used in a number of ways in the Quran, mostly leading to the belief that it is a personal struggle to maintain one's relationship with the creator by doing his will. Quoting another verse of the Quran, he states that the word is even used for non–Muslims in a verse of the Quran when they "strive [jahadaka] to convert their Muslim offspring back to disbelief" (Quran, 2:109).

Many of the extremists would regard this as a "politically correct," rather escapist route propagated by those who constantly pursue a policy of appeasement with the West. They continue to quote Hadith which undoubtedly support verses of the Quran glorifyings fighting in the cause of Allah and the consequent status of martyrdom bestowed on those who lose their lives fighting for Islam. They insist the other meanings of Jihad normally associated with the word are only peripheral. Whether Jihad is understood as a personal struggle or fighting in a war, the fact remains that the Quran exhorts believers to engage in battle, regardless of the terminology it employs for such exhortations. Whether the Quran uses the words *Qital, Harb* or *Jihad* to mean fighting in Allah's cause, extremists believe an armed struggle is imperative for the purpose of combating the enemies of Islam.

According to one Hadith of the Prophet, the greater Jihad is to battle one's evil inclinations, the lesser Jihad being to fight the enemies of Islam. Jihad can also be undertaken in a number of ways. It is spiritual, intellectual, social, political and military. Writes one columnist, "Imam Raghib Isphahani has said that Jihad is of three kinds: (1) Fighting the known enemy. (2) Fighting the devil and his promptings. (3) Fighting the unreasonable demands of one's own self."[2]

But as one examines the context of the verses of the Quran, there is little to support the contention that Jihad is largely a personal struggle rather than a militaristic philosophy. In recent times in particular, it has indeed come to be glamorized as a philosophy of warfare with promises from the divine as incentives both in the lives here and hereafter.

When examining the contexts within which the word Jihad is used, one can easily conclude that it can either mean a personal struggle or participation in battle to defend Islam. The hundred and fifty odd verses that use the word Jihad, however, while elaborating the ideological framework of Jihad, also restrict the conditions in which it is to be undertaken.

First, Jihad is never to be instigated by Muslims, according to the following verse:

> Fight in the name of Allah against those who fight you, but begin not hostilities. Lo Allah does not love aggressors [Quran, 2: 190].

The Quran again qualifies the conditions which justify Jihad, qital, harb, or fighting in Allah's cause, in the following verse:

> Permission to fight is given to those who are fighting them because they have been wronged, and surely Allah is able to give them victory. Those who have been expelled unjustly only because they said: "Our Lord is Allah" [Quran, 22: 39, 40].

The above verse appears to be a reference to the expulsion of Muslims from Mecca under severe persecution from the Meccan pagans. Their properties had been seized, their livelihoods were threatened because of embargoes and sanctions and they were under constant threat of losing their lives to acts of hatred.

Once a Jihad is declared, no restraint towards people who drive Muslims from their homes or persecute them is to be exercised. They are to be given treatment commensurate to the injury they inflicted as explained in the following verse:

> So when you meet those who disbelieve smite at their necks till when you have killed and wounded them, then bind a bond firmly [then take them as captives]. Thereafter [is the time] either for generosity [free them without ransom] or ransom until the war lays down its burden. Thus you are ordered by Allah to continue in carrying our Jihad against the disbelievers till they embrace Islam. But He lets you [fight] in order to test you some with others. But those who are killed in the way of Allah, He will never let their deeds be lost. He will guide them and set right their state and admit them to Paradise which He has made known to them [Quran, 47: 4–6].

Many in modern Muslim discourses bordering on extremism and militancy consider Jihad obligatory based on the wording of the above verse of the Quran. It is therefore surprising that Jihad is not listed as a pillar of Islam, although its proponents often regard it as a sixth pillar in times of crises. There are others such as Sheik Abdullah Bin Muhammad who consider Jihad a voluntary act to be considered more noble than the obligatory acts of reciting the *Shahada* (declaration of faith), praying, fasting, giving alms, and performing the Hajj. In his article entitled "Jihad in the Quran and Sunnah," Abdullah Bin Muhammad states:

> But as regards the reward and blessings there is one deed which is very great in comparison to all the acts of worship and all the good deeds — -and that is Jihad.[3]

The sheik derives his views again based on the Quranic statements such as the following which elevates Jihad to an act of piety:

> Those believers who sit back, not disabled by injury, are not equal to those who do Jihad in the way of God with their wealth and lives [Quran, 4:94].

Jihad is justified only under very severe conditions according to the classical theory of Jihad. First, it is meant only as a defensive war as is evident from the words, "Fight in the name of Allah against those who fight you, but begin not hostilities." Jihad must be undertaken only to restore justice and to wipe out oppression and persecution. One verse of the Quran mentions defending churches, synagogues and temples, suggesting that oppression against those communities must also be eliminated:

> If God had not allied one group of people to repel another, then there would have been pulled down cloisters and synagogues and churches and mosques, in which God's name is remembered [Quran, 22: 40].

The picture that emerges from highly suspect Hadith literature when read in conjunction with the Quran further glamorizes warfare against nonbelievers. According to one such Hadith, the Prophet of Islam is reported to have said, "Do Jihad against the idolaters with your wealth lives and tongues" (Mishkat book of Jihad, ch. 1 sec. 2).

Regardless of what Jihad means in the classical literature of Islam, it has come to connote warfare against individuals or nations striving to annihilate Muslims or Islam. An in-depth analysis is warranted on the current ideology of Jihad with respect to its earliest manifestations during the lifetime of the Prophet Mohammed. Looking at Jihad as an expressed precept during that pristine era of Islam will shed light on whether current jihadist posturing has deviated from both the theory and practice of Islam, or whether it is true to its original intent.

As mentioned earlier, the Meccan period marking the advent of Islam was fraught with perils for the nascent Muslim community. They were not in a position to retaliate against the onslaughts of the pagans, who were the main opponents of the newly rejuvenated radical monotheism of Islam.

In the second year of the Hijrah or migration from Mecca to Medina, however, circumstances began to change drastically for the Muslims. They were now better equipped to establish a society based on Islamic precepts. Defending the new values and beliefs would now become imperative; otherwise the ideology would die forever along with the handful of those who professed adherence to it.

Now that Islam has come under tremendous scrutiny as an ideology from both within and without, it is arguable whether warfare in Islam is only defensive, or whether it can also be launched as a preemptive strike.

The bulk of the Muslim narrative, scholarly and popular, suggests that warfare in Islam is strictly defensive. Non-Muslim historical accounts, on the other hand, give credence to the view that the small party of Muslims who moved to Medina routinely led unprovoked raids known as *Ghazwat* on Meccan caravans, justifying them on grounds that the Muslims too had suffered and been expelled at their hands.

History has it that skirmishes and raids of this nature escalated with attacks and counter attacks involving the Qureish of Mecca and the Muslims of Medina. This led to the first "war of Islam," known as the Battle of Badr, a small village on the outskirts of Medina.

Medina was situated just off the trade route of the Meccans. Word got out to Mohammed that a large caravan was on its way to Syria led by the leader of the Qureish, Abu Sufyan. Also fearful of reprisals to previous raids, the Prophet gathered an army of exactly 313 men including many of the early luminaries of Islam such as the Prophet's uncle Hamza, his cousin and son-in-law Ali, and his friends Abu Bakr and Umar who assumed the caliphate after his death.

When Abu Sufyan heard of the possible raid on his caravan, he sent word to Mecca to prepare an army to intercept the Muslim army in order to protect his caravan. He also decided to change his route towards Yanbu, a Western Arabian seaport. The Muslim army was duly apprised of this retreat by the pagan caravan and hurried towards the wells of Badr to preempt such departure. Dissent broke out among the Qureish on whether to fight the Muslims or go their way. However, since the Muslim army was already positioned to attack the Qureishi pagans, there was no option left but to engage Muslims in battle.

On the 17th of Ramadan in the second year of the migration to Medina, the Battle of Badr broke out near the wells. Ali, Hamza and Ubaday from the Muslim army emerged to take the lead in battle and crushed their opponents. Although the Meccan army far outnumbered the Muslims, as it was one thousand soldiers strong, it experienced a crushing defeat, taking several casualties when fighting broke out under a shower of arrows from both sides. The Battle of Badr was decisive in the history of Islam as a turning point towards future conquests. The Quranic account also assigns great importance to the battle as it is discussed at length in the chapter entitled "Al Anfal" (The Spoils of War), which also speaks of divine intervention that made victory for the much smaller army of Muslims possible:

> When you implored the help of your Lord, and He answered your prayer saying, "I will surely help you with a thousand of the angels, rank on rank" [Quran, 8: 9].

According to yet another verse of the Quran, the pagans retreated because they wrongly estimated the number of Muslims, again due to divine intervention:

> And remember at the time of your encounter, He made them appear to you as few in your eyes, and made you appear as few in their eyes, that Allah might bring about the thing that was decreed [Quran, 8: 44].
> And Allah had already helped you at Badr when you were weak. So take Allah for your protector so that you may be grateful [Quran, 3: 123].

The pagan Qureish soon vowed revenge. For the entire following year they amassed an army aided by neighboring tribal chiefs to avenge the deaths of their fallen sons and chieftains including Abu Jahal, Mohammed's arch-enemy during his struggling years in Mecca.

A year later, an army of five thousand Meccan soldiers marched towards Medina only to be met this time by a paltry seven hundred fighters from the Muslim army. The scene of the battle this time would be the vicinity of Uhud, the mountain believed to be one of the remnants of Mount Sinai, burnt after Moses demanded God reveal himself in physical form to him. The mountain is situated three miles north of Medina.

Again the Muslim army was able to crush the pagans despite their fewer numbers and again the pagan army began their retreat. The outcome of the battle, however, tilted against the Muslims, who, assured of their victory, busied themselves in collecting the spoils of war even though they had been advised by the prophet to refrain from leaving their positions. In particular, the fifty or so men who had been perched on the mountain to monitor the movements of the retreating Qureish army also left to join in the amassing of the newly acquired spoils.

Capitalizing on this moment, General Khalid Bin Walid, who had not as yet embraced Islam, changed direction towards the Muslims and attacked them from behind the mountain. According to the earliest historical accounts largely transmitted through Hadith, seventy Muslim men were martyred in the battle of Uhud. The Prophet, too, was injured, losing his four front teeth.

At one point during the battle, the Prophet's disappearance gave rise to the rumor that he too had been martyred. He had however been shielded and protected single-handedly by a woman called Umm Ammara, who sustained many wounds on his behalf.

The pagans were not as charitable as the Muslims in their treatment of the corpses. The Prophet had prohibited desecration of the bodies but the pagans mutilated and desecrated the bodies of many martyrs including the Prophet's uncle Hamza's corpse. Hind, the wife of Abu Sufyan, the Qureish chieftain, dug deep into his stomach and chewed Hamza's liver in revenge for her brother's death the previous year, as he had been killed by Hamza during the Battle of Badr.

It is not clear what occasioned the battle of Khaiber. Muslim sources narrate that the Jews of Medina had come to settle there after their expulsion from that city, but that they plotted and planned against Islam and Muslims. The Prophet therefore decided to march towards it in the sixth year of the Hijrah or migration, to engage in battle with the Jews who had sought refuge in the two forts at Khaiber. He reached the city by night but, holding true to his policy, he did not launch an attack till the next morning when the opposing army was well prepared. However, many of the fighting men from among the Jews were killed in battle and their women and children were taken captive by the Muslim army. The Jewish chief's daughter Safiyyah was also taken hostage. The Prophet later married her and gave her back her freedom as her dower or *mahr*.

Meanwhile the pagans of Mecca were still not satisfied with the revenge and another battle would be fought which would come to be known as the Battle of the Trench. During this battle, there was no bloodshed from either side as the Muslims had dug an enormous trench around Medina, which proved to be insurmountable for either side to engage in battle, due to its sheer size and depth.

The Battle of Tabuk was occasioned by a verse in the Quran prohibiting non–Muslims from approaching the holy precincts of the mosque at Mecca. It was launched against the Byzantine army situated at the city of Tabuk in northwestern Arabia. No actual battle, however, unfolded between the 30,000-strong Muslim army and the 200,000-strong Byzantine forces, for the Muslims had underestimated their strength.

Here, a brief historical perspective must be provided for the circumstances that occasioned the Battle of Tabuk. It would forever result in the barring of non–Muslims from entering the cities of Mecca and Medina. The relevant verse of the Quran reads:

O ye who believe, truly the pagans are unclean so let them not, after this year of theirs, approach the sacred mosque. And if ye fear poverty, soon will Allah enrich you, if He will, out of his bounty, for Allah is All-knowing, All Wise. Fight those who believe not in Allah or the Last Day, nor hold that which is forbidden which hath been forbidden by Allah and His Messenger, nor acknowledge the religion of truth from among the people of the Book [Jews and Christians], until they pay the Jizya with willing submission, and feel themselves subdued [Quran, 9:28].

This verse perhaps comes closest to giving credence to the view that Islam came to be spread by the sword. War was to be waged against the pagans and the "people of the book" till they either accepted Islam voluntarily or came to be "subdued" by accepting their inferior status in a Muslim state, by agreeing to pay the tax known as the Jizya. This was meant to compensate the Muslims who had been asked to prohibit the pagans from entering the precincts of Mecca and hence were deprived of the economic benefits such interaction would have generated, as the cited verse suggests.

The Muslim army marched towards Tabuk. Hadith narrate that many from among its ranks who were of weak will ultimately chose not to go to war. This is how the "hypocrites" were sifted from the sincere among the Muslims. Again according to Hadith, this was a battle to test the will and sincerity of Muslims in Allah's cause.

While these battles were being waged, Muslims also devoted themselves to building their institutions and their community in Medina. It would be eight years after their migrations from Mecca to Medina that the Muslims would once again enter Mecca triumphant, with ten thousand soldiers to establish Islam in its birthplace.

The 10,000-strong Muslim army reached the outskirts of Mecca on the 10th of Ramadan in the eighth year of the Hijrah or its equivalent, February 21, 630 CE. The Meccans lay besieged by the army. After some deliberation they concluded that it would be futile to try to repel the Muslim army. Abu Sufyan, now convinced of divine intervention in the military, political and spiritual success of Mohammed and the Muslims, also embraced Islam. Consequently, the Muslim army was allowed to march into Mecca in a bloodless victory over the Prophet's home city.

When he entered its precincts triumphant, the pagans watched from inside their homes, fearful of the Prophet's wrath due to their past misdeeds. The Prophet, however, immediately declared a general amnesty for pagan and Muslim alike. His task, though, was not complete yet, as he had to purge the city of its idolatrous past. He then entered the cubical structure called the Kaaba which until then had housed 360 idols including the pictures of Jesus and Mary. Tradition has it that he destroyed all the idols and pictures except those of Jesus and Mary.

Muslims fervently believe that the conquest of Mecca was prophesied in the Bible in the following verse, particularly because of its reference to Mount Paran which is believed to be situated near Mecca, and because of the fact that the Prophet had returned to his hometown accompanied by ten thousand soldiers:

> And he said, The LORD came from Sinai, and rose up from Seir unto them; he shined forth from Mount Paran, and he came with ten thousands of saints: from his right hand went a fiery law for them [Deuteronomy 33:2].

After his victorious return to his hometown, however, the Prophet chose not to resettle in Mecca but returned to Medina, for now it had come to be known as *Medina tun Nabi,* or the city of the Prophet. But after the conquest of Mecca, idolatry vanished from Arabia, bringing the Prophet's message of monotheism to fruition. He died at the age of sixty-two in 632 CE after a brief illness.

The historical account makes one wonder about the validity of the belief that fighting in Islam is purely defensive. Tabuk and Khaiber were clearly initiated by the earliest armies of Islam based on Quranic commandments. Even skirmishes before the Battle of Badr were justified based on the Quranic law of equality, derived from Talmudic law which afforded bands of Muslims to raid pagan caravans. The following verse of the Quran expounds the law of equality:

> O ye who believe! The law of equality is prescribed to you in case of murder: The free for the free, the slave for the slave, the woman for the woman. But if any remission is made by the brother of the slain, then grant any reasonable demand, and compensate him with handsome gratitude. This is a concession and a Mercy from your Lord. After this whoever exceeds the limits shall be in grave penalty [Quran, 2:178].

According to the *Islamic Glossary Home: University of Southern California Compendium of Muslim Texts,* "Jihad is not a defensive war only, but a war against any unjust regime. If such a regime exists, a war is to be waged against the leaders, but not against the people of that country. People should be freed from the unjust regimes and influences so that they can freely choose to believe in Allah."[4]

The same notion must have inspired George W. Bush to lead the war against Saddam Hussein's tyrannical regime. Bush claimed he would bring democracy to the country where the Shia majority suffered severe discrimination, as dissident voices were crushed with impunity by Saddam. According to some, it was Bush's pietistic zeal that led him to attack Afghanistan and free its people from the tyranny of the Taliban who had imposed a very strict and punitive interpretation of Islam, particularly on Muslim women. Again the UCLA compendium explains:

> Not only in peace but also in war Islam prohibits terrorism, kidnapping, and hijacking, when carried against civilians. Whoever commits such violations is considered a murderer in Islam, and is to be punished by the Islamic state. During wars, Islam prohibits Muslim soldiers from harming civilians, women, children, elderly, and the religious men like priests and [rabbis]. It also prohibits cutting down trees and destroying civilian constructions.[5]

Another Quranic verse sanctions killing but only through "just cause" and includes a dire warning that limits must not be exceeded, which would tend to support the verse above.

> Do not take life — which Allah has made sacred — except for just cause. And if anyone is slain wrongfully, we have given his heir authority [to demand retaliation or forgive] but let him not exceed bounds in the matter of taking life, for he is helped [by the law] [Quran, 17:33].

The view expressed by the UCLA compendium is also derived from the narration in Hadith below:

> Narrated Abdullah: During the *ghazwat* [military expeditions of the Prophet] a woman was found killed. Allah's apostle disapproved the killing of women and children" [Bukhari: Muhammad Muhsin Khan, Vol. 4, no. 257].

The theory *of jihad, qital* or *harb* that emerges based on its various definitions, nuances and interpretations of the injunctions of the Quran and citations from Hadith, suggests it is to be fought not only in self-defense but also to eradicate oppression. Of course the rules of engagement are to be clearly observed, ensuring that no weak parties will be attacked in the process. Sayed Qutb, an influential exegete and foremost ideologue of the modern jihadist movement, expounds his theory of Jihad in his book *Milestones,* confirming the view that Jihad can be undertaken preemptively as well:

> If we insist on calling Islamic Jihad a defensive movement, then we must change the meaning of the word "defense" to "defense of man" against all those elements which limit his freedom. These elements take the form of beliefs and concepts, as well as of political systems, based on economic racial or class distinctions.[6]

Sayed Qutb, in his understanding of Jihad, has expounded the agenda that most Islamists (i.e. those who believe in the supremacy of Islam as a faith) espouse. In fact Sayed Qutb is deemed the founder of modern jihadist ideology. He has succinctly and forcefully declared Jihad on all forms of "oppression," economic, political and ideological — in essence anything that doesn't conform to his conservative view of Islam.

Taken in this general sense, Jihad can be waged at any time when Muslims feel they are suffering oppression at the hands of forces that curtail their freedom of religion. Although Islam is not to be imposed by force, as "there is no compulsion in religion" according to the Quran, those who practice Islam must be freed from any tyranny that prevents them from practicing their faith. One translation of the Quran is particularly supportive of Jihad to establish Islam's supremacy across the world. It is posted by the Muttaqun Foundation (www.muttaqun.com):

> And fight them until there is no more "fitnah" [disbelief and worshipping of others along with Allah] and [all and every] kind of worship is for Allah [Alone]. But if they cease, let there be no transgression except against the Zalimun [polytheists and wrongdoers] [Quran, 2:193].

The words in brackets are explanations by the translators rather than actual words of the Quran. They need to be examined for fidelity to the text as well as with other more accepted translations of the Quran such as that of Abdullah Yusuf Ali as follows:

> And fight them on until there is no more Tumult or Oppression and there prevail Justice and faith in God. But if they cease, Let there be no hostility except to those who practice oppression [Quran, 2:193].

It is imperative to note that it is the manner in which the Quranic message is understood that can lead to a Jihadist or Islamic-imperialist mentality. Modern discourses on Jihad, terrorism and Islam often express puzzlement over the disparity between the theory of Jihad in Islam, which strictly prohibits terrorism, and the ideologies developed by terrorist networks, many of whom quote verses of the Quran to legitimate their agenda.

Like any other religious text, the Quran is subject to various readings suited to the character and dispositions of those wishing to understand its message. Yet one must ask, if Islam is so explicit in forbidding the slaughter of innocents, what is it that drives terrorists to kill so mercilessly and indiscriminately?

A look at the evolution of the jihadist outlook and its recent manifestation in the madrassahs of Pakistan, considered training grounds for the terrorist networks across south Asia and the central Asian former Soviet republics of Kazakhstan and Turkmenistan, can perhaps help address the confusion. An examination of the ideologies and attitudes that instill a brutally militant outlook is therefore warranted.

While Christian fundamentalism was evolving in the late nineteenth and early twentieth century as a response to disintegration from within Christianity and secular forces from without, Islamic fundamentalism emerged from the need to resist Western domination and from Islam's own deviations from what fundamentalists saw as the true message or doctrine. Hassan al-Banna, the founder of the Ikhwan Al Muslimeen or the Muslim Brotherhood, impressed the need upon Muslims to revert to the pristine tenets of Islam if a lasting solution to their problems was to be found. Keeping as his model the early Medinan society of Islam, which had flourished under the leadership of the Prophet Mohammed, he came to the conclusion that Islam would have to evolve into a political force in order to defeat the modernist challenge from within and the colonialist challenge from without. The seeds of Islamism, which promotes Islam's ascendancy as an ideology across the world, were first laid in al-Banna's philosophy in modern times. Al-Banna, influenced by the fact that the early Islamic period did not recognize a dichotomy between religion and politics, confronted the Egyptian monarchy for its "un–Islamic practices" of promoting dynastic rule. Al-Banna was assassinated in 1949.

Islamism, often known as political Islam, also incorporates in its world-view messianism which both predicts and guarantees the predominance of Islam as a global force. It becomes an obligation for able-bodied Muslims to launch a Jihad, whether militant, through the pen or other means, to see that this ultimate aim comes to fruition. Western values are increasingly seen as morally decadent and ones that have to be countered by Wahabi Islam's extremely austere standards of morality. Muslims also believe in the absolute truth of the message revealed to the Prophet Mohammed. As "God's final communication" to man, they believe, the Quran is free of all doctrinal adulteration of the previous messages, which according to them had undergone change over time. Not only is it crucial to establish the Quranic standards of decency everywhere, it is equally important to establish correct belief among humanity — for their own good, because Islam is the only "true" or "straight" path to salvation.

The aforementioned Sayed Qutb, who was the Muslim Brotherhood's most articulate and innovative thinker, carried the task of the movement forward in the sixties after Hassan al-Banna. He saw the world community as a division between the community of the believers (Ummul Mumina) and the community of the ignorant (Ummul Jahilliya). Qutb often directed his anger against his own communities in Egypt, alleging Muslims of his time were no longer authentic Muslims. According to him they had abandoned the pristine spirit of Islam, which was a "complete way of life" as a political, social and religious force. Simple attestations of the creed "there is no

God but God and Mohammed is his Prophet" were not enough to qualify as a Muslim, according to Sayed Qutb. Muslims would have to incorporate Islam's value system in each and every aspect of their lives, particularly if Islam and Muslims were to regain their past glory and dominate the world in the end times.

The entire society, its governance and its laws would have to be based on religious precepts. Shariah law would have to dominate any government run according to Islamic principles of "democracy."

Political Islam as expounded by Hassan al-Banna and Sayed Qutb was also a precursor to Pan-Islamism in its agenda to unify Muslims against external threats. The name "Muslim Brotherhood" was symbolic of this move to revert to the days of the caliphate, when the Muslims of the world lived together as one political and religious entity. True to its agenda of launching a Jihad against any threats to Islam or Muslims, the Brotherhood and its members also joined the Palestinian struggle against Israeli occupation.

The *Ikhwan ul Muslimeen* developed into a very organized, highly militant group which kept meticulous records of its membership. It systematically planned assaults on government interests. Consequently many of the members suffered incarceration during Egyptian leader Gamal Abdel Nasser's regime after a few attempts were made by the group on his life. The group hence remained banned for the years 1954 to 1984, after which it was allowed as a strictly religious group that would have to renounce its political agenda. Ayman al-Zewahiri, Osama bin Laden's lieutenant, was a member of the group. He was imprisoned in Egypt before being released and exiled to Afghanistan.

During such time as the Muslim Brotherhood's career in Egypt was going through periods of ascendancy and decline, Maulana Maududi of Pakistan was also expounding his Islamist philosophy and working hard to translate it into a political movement. Originally opposed to the idea of Pakistan based on the notion that Muslims must remain one political community rather than separate themselves from the Muslims of India by asking for a state of their own in Pakistan, Maududi subsequently formed the Jamaat-e-Islami or the Islamic Party with a pronounced political agenda in Pakistan. The Jamaat was also divided into sub-groups which involved the participation of women and students, like the Jamiat Tulaba Islam or the Party of the Students of Islam. Their oftentimes militant zeal was rooted in the belief that they were inspired by God-given authority. According to author Lloyd Ridgeon in his book *Crescents on the Cross*, "Jihad is the ultimate expression of Islam, it is the pinnacle of faith" as far as Maududi is concerned. Such idealism translated into activism would achieve the apocalyptic goals of establishing true Islam everywhere, whether in seats of power, in the social insti-tutions or in the hearts of men. Propagation of the faith was therefore a major component of the fundamentalist Islamic zeal. Every fundamentalist group has a Dawah (invitation to Islam) wing which attempts to attract non-practicing Muslims and non–Muslims to Islam, in the interest of fulfilling the apocalyptic vision of Islam's supremacy across the world.

Islamic fundamentalism is not always militant. The Tablighi Jamaat (Islamic Missionary Party), which is comprised of an enormous network of devout Muslims, believe their Jihad must be undertaken in a pacifist man-ner by convincing people of the value of Islam in their lives. Based in the small city of Raiwind, Pakistan, their missionaries travel to different parts of the world in groups for a duration ranging from three days to three months at a time in the hope of gaining new converts. The Tablighi Jamaat's pacifism can also be attributed to their firm belief that Islam is destined to win as an ideology because the Quran and Hadith predict so, even if this goal is not reached militarily.

While the ideological framework for the new Islamic militant zeal was germinating in Egypt and Pakistan with Maududi, Hassan al-Banna and Sayed Qutub as its founders, the Islamic world was either subjugated under European colonial rule or under the domination of the Bolsheviks. Com-munism was vehemently opposed to religion in general and Islam in partic-ular, as it was seen as far too reactionary a force. After the dissolution of the Ottoman Empire, it seemed the entire Islamic world was plunged into the darkest period of its history. But Islam continued to be practiced surrepti-tiously even under Soviet rule in the central Asian countries that would gain independence after the collapse of the Soviet Union in 1989.

These Islamic forces, suppressed for so long, would reemerge with full gusto not only in the central Asian republics but elsewhere in the Islamic world as well. Islamic revivalism and its current political posturing came to be manifested in militant Islamic groups leading a Jihad against Soviets both in the former Soviet Republics and Chechnya. The Soviet invasion of Afghanistan in 1979 sparked the jihadist zeal in that country which lasted for ten years till the Soviets were finally ousted. Concurrently, Zia-ul-Haq of Pakistan launched his campaign to "Islamize" Pakistani law, politics and society. In Algeria, the first Islamist party also showed signs of winning the electoral vote, but the party was banned in an unprecedented move, stifling any strides towards democracy.

Amidst Sunni revivalism, Iran also experienced its own Islamic revolu-tion as a champion of Shia Islam when Ayatollah Ruhollah Khomeini returned from his exile in France to assume leadership of his country after deposing the Shah of Iran. After years of suppression, Islam as an ideology and seminal force had emerged triumphant all across the Islamic world among its adherents. After the end of the Cold War, the Christian world in the West would see a new threat emerging from the populous Islamic countries of the Middle East, south Asia, central Asia, North Africa and southeast Asia. The reemergence of Islam as a seminal force in people's lives appeared to be a coordinated movement with respect to its timing. As discussed later, a loose connection between the various jihadist movements would be established in terms of funding, ideology, networking, cooperation and the general goal towards an Islamic solution.

Once again, after many years, Islam as a faith was able to "unite" peoples of different ethnic backgrounds, those who spoke different languages, wore different clothes and belonged to separate polities. All this seemed to be coming true in line with the prophecies that predicted the ultimate triumph of Islam when its peoples would unite against a common enemy, in this case the West and its hegemony in Muslim lands.

The year 1994 also marked the Taliban's rise to political power in Afghanistan. Mullah Mohammed Omar, who is currently said to be in hiding with Osama bin Laden, was its founder.

Mullah Omar had been trained in a Pakistani madrassah in the Frontier Province of that country. Along with fifty other students or "Taliban," Mullah Omar ventured to gain control of the country, inspired by a purported dream in which the Prophet Mohammed appeared to him, urging him to launch a Jihad against the tyranny of the civil war perpetrated by Afghanistan's warlords. Initially he would gain control of the provinces of Urzgan and Zabol, but as more Taliban heard of these victories, they joined forces with the jihadist army and gained control of Kabul in 1996.

The Taliban were distinct from other Jihadists in their dress and demeanor. They established the most barbaric version of Shariah law in the country, beating and even beheading women who appeared in public without a veil and banning, among other things, kite flying as "un–Islamic."

The Taliban would come to play a pivotal role in the rising popularity of the international jihadist movement led by Osama bin Laden. As an umbrella organization, the Taliban would provide safe haven to the militant group Al-Qaeda, militant movements from Pakistan such as the Lashkar-e-Tayyaba, and the IMO from the central Asian republics.

Not only was the Taliban an umbrella organization providing safe haven to militants, Mullah Omar also declared himself the Caliph, thereby giving the Islamic world a hope for political unity.

Prophetic Hadith had previously spoken of Islam's armies rising from the Khorasan valley in the latter days. The army was described as men with beards wearing black turbans. The Taliban accordingly issued an ordinance requiring all Afghan boys to wear either black or white turbans according to their level of education. At the same time, Western clothes were shunned and deemed un–Islamic. The Taliban wore distinctive attire that undoubtedly appeared to fulfill this prophecy to the letter. The radical Shiite leaders under Ayatollah Khomeini also wore black turbans, perhaps again to realize the prophecy as follows:

> Muhammad, son of al Hanaffia, said: "The Black Banners will come out of the children of Al Abbas. The other black banners will come from Khurasan. Their turbans will be black and their clothes white. At their front will be a man named Shuyab, the son of Salih, from Tamim. They will defeat The companions of the Sufyaani until he comes to the House of Jerusalem where he will establish his power for the Mahdi, and he will be supplied with three hundred (men) from Syria after his arrival and the matter will be settled for the Mahdi in seventy-two months (six years).[7]

After the attacks of September 11, 2001, many Muslims recalled this prophecy suggesting the triumph of Islam was now close because the army of men with black turbans had already emerged from the valley of Khorasan, located in northeastern Iran.

The Taliban were nurtured in the madrassahs of neighboring Pakistan which currently houses close to 15,000 all across Pakistan, a phenomenal growth from the mere 130-odd madrassahs at the time of Pakistan's separation from India. The following chart taken from the Institute of Policy Studies, a Jamaat-e-Islami think-tank, will reveal the pattern of the growth of these madrassahs in Pakistan.[8] This estimate is, however, considered very con-

Table 1. The Growth of Madrassahs in Pakistan from 1947

Provinces/Region	1947	1960	1980	1988	2000
Punjab	124	195	1012	1320	3153
NWFP	59	87	426	678	1281
Sindh	21	8	380	291	905
Baluchistan	28	70	135	347	692
AJ Kashmir	4	—	29	76	151
Islamabad	—	1	27	47	94
Northern areas	12	16	47	102	185
FATA	—	—	—	—	300
Total	**248**	**496 [*sic*]**	**2056**	**2861**	**6761**

servative and current government estimates place the number to be closer to 12,000, even according to President Musharraf's autobiography.

The madrassahs provide an alternative to the public education system which Pakistan, due to its paucity of resources, has not been able to deliver to all its citizens. The alternatives provided by the madrassahs include basic studies in Quran and Hadith and the learning of the Quran by rote, even its memorization from cover to cover. The Pakistani government's madrassah reform effort to introduce modern subjects has been stalled since the summer of 2006 and instead, the focus has shifted to reforming the curriculum of regular government schools. Most of the madrassah attendees are boys from among the impoverished masses who cannot afford even the slightest expense involved in educating their children in the government-run schools.

In a recent World Bank study, however, the view that only the downtrodden attend madrassahs was duly challenged. Said Saeed-ur-Rahman, a British-born Muslim of Pakistani origin: "It's a misconception that students are downtrodden, poor, dead-enders."[9]

The World Bank study's conclusion is based on the number of foreign attendees of madrassah education. Many repatriates also join madrassahs to supplement their education with religious knowledge. Their presence is perceived as a moderating influence on the rest of the students, although the Pakistani government has had to put a moratorium on admitting foreign students after it discovered that one of the bombers in the July 7, 2005, attack on London had attended a local madrassah.

The indoctrination in madrassahs occurs as part of the madrassah curriculum, as well as part of the conscious imparting of values. Children are taught about the absolute truth of the Quran, Hadith and the rulings of the classical jurists of Islam. The students are then employed in various affluent homes to tutor children in learning the Quran by rote. This involves reading the text in Arabic without understanding its content. A madrassah education is therefore not confined to the walls of the mosque or other facilities housing them, but is disseminated through the different strata of society.

This would give the false impression to readers that madrassahs are unified and united in their struggle against "anti–Islam" forces. On the face of it, the madrassah curricula appear to be standard and uniform; however, suffice it to say that there are numerous differences in how the materials and contents are interpreted. Although the madrassahs represent a very conservative stream of Islamic thought, they differ profoundly with each other in their sectarianism, their degree of devotion to the Prophet of Islam and their political or militaristic agenda.

The madrassahs of Pakistan represent the Deobandi, the Barelvi, the

Salafi, and the Shia schools. The Barelvi subset within the larger Sunni sect of Islam is noted for its reverence for the Prophet Mohammed. They believe that those who do not accord him the status of being God's first and only chosen creation are not true Muslims. The Wahabis in particular are in absolute disfavor with the Barelvis, as the Wahabis do not consider the Prophet to be worthy of respect any greater than their "elder brother." According to the Barelvis, this amounts to an attempt to disparage the image of the Prophet and needs to be countered even by force. A brutal manifestation of the rivalry between the Wahabis and Barelvis in March 2006 occurred in Karachi, Pakistan, at a Barelvi celebration. Sixty people died.

The Wahabis consider the Barelvi veneration of the Prophet misguided and bordering on "Shirk," which is deemed the most heinous crime committed against Allah, as it affords other entities equal status with Allah. Much of the Barelvi litany depicts the Prophet as being synonymous with God, which the Wahabis consider heretical and blasphemous because it goes against Islam's central doctrine based on radical monotheism.

Enmity against the Shia is shared by all the Sunni madrassahs. And it is here that a clear link between madrassahs and militancy is established, although these seminaries have in recent times also been linked to acts of international terrorism, especially in their role in preaching a jihadist ideology and promoting the movement worldwide.

But Jihad is also to be pursued internally, against the forces of disintegration from within. The doctrinal purity of the faith, according to the fundamentalists, must be upheld at all times. Muslims who deviate from the "true," obvious and literal message of the Quran must be weeded out because they pose a greater threat to Islam than outsiders would. Ahmadis and Shias are therefore often targeted by the militaristic jihadist zeal of the madrassah graduates, as are Muslims who espouse a more liberal and secular understanding of Islam.

As for the perception that the madrassahs are breeding grounds for jihadists, one needs to examine political events after the Soviet withdrawal from Afghanistan. As mentioned earlier, a flood of Islamic revivalism shook the south Asian, Asian and central Asian Islamic states. The Darul Uloom Haqqania, in Akora Khattak, Pakistan, where Mullah Omar of the Taliban was trained, has a clear linkage with the global Jihad as it has surfaced on the international scene. Not only is the madrassah notorious for producing the Taliban, its president is now also in direct control of seats of power as an elected member of the Pakistani legislature. Many of the madrassah's alumni are also his colleagues who have attempted to introduce a very stringent interpretation of Islam in the Frontier Province of Pakistan.

After their debacle in Afghanistan at the hands of the American forces, the Taliban are regrouping with fresh recruits from these madrassahs not only from among the Pakistani population but also from foreign students arriving from the central Asian republics. One well versed in the prophetic tradition of Islam and Christianity would undoubtedly see a connection between the forces of the caucuses as the Gog and Magog.

Although internally Pakistani madrassahs suffer from disunity and sectarian rivalry, Madrassahs in the Frontier Province are united in their goal of international Jihad against the forces of oppression, in this case what they consider Western imperialism. The students, who are inspired by the ardor of youth, express the jihadist outlook unreservedly. For a link to be established between madrassahs and Jihad, a link has to be established also with Jihad and terrorism. Many have suggested there is no direct link between madrassahs and international terrorism; however, this thesis will not hold true when one examines the jihadist mindset in greater depth.

Unfortunately none of the madrassah-trained jihadists acknowledge the stringent conditions required for "righteous Jihad," as specified in the classical theory of Jihad. Having acquired their scanty knowledge only through rote and memorization, they are not fully familiar with the concepts and applications of religious precepts. The true understanding that comes from analysis and critical thinking is missing from the jihadi mindset. Jihad therefore has become synonymous with terrorism. The only means of combat that the jihadists are familiar with is unrestricted militancy, and therefore an immediate connection is made between Jihad and terrorism.

The law of equality mentioned earlier is also invoked, despite rules to the contrary, prohibiting attacks on noncombatants, that are expounded in the classical theory of Jihad. The jihadists have therefore led struggles against the Russian government and its intransigence over the Chechnyan conflict, against the Israeli occupation of Palestinian territories, against the Indian government's policy in the disputed Kashmir region, and against other threats to Muslim thought in other parts of the world. The law of equality permits them to attack their provocateurs in like manner. If Muslim children are being killed, then the law of equality would allow the killing of enemy children. Jihadists therefore do not believe they are violating any core doctrines of Islam, as they feel they are only defending themselves and only inflicting injury commensurate with the injury they received.

Thus Jihad in modern times has assumed an extremely virulent form that stops at nothing to achieve its agenda. From the mosque pulpits, to the madrassahs of Pakistan, to the militant strongholds of central Asia, to Western streets where Muslims protest the publications of objectionable cartoons of the Prophet Mohammed, the Islamic world is seething with hatred for all things "un–Islamic." Modern Jihad, thus popularized, is being undertaken "through the pen" on internet forums, on websites, in religious discourses, on the streets, in terrorist attacks and through militant resistance in various parts of the Islamic world.

Author Noah Feldman, however, in his book *After Jihad*, provides hope in the notion that Islamic militants are increasingly resorting to democratic and political means to further their agenda:

> The Islamists' call for democratic change in the Muslim world marks a funda-
> mental shift in their strategy. For more than a decade after the Iranian Revolu-
> tion of 1979, many Islamists sought to emulate the Iranian model by
> Islamizing their own countries through revolutionary transformation of violent
> Jihad. This violence was never embraced by every Islamist, but it was very
> much in the air, and few Islamists were prepared to condemn it."[10]

He further concludes:

> A proliferation of so-called jihadi organizations throughout the Muslim world
> occurred during the 1980s, and the one that emerged as most prominent,
> Osama Bin Laden's Al Qaeda, culminated its Jihad with the horrifically suc-
> cessful attack on the World Trade Center and the Pentagon. But September
> 11th and the sporadic attacks which have followed are the last, desperate gasp
> of a tendency to violence that has lost most of its popular support.[11]

As mentioned earlier, the Taliban recently gained considerable control over seats of power in Pakistan's northwest Frontier Province. If Jihad is to be understood merely in terms of terrorist activity, Noah Feldman's thesis may be correct, as attacks have declined both in number and severity. How-ever, if it continues as a movement to promote Islam either militarily or legally, it will continue to grow in strength.

The *Daily Times* of Pakistan, a popular English journal read by the English-speaking intelligentsia of Pakistan, publishes frequent reports of Tal-iban brutality in the areas now under its political control. In a recent edi-torial entitled "Taliban, Pakistan and Modernity" the journal noted that the "local Taliban" in South Waziristan executed a twenty-five-year-old man over charges of immoral conduct according to their interpretation of "Islamic law and Shariah."[12]

The Pakistani government is simply turning a blind eye to the brutal-ity, as it wishes to preserve its own clout with the militants. Even if Jihad is not taking the shape of terrorist activity, it will certainly translate into acts of brutality through legal means, or the military machinery of governments if the Islamists are empowered through democratic means. Their presence is strongly felt each time the proverbial clash of civilizations surfaces between

Islam and the West. The Taliban in Afghanistan demanded death for Abdul Rahman, a forty-one-year-old Muslim who converted to Christianity; they came out into the streets in throngs as a manifestation of this clash of cultures. The spirit of Jihad is alive and kicking; it may assume different shapes, but it will certainly not die.

According to Dr. Anis Ahmed, a longstanding veteran of the Jamaat-e-Islami founded by Maulana Maududi, "all this madrassah reform is about trying to stop the spirit of Jihad that distinguishes Muslims from other Faiths, and that they will not stop."[13]

The Islamist mindset will not abandon Jihad in its various forms, whether militant or benign. In this mindset, Muslim lands are under foreign domination and control; Kashmir, Chechnya and Palestine are embroiled in a freedom fight; Islam has evaporated from the hearts and minds of people and must be revived; society is morally corrupt; and the legal systems in Muslim countries are un–Islamic, for Shariah law must rule Muslims. Muslims also need to unite as a single polity under a new caliph if they are to repel external onslaughts; and last but not least, Islam has to be propagated all across the world as the absolute and unadulterated Word of God, for prophecies predict that this will be so.

Thus Jihad and Islamic revivalism go hand in hand. *Tajdid*, or renewal, a concept that pervades religious discourse among the conservatives and radicals of Islam, calls for all of the above before Jihad will be abandoned. It wishes to take Islam and Muslims back to the time of the Prophet Mohammed by replicating seventh century Arabian society. The sprit of *Tajdid* has manifested itself on websites in various movements such as the "Party for Islamic Renewal." Never before has the spirit of Jihad surfaced the way it has in contemporary politics, and it is all linked to seeing an apocalyptic agenda brought to fruition. Very recently, the militant Hamas party won a victory in the Palestinian territories and formed a majority government. The Muslim Brotherhood and Hezbollah have also won considerable clout in seats of power.

The spirit of Jihad is rife among the Taliban as well. Recent spates of violence, which included an attack on a Canadian military base, indicate the resilience of the Taliban fighters driven by a desire to impose puritanical Islam and regain their control in the country. Jihad, therefore, continues to manifest itself in several ways.

Ahmadinejad, the recently elected president of Iran, has also stepped up his jihadist and apocalyptic rhetoric against Israel and the West. As part of his rhetoric, he recently organized a conference to deny the Holocaust ever occurred. Ahmadinejad is convinced victory is his because the time for the Mahdi to arrive has come. The messianic overtones of his statements are testimony to the power of prophecy to affect the politics of today.

Regarding Ahmadinejad and those professing apocalyptic faith, columnist Charles Krauthammer writes:

> This atavistic love of blood and death and, indeed, self-immolation in the name of God may not be new — medieval Europe had an abundance of millennial Christian sects — but until now it has never had the means to carry out its apocalyptic ends.
>
> That is why Iran's arriving at the threshold of nuclear weaponry is such a signal historical moment. It is not just that its President says crazy things about the Holocaust. It is that he is a fervent believer in the imminent reappearance of the 12th Imam, Shi'ism's version of the Messiah. President Mahmoud Ahmadinejad has been reported as saying in official meetings that the end of history is only two or three years away.[14]

Iran's nuclear aspirations are also cause for alarm, as Ahmadinejad's apocalyptic agenda may very well bring about a nuclear holocaust. In his rhetoric he is only matched by George W. Bush, the president of the most powerful nation in the world. He too is driven by a missionary, fundamentalist zeal. The clash of apocalyptic religions with crusaders and jihadists thus positioned to conquer the world may very well spell doom for its six billion inhabitants.

CHAPTER EIGHT

Osama bin Laden and His Terrorist Agenda

Images of Osama bin Laden waving his branch to assemble goats just outside a cave in Afghanistan often occupy a prominent place across Western television screens. They almost appear farcical when one examines this avowed enemy of America's formidable agenda. The media appear to have a sense of humor about these things. Comical is the fact that a frail raggedy man, barely able to survive his kidney disease, has taken on the most powerful military nation of the world, the United States of America. This gangling man with a turban, a long unkempt beard and a permanent smirk as he herds the goats is quite telling of the irony behind the recent war on terror—a David and Goliath scenario, so to speak. How such a man became America's archenemy is a question certainly worth exploring. Perhaps he is driven by an assurance of Islam's ultimate triumph as demonstrated in its eschatological literature. This chapter attempts to examine the beginnings and makings of Al-Qaeda, the influence it wields on modern jihadist ideology, and its recent manifestations in international terrorist organizations.

According to Yossef Bodansky, Osama bin Laden is "not an evil 'Lone Ranger' but rather a principal player in a tangled and sinister web of terrorism-sponsoring states, intelligence chieftains, and master terrorists. Together they wield tremendous power throughout the Muslim world and wreak havoc and devastation upon their foes."[1] In his book entitled *Bin Laden, the Man Who Declared War on America*, Bodansky goes on to state: "Bin Laden is not a man to be ignored, for he is at the core of Islamist international terrorism."[2]

Perhaps the author of the above book makes too extreme a claim when he suggests Bin Laden wields "tremendous power throughout the Muslim world."[3] A significant portion of the Muslim world routinely and forcefully condemns bin Laden's mission as criminal and immoral. The Muslim Canadian Congress, for example, a very progressive Muslim organization founded by author/activist Tarek Fatah, has been unequivocal in its denunciation of Islamist terror. Many express dismay at the fact that bin Laden has given the entire Muslim world a bad name through his heinous crimes. The educated among Muslims in particular do not subscribe to bin Laden's version of Jihad or to the Islamist agenda which strives to impose Islam on the rest of the world, either through force or persuasion. They are themselves targets of Islamist wrath, for according to the militants, those who do not actively participate in a Jihad are seen as colluding with the West, in allowing Western dominance over the Islamic world. Any moderate, therefore, even by default, becomes an "infidel," and to kill such a one is hardly a crime.

The previous chapter explored the rationale behind the twisting of classical Islamic philosophy by drawing parallels between conditions existing in pre–Islamic Arabia and those dominating the political scene today. A look at Osama bin Laden's writings and pronouncements will shed further light on the issue, showing what transformed him and why he feels compelled to launch a Jihad not only against the West, but also against his own government in Saudi Arabia and against other puppet regimes in the Muslim world, as well as the forces of moderation and progress within the faith, which according to bin Laden weaken the foundations, strength and solidarity of "true Islam" and its proponents.

Osama bin Laden was born on March 20, possibly in the year 1957, although birthdays are hardly occasions of significance in the Islamic world. Subscribing to an otherworldly approach to almost every aspect of existence, orthodox Muslims rarely record birthdays, particularly in rural settings. The year 1957, however, seems a plausible date for this influential man's entry into the world.

It is also more than likely that bin Laden's father eventually lost track of the births of his fifty-one children. Bin Laden is the son of a Yemeni father and a Saudi mother; his father, Mohammed Bin Laden, moved to Saudi Arabia, settled in the holy city of Medina, formed a construction company there and embarked on a rollicking business under the patronage of the Saudi government. His company would soon grow to be worth billions of dollars, enabling him to provide his many children with the best of education in the choicest academic institutions of the world. Although he died when Osama was a mere thirteen years old, the family business continued to flourish and Osama continued to live a life of luxury, privilege and opportunity, completing his engineering degree at King Abdul Aziz University in Jeddah, Saudi Arabia.

Osama then proceeded to take over the family business. Soon the young entrepreneur would partake of the honor of rebuilding Islam's two holiest sites, the grand mosque in Mecca housing the Kaaba and the Prophet's Mosque in Medina, where Islam's venerated founder is buried along with his two most trusted friends.

Brought up in a strict home environment of Wahahism — a puritanical sect of Islam found in Saudi Arabia — Osama experienced a spiritual rebirth after lascivious sexual escapades and began to associate more and more with the devout among his community. Many of these were Islamists committed to reviving the purity of the faith and bringing about its prophesied victory over the many perceived forces of evil, for they regarded themselves as end-time companions of the Prophet — in spirit at least.

Osama duly renounced his old "sinful" ways and gradually chose to adopt a more austere lifestyle governed by the Quranic philosophy that the life of this world is a mere pastime and a testing ground for true believers. All the rewards were to be gained in the hereafter, not the least of which was closeness to Allah. The promise of seventy-odd virgins for martyrs in Allah's cause was an added bonus and more of a reward system for the young ones who would sacrifice pleasures in this life for a higher end.

Osama became more engrossed in the texts and literature of Islam. As he immersed himself in Islamic study, he developed abhorrence for the moral freedoms of Western societies seeing a connection between the economic dysfunctionality of Muslim nations and Western affluence, Osama blamed the West for the Islamic world's sorry plight. In this he was joined by many in Saudi academia who shared their disgust of the West and insisted that only a reversal to strictly Islamic values would provide a solution to the myriad problems of Muslims.

Osama's ideological transformation came at a propitious time. It coincided with the rebirth of the Muslim Brotherhood in Egypt. In Iran, the Shia Islamists also made a comeback in 1979 under the leadership of the charismatic Ayatollah Khomeini — an event that was cheered as Islam's triumph over the West, for the deposed Shah was a mere American puppet. Islamists were now poised to take on the entire world, particularly the forces of imperialism, through the sheer strength of their faith. Hadith had predicted that evil in the end times would be destroyed only by pronouncing "Allah-o-Akbar" or *God is great*, and the wicked empires would crumble to the ground through the sheer power of the words!

While Khomeini was busy warming up to his new role as Iran's spiritual leader, deriving his mandate from God as the *Wilayat Faqih*, or the anointed just ruler and scholar of Islam, Juhayman al-Utaybi attacked the grand mosque at Mecca in order to realize the prophecy of the return of the Mahdi in the same year. He was followed by close to four hundred men, an indication that the Islamist zeal was rife among the youth. Osama continued to find inspiration in such events although at that moment he chose not to join in the rebellion. A rash of copycat events throughout Saudi Arabia with Islamist youth storming smaller mosques occurred that year.

Such cataclysmic upheavals throughout the Islamic world, which were also symptomatic of general economic, political and social decline, had greatly affected Osama bin Laden, who considered puritanical Islam the only anchor on which the Muslim nation would ever hope to reclaim its past glory. The year 1979 would also mark the Soviet invasion of Afghanistan, another Muslim nation subjugated by Christendom. Osama was now ready for a formal Jihad, particularly as the new invaders had started a deliberate campaign to obliterate not only the Islamist movement, but Islam within Afghanistan.

General Mohammed Zia-ul-Haq of Pakistan, who was himself deeply committed to Islamist ideology, was equally disturbed at the new developments. He would later come to be known among his admirers as the "Shaheed Jihad Afghanistan" or the Martyr of the Jihad of Afghanistan. His jihadist zeal was outlined in a conference of foreign ministers of thirty-five Muslim states who refused to recognize the puppet government the Soviets had installed in Afghanistan.

Bin Laden soon arrived in Pakistan with the express purpose of leading a Jihad against the Soviets. Finding support for his mission from Pakistan's devout Muslim military dictator, he gathered Pakistani and Afghani jihadists and established a training camp in Afghanistan. There he was soon to be joined by another influential Islamist by the name of Abdullah Yusuf Azzam, who would formulate an ideology of terror and establish the militant organization called the International Legion of Islam. Bin Laden and Azzam continued to work together, the latter providing the intellectual thrust and the former helping with finances.

Not only did Osama finance the travel expenses of the Mujahideen or the warriors of Islam, he also went about building the nation's infrastructure by constructing roads to facilitate the war machinery against the Soviets. During this time he traveled back and forth from Afghanistan to Saudi Arabia to replenish his supplies and funds. The movement, however, did not gain momentum until the mid-eighties, when thousands of Islamists from Arab nations and neighboring Pakistan began to join the struggle. It is also at this point that Osama was joined by his right-hand man, Ayman al-Zawahiri, who had fled Egypt after President Hosni Mubarek's crackdown on Islamic militants.

With the best and most loyal brains at his disposal now, Osama bin Laden was fortified in his effort to purge the Islamic land of Afghanistan from "infidel" rule. President Zia-ul-Haq of Pakistan continued providing tactical support through the country's intelligence agency, the ISI, as well as through ensuring a continual flow of manpower. The government of Pakistan also provided weaponry and military training which would eventually extend to Islamists from all over the Muslim world, not just the Afghans and the Pakistanis. At that point, Pakistan would also become home to some two million Afghan refugees, many of whom would come to operate flourishing businesses in Pakistan for goods they smuggled from Afghanistan.

Washington too was now supporting the Afghan Jihad against the Soviets. President Jimmy Carter had initially offered thirty million dollars in aid to the Mujahideen to oust the Soviets in an attempt to curb Communist influence. During the Reagan administration the figures rose to $700 million covering aid, arms and equipment. Bin Laden personally took part in the battles as a combatant during the Afghan resistance against the Soviets.

The Soviets were ousted in 1989. The Soviet Union itself would later collapse. Bin Laden was now convinced more than ever that the Jihad was the will of Allah and ultimate victory was the Muslim's right.

His conviction was based on an apocalyptic vision of the future when he stated in his letter to America, quoting verses of the Quran:

> The Nation of Victory and Success that Allah has promised:
> "It is he who has sent his Messenger (Mohammad peace be upon him) with guidance and the religion of truth (Islam), to make it victorious over all other religions even though the Polytheists hate it [Quran, 61: 19].
> "Allah has decreed that 'Verily it is I and My Messengers who shall be victorious.' Verily Allah is All-Powerful, All-Mighty" [Quran, 58: 21].[4]

Deriving his inspiration directly from scripture prophesying glory for Muslims, Osama joined hands with the Taliban to further the spread of Islam by removing any traces of foreign rule from both his homeland in Saudi Arabia and other Muslim nations. He began building his terrorist network with the help of the Taliban and soon formed a coalition of militant organizations ranging from the Lashkar-e-Tayyaba in Pakistan to the Safi group for Proselytism and Combat in Algeria. The militants were hoping to revive the institution of the caliphate by unifying all Muslims once again under a single ideology, that of Islam or more specifically Wahabi Islam. In the spirit of "Tajdid," or renewal of the original Islam so zealously advocated by Islamic revivalists, Osama bin Laden would launch his mission of establishing a global government under the banner of Islam. Often lamenting the dismemberment of the Ottoman caliphate at the hands of "Christian infidels," Osama hoped to unite the Islamic nation once again in a movement that would germinate in Afghanistan.

The new coalition would come to be known as the International Islamic Front. Their first international assault would result in the bombing of the American embassy in Kenya, killing three hundred people, while Osama and his right hand men sought safety in a Pakistani madrassah, anticipating U.S. retaliation.

But the most active phase of bin Laden's Jihad began after his arrival in Afghanistan. Mullah Omar, who gained control in 1996 of Kabul, the country's capital, was now in a position to welcome the arch-jihadist with open arms. He was going to protect bin Laden against all threats, internal and external, even at the risk of losing his own life under the Pashtun "melmastia" pact. Those who entered this pact were required to display absolute loyalty to the signatories. Little wonder that the Taliban did not cower under U.S. pressure to give up bin Laden after the 9/11 attacks and a war had to be fought instead to oust both the Taliban and the Al-Qaeda interests they were protecting.

Ever ready for a showdown with Americans and Westerners, bin Laden, firmly believing in the millenarian outcome of the conflict, busied himself in the manufacture of weaponry. In this quest, he would not rule out human beings as weapons also. But where would bin Laden garner such support? Would anyone wish to sacrifice his life for this cause?

The widespread support for the global Jihad would once again find a basis in the belief that Islam would gain supremacy in the world and that Allah's soldiers were certainly on the path of righteousness. The attainment of glory and victory for Islam was an attractive concept. It demanded the ultimate sacrifice which would be duly rewarded by Allah in the hereafter. Hadith were replete with promises of wide-eyed virgins awaiting the martyrs as they entered a luscious paradise.

Thus was death glorified. Allah even stated in the Quran that the martyr's death was not really a death, but a living testimony and triumph of the "True Faith."

The Quran states:

> Think not of those who are slain in Allah's way as dead. Nay, they live, finding their sustenance from their Lord. They rejoice in the Bounty provided by Allah. The martyrs rejoice that on them there is no fear, nor have they cause to

grieve. They rejoice in the Grace and the Bounty of Allah, and in the fact that Allah suffereth not the reward of the Faithful to be lost [in the least] [Quran, 3: 169–71].

Not only would Osama garner support for his cause from young men eager to seek their heavenly reward, he would also count on the almost universal resentment of Muslims against American expansionism, the Israeli occupation supported by the Americans, and to some extent, Christian proselytizing in Muslim lands through charitable organizations. Although such widespread resentment would not always or inevitably translate into violence, it nonetheless provided Osama with a vast pool of potential jihadists. According to Paul Williams, author of *Osama's Revenge*, "Ninety-five percent of educated Saudis between the ages of twenty-five and forty-one supported bin Laden's Jihad against Americans and a major Gallup poll showed that a majority of the world's Muslim population possessed an unfavorable opinion of the United States."[5]

Young Muslim men were answering Osama's call to Jihad in throngs. Not only were Afghanistan and Pakistan producing these soldiers, but Europe itself was home to potential militants with the largest concentration in France, estimated at forty thousand men.

For the first time in history, the Shia and the Sunni would also unite, at least in purpose, to fight a common enemy. Islamic Jihad, Hezbollah and Al-Qaeda, though not allied to each other formally, were nonetheless involved in the same global jihadist movement against the infidels in the hope of achieving their version of the prophesied apocalyptic world. The Shia militant organizations based in Palestine launched offensives against the Jewish state. Al-Qaeda concentrated its resources on dismantling the power of anyone seen to be supporting them.

Along with the men from across Europe who joined his cause, bin Laden also had a ready-made army at his disposal in the Taliban militia. Together they formed a formidable apocalyptic alliance of terror. Bin Laden and his Taliban allies offered their hospitality to young jihadists from all across the world. Terrorist groups from neighboring countries such as China and Pakistan as well as the central Asian countries joined in the struggle.

With the human arsenal at his disposal, Osama proceeded to acquire other weapons to see his global Jihad through, from conventional to nuclear arms. In this he found a very useful and willing ally in Pakistan's most renowned nuclear scientist, Dr. Abdul Qadeer Khan, who had channeled his religious zeal into building the proverbial "Islamic bomb."

As a result of this alliance, Osama and his followers acquired the needed knowledge to build dirty bombs to be transported in suitcases across the oceans. Unauthenticated Arab sources suggest these may number around twenty and the donors may be Chechen rebels. There is speculation that the suitcase bombs are being stored at two separate locations in Afghanistan.

Since the Taliban too were Osama's avowed allies and the recipients of aid from neighboring Pakistan, a constant supply of conventional weaponry was regularly transported across the border. But the Taliban's "melmastia" pact with bin Laden had done much more for the leading world jihadist. Now the entire country was at bin Laden's disposal with its rugged mountainous environment providing the ideal terrain for fully functioning terrorist training camps.

Dr. Paul Williams, while alluding to other means available to Osama bin Laden in regards to weapons production, makes the following observation about factories and their scope in his book *Osama's Revenge;*

> By 1999 he had established a well-equipped and fortified weapons factory in Kandahar for development and production of chemical weapons with the help of Pakistani ISI officials. Viruses causing deadly diseases, such as Ebola ..., were imported from Russia ; botulinum biotoxin was obtained from the Czech Republic and deadly anthrax from North Korea. At the weapons factory, Al-Qaeda operatives were trained to grow "lethal biological cultures" that could be used to poison water supplies along with the means of releasing lethal gases in major metropolitan areas.[6]

Osama's Jihad was therefore multi-pronged. Williams further elaborates on the volume, extent and range of the weaponry:

> A second base for the development of weapons of mass destruction was created in Zenica, Bosnia Herzegovina where an isolated farm house was converted into a "research centre" for advanced weaponry . Much of the research was devoted to the creation of human bombs — individuals who could carry and spread an incredibly virulent form of bubonic plague that remains resistant to treatment with choramphenicol or one of the tetracyclines."[7]

Thus bin Laden would stop at nothing to see his agenda through. And with all the necessary arsenal at his disposal, bin Laden declared: "Acquiring weapons for the defense of Muslims is a religious duty. If I have indeed acquired these weapons, then I thank God for enabling me to do so."[8]

All devout Muslims are "Islamists" in a loose sense, since they aspire to see Islam not only prevail over other ideologies and religions throughout the world, but obliterate them if possible. According to the overwhelming majority, this outcome is desirable only through persuasion. Bin Laden and his militant followers, however, feel such an approach has failed Muslims entirely. Fighting, Jihad and terrorism are the only options left for them that will fulfill the objectives of the *Ummah*, which envision the culmination of the global rule of Islam under a caliph. According to Daniel Benjamin and Steven Simon, authors of *The Next Attack*, this apocalyptic vision runs along the following ideological lines:

> At the core of bin Laden's thinking is an understanding of history as an unending conflict between Islam and "world infidelity." Drawing on the work of the twentieth century Egyptian Islamist Sayyid Qutb, the medieval Muslim commentator Taki al Din Ibn Taymiyaya, and a group of contemporary Saudi apocalypticists, bin Laden and his fellow radicals believe that waging this battle is the highest activity man can undertake, and they argue that this is part of the original message of Islam. Their struggle is therefore also about returning the faith to its original state and purifying it of all that has corrupted it in the centuries since the time of the Prophet Muhammed and his immediate successors, known as the four "rightly guided Caliphs." In this reformed Islam, Jihad — understood as driving non–Muslim forces from Muslim lands — belongs at the sacramental center of life. As more Muslims embrace this vision and join the struggle against world infidelity, not only will the heterodox innovations that have crept into the faith be eliminated, but the believers will turn the tide against the infidels. Reform and revival will be rewarded when a global order is established with Islam triumphant.[9]

Osama quotes profusely from the Quran in order to give legitimacy to his view on Jihad, something which moderate Muslims often balk at, as they feel it implicates the Quranic message as embodying a hateful ideology. But it is bin Laden's interpretation of verse 2:191 of the Quran which allows for the jihadist agenda to encompass many political and military struggles. The verse reads:

> and fight the pagans altogether as they fight you altogether. And fight them until there is no more tumult and oppression, and there prevail justice and faith for Allah.

When persecution becomes subordinated to killing, as in the case of the above verse, it can give the jihadist a variety of options as to what may be understood as persecution. Though the intent of the Quranic verse was hardly to incite terror, nor is the Quran the only scripture susceptible to manipulation in this fashion, the general purport of the terminology leaves the field wide open for a number of interpretations. It is on such verses that bin Laden and his jihadist camp rely.

His philosophy also rests on the eye-for-an-eye retributive law which allows the victim to seek revenge in equal manner, though the conditions of Jihad postulated in the Quran always warn Muslims never to "transgress" in the manner of retaliation. Again bin Laden feels that his Jihad does not entail such transgressions. Rather, it is obligatory on Muslims to retaliate. He makes this clear in his "Letter to the American People" as follows:

You attacked us in Somalia; you supported the Russian atrocities against us in Chechnya, the Indian oppression against us in Kashmir, and the Jewish aggression against us in Lebanon.

Under your supervision, consent and orders, the governments of our countries which act as your agents, attack us on a daily basis....

You steal our wealth and oil at paltry prices because of your international influence and military threats. This theft is indeed the biggest theft ever witnessed by mankind in the history of the world.

Your forces occupy our countries; you spread your military bases throughout them; you corrupt our lands, and you besiege our sanctities, to protect the security of the Jews and to ensure the continuity of your pillage of our treasures....

You may then dispute that all of the above does not justify aggression against civilians, for crimes they did not commit and offenses in which they did not partake:

This argument contradicts your continuous repetition that America is the land of freedom, and its leaders in the world. Therefore, the American people are the ones who choose their government by way of their own free will; a choice which stems from agreement to its policies.... This is why the American people cannot be innocent of all the crimes committed by the Americans and Jews against us.

Bin Laden also quotes Islamic scholars of old, who had legitimized Jihad in the eventuality the religion was faced with external threats. His view that American and infidel forces are involved in a conspiracy against Islam is evident in the following statement of bin Laden as it appeared in his statement about the "Jihad against Jews and Crusaders":

All these crimes and sins committed by the Americans are a clear declaration of war on Allah, his messenger, and Muslims. And Ulema [scholars] have throughout Islamic history unanimously agreed that the Jihad is an individual duty if the enemy destroys the Muslim countries. This was revealed by Iman Bin-Qadamah in "Al Mughni," Imam al-Kisa'i in "Al-Bada'i," al-Qurtubi in his interpretation, and the shayieh of al-Islam in his books, where he said: "As for the fighting to repulse [an enemy], it is aimed at defending sanctity and religion, and it is a duty as agreed [by the ulema]. Nothing is more sacred than belief except repulsing an enemy who is attacking religion and life."[10]

While most moderate Muslims consider this a manipulation of religious texts, classical sources and commentaries, it is easy to see how bin Laden turns a "righteous Jihad," which is theoretically a war fought in self defense, to an ideology of terror. He insists, therefore, that it is Muslims who are being attacked. By retaliating he is not violating Islamic precepts; he is only fighting a defensive war. While ordinary Muslims believe the verses of the Quran referring to Jihad are contextual and speak to circumstances of the time, bin Laden insists the contexts and scenarios that originally necessitated Jihad have been recreated in modern times, legitimizing his stance. Thus the fine line that sets apart a "righteous Jihad" is often crossed into the realm of terrorism.

What is often sidelined in bin Laden's terrorist ideology is the pristine Islamic narrative on Jihad which explicitly prohibits the killing of innocent people, described clearly as the old, children, women, and the infirm as well as non-combatants. Abu Bakr, the first caliph of Islam, declared that livestock, trees, plantations and ecosystems were not to be disturbed, let alone innocent human beings.

On the other hand, bin Laden was often found quoting Ibn Taimiyya, the 13th century scholar, who said: "To fight in the defense of religion and belief is a collective duty; there is no other duty after belief than fighting the enemy who is corrupting the life and the religion."[11]

Many young men and women buy bin Laden's arguments of the legitimacy of Jihad by any means whatever in modern times, as they feel they are in a state of perpetual warfare. When Osama quotes Ibn Taimiyya to the effect that the danger to their religion is greater by not taking up arms, they are easily swayed into fighting in Allah's cause, as it also comes with profuse rewards in the hereafter.

The above fervently explosive jihadist zeal, with willing fighters, arsenal and presentiments of future glory, would result in a series of terrorist attacks all across the world. Of the long list of suspected terrorist attacks by Al-Qaeda after its weapons production and military machinery was so creatively put in place by bin Laden, a few deserve special mention.

One: The US embassies in Nairobi, Kenya and Dar-us-Salam, Tanzania, suffered massive explosions in August of 1998. The attacks claimed 224 lives. There were close to four thousand reported injuries. This was the first massive attack by Al-Qaeda.

Two: The year 2000 saw the bombing of the USS *Cole* on the coast of Yemen on Oct 12, killing 17 soldiers and injuring 39 others. This was executed as a suicide attack by Abdullah Ibrahim Thaur.

Three: Much of the brain power of Al-Qaeda and the newly established International Islamic Front had survived to plot and plan the next attack on American and Western interests that attack took place on American soil one horrific day in September 2001 when three thousand unsuspecting civilians lost their lives. The World Trade Center buildings in New York were destroyed; the Pentagon was badly damaged; and the world was forever changed.

Soon, a rather bizarre interpretation of verses 109 and 110 of chapter nine of the Quran was circulated among Muslim apocalypticists. They read:

Is the man who lays the foundations of his sanctum on his allegiance to God and the wish to seek his favor better, or he who lays the foundation of his building on the edge of a bank eroded by water, which will collapse with him into the fire of Hell? But God does not guide the people who are willfully unjust. The edifice they have built will always fill their minds with perturbation [which will not cease] till their hearts are rent to pieces, for God is all-knowing and all-wise [Quran 9:109–110].

The Quran, apart from being divided into chapters of varying lengths, is also divided into thirty equal parts called "juz." Coincidentally, the cited verses appear in the *ninth* chapter of the Quran and the *eleventh* juz. Concordances were immediately drawn in the minds of apocalypticists about this bizarre coincidence of the numbers 9/11 conforming to that fateful date in 2001. The extremists were convinced the Quran had prophesied 9/11.

After 9/11 the world became much more vigilant, but Al-Qaeda's insidious plotting resulted in the 2002 Bali bombings in Indonesia killing 202 people. The perpetrators of the violence had expressed allegiance to Al-Qaeda's mission. It appears that bombs were carried in a backpack which caused a minor explosion followed by a much more powerful car bomb explosion. Jemaah Islamiya, a cell linked to Al-Qaeda, and its leader Abu Bakr Bashir claimed responsibility for the attack.

Terrorist assaults also manifested themselves in a 2004 standoff in Baslan, Russia, when Chechen rebels held hostage twelve hundred children. The rescue effort was able to retrieve only some of these innocent hostages. Many of the children perished in the siege. All the assailants were either killed or captured. But the new jihadist ideology continued to surface in many parts of the world where Islam and Christianity were to come into contact with each other.

Western targets, particularly after the 2003 U.S. invasion of Iraq, became particularly vulnerable. On March 11, 2004, bombs exploded in a busy commuter train station in Madrid, Spain, killing 200 and injuring 2000 commuters. Spain pulled out its troops from Iraq shortly after the attacks.

The Saudi monarchy, too, has been the target of Al-Qaeda's rage. Again inspired by apocalyptic zeal to reinstate the caliphate, Osama would have to depose the Saudi monarchy he regards as being utterly corrupt and a puppet of America.

It is crucial to examine the future and scope of Al-Qaeda in our constantly changing world. As mentioned earlier, author Noah Feldman, in his book *After Jihad: America and the Struggle for Islamic Democracy*, makes the rather fanciful prediction that terrorism will be replaced by extremist control of political seats of power. Once they have this power at their disposal, they will not have a desire to achieve their goals through terrorist assaults.

There are several snags to this theory. First, Muslim rage over unresolved political disputes such as the Israeli-Palestinian issue is not likely to decrease. On the contrary, the longer these issues take to resolve, the greater chance there is for more Muslim youth to be radicalized in the name of religion, because these terrorist groups have a religio-political agenda. They see politics as a tool to further the religious cause. The two are interlinked.

Those who perpetrate acts of violence at the grassroots level do not always aspire for political power since they do not consider it within their reach. They are simply driven by a religious zeal which strives to make a strong statement against Western domination, Israeli occupation or perhaps something more threatening to them, such as the infiltration of western values in Muslim societies. It must be borne in mind that terrorist command and control are not as centralized as many believe. Al-Qaeda, Hamas, Islamic Jihad or Hezbollah are providing the ideological thrust to the jihadist movement, but many splinter groups act on their own accord, striving to acquire means and know-how through private sources and individual effort.

The recent discovery of terrorist cells, both in Canada and the United States, gives credence to the above contention. Seven men arrested from the Miami region in June 2006 professed a mixture of Christianity and Islam and associated themselves only loosely with Al-Qaeda ideology. Seventeen Muslim men arrested from the Toronto area that same month also acted on their own initiative. Their leader, Imam Jamal, was preaching hatred and vengeance to local teenagers disillusioned with the Canadian government's role in Afghanistan, or the treatment of Muslim men incarcerated under security certificates.

The view that terror will decline due to extremist access to power rests also on the contention that they will indeed assume that political power. The political dynamics of Muslim countries suggest this is an unlikely scenario. It is true that Hamas in January 2006 won a sweeping victory in the Palestinian authority; the Hezbollah, a Lebanese terrorist militia, have acquired seats in the parliament of Lebanon; and the Taliban gained control of much of Afghanistan in 1996. Nevertheless, these governments do not enjoy long term popular support due to their fundamentalist understanding of Islam as well as the draconian measures they adopt to suppress moderate views and practices. When the Taliban was deposed by the U.S., there was mass jubilation on the streets of Kabul. Schools were reopened for girls, and though women continue to be marginalized, steps were nonetheless taken to integrate them in the social and professional life of the country.

Hamas' victory in Palestine is seen more as a rejection of the Fatah faction rather than an endorsement of the Hamas agenda. Besides, Hamas' control of political power has not seen a decrease in terrorist assaults on Israeli targets — proof that centralized control of terrorist activity is not crucial to this movement, nor is access to political control a substitute.

Particularly relevant to the Israeli-Arab dispute is the role of the Hezbollah or "the party of God." A resistance movement formed after the Israeli occupation of Lebanon in 1982, the Hezbollah have grown to be a powerful force, politically, militarily and economically. Their main ideological difference with Al-Qaeda is of course based on sectarian division, Hezbollah being Shia, but their ultimate objective is to guarantee the security of Lebanon, though Israel remains the Hezbollah's common enemy with the Palestinians.

During the July 2006 conflict between Israel and Lebanon, the Hezbollah held on to their posts till the very end against what was deemed the strongest military power in the region. The Shia group gained immensely in stature all across the Islamic world as a result. Polls showed 89 percent support of Hezbollah even among Sunni populations. Among Lebanese Christians their support soared to 80 percent for Hezbollah.

The other hotbeds of terrorist ideology, such as Pakistan, will likely not see terrorist control of the political reins. Although extremism is rife in many parts of Pakistan, political control of groups such as the Taliban remains confined to the Waziristan area of the country. The bulk of the population espouses a moderate view of Islam and would balk at any possibilities of their freedoms and privileges curtailed because of restrictions posed by fundamentalism. Moreover, ostensibly moderate regimes such as that of Pakistani president Pervez Musharraf enjoy the support of the United States. Many of the corrupt monarchies of the Middle East like the Saudi clan have been able to hold on to power due to such support. Elsewhere in the Arab world, elections were held in Algeria with the Islamists poised to win a majority, but they were canceled in order to prevent such a scenario from unfolding.

Hypothesizing Al-Qaeda's control over seats of power, one would have to conclude that the terrorist organization would resort to launching state sponsored terror which would prove to be far more lethal than any terrorist assaults the world has witnessed thus far, if indeed it ever gained control over government.

The state machinery will afford these militant groups the necessary tools, equipment and financial resources to further their agenda. Perhaps it is for this reason that attempts have been made to prevent Islamists and Muslim extremists from gaining political control in their respective countries.

Bin Ladenism and Al-Qaeda may be obliterated, but unless the root causes of terror are addressed honestly, the terrorist agenda is likely to stay and further infiltrate the masses with splinter groups acting independently. As mentioned earlier, the militants are also driven by an apocalyptic agenda dominating sections of their religious texts. Wars are inevitable, so the scriptures and religious texts say. There is no other way to see God's kingdom established on earth. The Muslim extremists are convinced it is their version of apocalyptic events that will come true, as they wish to establish Shariah law everywhere in the world after Islam has gained ascendancy, and Shariah law claims to uphold the sovereignty of God alone. This according to the Islamists is the only genuine kingdom of God that can be established, because according to them it embodies the only genuine doctrine or understanding of what it means to establish the kingdom of God. Islam's political ideology does not allow for the sovereignty of human beings or nations. Only God is the sovereign ruler of the world. It is only when his sovereignty is thus realized and acknowledged through establishing Islam's apocalyptic vision that the true meaning of the kingdom of God on earth will be realized.

Bin Ladens will come and go, but the ideology is permanent. Unless a concerted effort is made to challenge it from within the Muslim quarters also, extremism and its violent manifestations will continue to occur. Even funding of groups like Al-Qaeda and Hamas is not dependent on charities or donations. The massive appeal of the movements is itself a continuing source of funds, and the loose controls often afford members the opportunity to fund their offensives covertly, through individual donations.

According to Daniel Benjamin and Steven Simon, "Amidst the many al Qaeda–related attacks of the period since 2001, the phenomenon of self-starting terrorists began to appear."[12] The authors draw the startling conclusion that the West is therefore losing the war against terror. Extremist elements among Muslims would see this as a realization of their apocalyptic goal.

CHAPTER NINE

The World Today

The world today is a seething bed of local, regional and global conflicts with a potential to erupt at any given time into a catastrophic confrontation of wills, ideologies, military might and religious dogma throughout the world. Some conflicts are of greater global significance, such as the Arab-Israeli dispute because of its potential effects on world oil supplies. Others may offer small countries the chance of aligning themselves with the major contenders, thus tipping power balances in favor of one side or the other, for the world today is extremely volatile in its shifting loyalties. Many would see doomsday scenarios in the current turmoil the world faces.

In the United States' decision, for example, to go to war in Iraq in 2003, "the coalition of the willing" entering with the U.S. was largely made up of Eastern European nations. Although these nations had only recently come under the umbrella of American influence, their presence nonetheless conferred upon the war a degree of moral legitimacy.

Added to the global political turmoil is the continuing growth of multinational conglomerates sucking the resources out of the world. The political process in many countries is now subordinated to the interests of these global forces, which have nothing but their own economic interest at heart. Apocalypticists would see a fulfillment of prophecy in these emerging global forces as the prophesied diabolical kingdom under the Antichrist.

The interests of the major players in the new stage of world politics are in such tremendous conflict with each other that many believe this conflict must lead to a war of cataclysmic proportions, either to change the current world order, or to completely wipe out the establishment that is forcing the

131

world towards annihilation. The magnitude of such global conflict seems to have been predicted in the religious texts of both Christianity and Islam. "Nation will rise against nation," the Bible had said (Matthew 24:7), and "there will be much *harj* (killing)," the Prophet Mohammed had predicted (Bukhari: Muhammad Muhsin Khan, Vol. 9, no. 184).

The struggle for the control of oil resources, the disputes over fresh water supplies, the ideological warfare between Islam and the West, China and India as newly emergent world powers, all seem poised to play a role in shaping the world in the twenty-first century. And in the troubled world today, these forces have not only converged, they are gathering momentum, spelling a dreadful scenario of mass destruction, widespread poverty and misery of untold proportions.

The strategic importance of various world conflicts will determine how volatile or explosive these are. On the global arena, the Israeli-Palestinian conflict continues to attract the attention of the world for several reasons. Oil in the Middle East and western dependence on cheap crude continues to shape the dynamics of the regional politics of the Middle East, the effects of which are felt beyond the borders of the region. The assumption that the United States is in Iraq in order to gain access to its oil reserves finds credibility among Muslim masses all over the world. The view that the U.S. is in Iraq also to protect Israel's hegemony in the region is also quite widespread. Any nation perceived to be a threat to Israel's security, according to prevalent Muslim sentiment, is attacked, its infrastructure destroyed and its government destabilized.

Saddam's Iraq, Muslims believe, posed such a threat to Israel's security and hegemony in the region. According to Samuel Huntington in his book *Clash of Civilizations*, the only Arab state with the capability to challenge Israel was Iraq.[1] Not only was Saddam funding the Palestinian resistance against the Israeli occupation by enticing young militants with huge sums of money, his commitment to weapons accumulation was a cause of much concern for the Bush administration. The fact that Bush is an avowed evangelical Christian gives many Muslims reason to believe that he is influenced by his apocalyptic Christian belief in supporting Israel by destroying Iraq. They draw parallels between the invasion of Iraq in 2003 with the control of Palestine by Jewish immigrants in 1948. Many Muslims believe the Jews connived to buy land off poor Palestinian peasants in the years leading to the creation of Israel. Now that Iraq is economically destroyed, many Jews and "infidels" are buying property in Iraq to set the stage for a permanent presence in the country. Many like Osama bin Laden therefore contend that the U.S.–led wars in Afghanistan and Iraq in fact represent a modern crusade against Islam. The resentment against both Israel and the United States grows in leaps and bounds.

The truth about Iraq is two-sided depending on whether one is a devout Muslim holding views discussed above, or an evangelical Christian. The evangelicals are also influenced by the apocalyptic belief that anyone who opposes Israel is not on God's side and will incur his wrath. God, as they see it, promised Israel that whoever would bless her would be blessed by God and whoever would curse her would be the recipient of God's displeasure (Gen. 12, 1–3).

They also believe Bush can do no wrong in going into Iraq. As a Christian man, he had nothing but the best interest of the Iraqis at heart, many evangelicals contend. He desired only to free them from the tyranny of Saddam; he aspired to introduce democratic rule in the Middle East; and he wanted to protect the American people from another possible terrorist attack — for Bush, they believe, went into Iraq under the presumption that Saddam may have forged links with Al-Qaeda.

But even educated and moderate Muslims would question that view. Certainly Saddam was a tyrant, but he was able to hold the different factions living within the borders of his country together, though Shias and Kurds were kept at bay with an iron fist. Iraq was also prosperous and peaceful, they say, with many social programs in place, particularly for Iraqi women. Now it has sunk into a state of near-anarchy. The Islamists have launched a virulent campaign of terror in the country, against both foreign forces and indigenous people who do not subscribe to their brand of Islam. They also wish to introduce Shariah law in Iraq which will greatly harm the cause of women's rights in the country. And many Muslims, even those of the liberal, moderate and secular persuasions, conclude that the war in Iraq is the greatest modern-day crime against humanity. The pulse of the Muslim world is more accurately taken by recognizing the anger among its moderate and liberal segments rather than its fundamentalists.

Furthermore, they scoff at any suggestions that the invasion was altruistically motivated in bringing about democracy, which many feel must grow out of the cultural ethos of the indigenous people. They also insist Saddam's regime would have imploded in time. Few are convinced that this was not a war of aggression to gain control of Iraqi crude. Resentment therefore is widespread among Muslims of all stripes against the 2003 American invasion of Iraq.

Although Iraq is a comparatively recent dispute between Muslims and what many among them refer to as the "Crusader-Zionist" alliance, it is the Palestine issue that continues to fester and seep till it begins to erupt in newer and bloodier conflicts and wars. Israel's incursions into Gaza are routine and terrorism against Israeli targets is unrelenting. Emotions are so much on edge in the region that the slightest provocation on either side can give the adversaries a pretext for military action.

In June 2006, the capture of the Israeli soldier Gilad Shalit by Hamas sparked a full-fledged Israeli military assault on Gaza, destroying the infrastructure of the territory, leaving its citizens without water, power, food and medical facility for days on end. While the firing of Qassam rockets from Gaza — which has occurred ever since Hamas, the terrorist Palestinian group, took control over seats of power — seemed to be the real cause behind Israel's incursion, the fallout on Palestinian citizenry in terms of the heavy casualty inflicted by Israel's military might invites criticism both from Arab and Muslim nations against the Jewish state. Israel is clearly seen as the aggressor and the United States' reluctance to condemn Israeli assaults exacerbates the animosity of the Muslims against both nations.

The 2006 conflict between Israel and the Palestinians expanded into Lebanon, killing an estimated one thousand Lebanese civilians in a matter of a month. The provocation came from the capture of two other Israeli soldiers by the Shiite militia, the Hezbollah or the "Party of God." While Hezbollah insisted their aim in capturing the soldiers was a prisoner swap and that it did not wish for the conflict to expand into a full-scale war, Israel began a full-scale military offensive against Lebanon, destroying the country's airports, bridges and roads in the attempt to destroy the Hezbollah's military capabilities. It is believed that Hezbollah is being funded both by Iran and Syria, with armaments being allowed into Lebanon from Iran via Syria.

Hezbollah also demonstrated its military strength to the world by firing katyusha rockets into Israeli cities as far south as Nahariya and Haifa, killing close to 170 Israelis and wounding more than a thousand.

First the invasion of Iraq by the Americans and recently Israel's incursion into Gaza and Lebanon reinforces the Muslim apocalyptic scholar's stance that the "crusader" forces will invade all of Syria, Lebanon, Palestine, parts of Northern Saudi Arabia, Iraq and Jordan which comprise "Greater Israel." Concordances between modern events and ancient apocalyptic literature are often cited as inevitable outcomes of wars that will eventually turn into victory for Muslims. This hopeful anticipation has instilled in the modern jihadists the religious zeal to never give up their struggle to liberate Palestine, to free Iraq, and to drive "infidel" forces out of Saudi Arabia, Afghanistan, Kashmir, Chechnya and wherever else Muslims happen to be oppressed.

And it is in recognition of the above that Israel's latest offensive in Lebanon, seen as far too disproportionate a response by some, has been justified by others on the following grounds. The Hezbollah, Al-Qaeda, Hamas and the fanatical regime of Iran under Ahmadinejad will never give up their animosity towards the Jewish state. It is therefore necessary to send a strong message to these nations that if they mess with Israel, not only the actual perpetrators but the innocent citizens of these countries will suffer as well. By doing so Israel hopes to sway public opinion against terrorist groups who support suicide attacks against Israel.

The military response, although acknowledged by most to be disproportionate, is still seen as justifiable, given the fact that Israel is defending its citizenry and its borders from future assaults by Hezbollah and Hamas.

The involvement of Hezbollah in the latest conflict is also likely to expand into Syria and Iran as the two countries are seen as suppliers of weaponry to Hezbollah. With the involvement of Iran also comes the threat of nuclear warfare. In fact the threat of conventional warfare turning into nuclear war is ever present. Iran itself has been labeled a "rogue" state. Even mechanical or human error can potentially ignite such a localized nuclear war. Moreover, as volatile as world politics is today, localized wars can easily turn into global conflicts.

Many Muslims, like evangelical Christians, feel the final conflict will be fought between the forces of Islam, Judaism and Christianity in the Middle East, and as predicted, the stage for this conflict is being set right where it is supposed to occur. And because both sides feel they are justified in their claims to the land promised to Abraham's descendants in scripture, they strongly believe only a final military conflict will resolve the issue.

Little wonder that since 1948, ever since the state of Israel came into existence, very little progress has been made towards peace, which remains ever elusive in light of the recent events. In fact, the continuing tensions have led to the further radicalization of militant groups and right wing politicians. In Israel, the right wing Likud party controls decisions. Its stance towards Palestinian overtures remains uncompromising. In Palestine, Hamas, which is a terrorist organization with an express agenda to destroy Israel and reclaim all of historic Palestine, also does not believe in any compromise, though it appears to be slowly capitulating because of economic sanctions against it, which only affect the ordinary civilian living in the Palestinian territories. Hamas recently conceded to a tacit approval of recognizing Israel's right to exist. All sides in this dispute are now poised to play a militant role driven by religious and nationalistic zeal. Hamas also wants to establish Islam in Palestine and the rest of the world. George W. Bush, on the other hand, is helping Israel hang on to control in all the sites important and historically relevant sites to that country.

Peace will not be achieved in the region especially when the two sides now holding the seats of power are far more entrenched in their hatred of each other. The great orthodox Islamic scholar Abul Ala Maudidi, typifying apocalyptic zeal, asserts:

> Now if a person looks at the affairs of the Middle East and studies them in the light of the background of the Holy Prophet's prophecies, he will at once perceive that the stage is fully set for the emergence of the Dajjal who would arise as the "promised Messiah" of the Jews as foretold by the Holy Prophet (Peace be upon him).[2]

Zakiuddin Sharfi, yet another authority on Islamic prophecy, makes the following observation about world events and their possible outcome:

> A specter is haunting the globe, the specter of a nuclear world war. Experts in international relations who know, due to their life long studies, the trouble points and bones of contention among the nations, scholars of Christian and Jewish faiths who know the biblical prophecies, and knowledgeable Islamic leaders such as Maududi all agree on one thing (in spite of their obvious difference in sources of obtaining the truth): that the Middle East is already in great turmoil ready to engulf the globe into a bloody confrontation unparalleled in history.[3]

As tensions continue to mount, the radicalization of the two warring groups will increase in proportion. Islamism and Zionism will exacerbate an already bloody conflict. Zionism strives to acquire all of Syria, Lebanon, Jordan, Iraq, parts of Turkey, the Sinai, and the northern part of Saudi Arabia including the city of Medina. Muslim lands are therefore the primary target of the Zionist mission. No wonder Islamist forces see the modern invasion of Iraq as part of the overall "Crusader-Zionist" expansionist agenda. Islamism on the other hand has designs all over the world, again either through force or persuasion, but sees the resolution of the Middle East conflict in Islam's favor as the starting point of its ideological and political expansion.

Zakiuddin Sharfi notes in apocalyptic language, "The Jews will be destroyed putting an end to their treacherous community. Whereas with the destruction of the Cross, all the religious communities will merge into the single community of Islam."[4]

This turn of events in the Middle East is reminiscent of the early days of Islam. Jews and Muslims were in direct confrontation with each other in the northern city of Medina. While many of the Jewish tribes of Medina had converted to Islam, there were a few, such as the Bani Nadir and Bani

Khuraiza, who remained the Prophet's most formidable adversaries. The modern conflict between Jews and Muslims is somewhat of a *déjà vu* after centuries of peace, or at least the semblance of peace, between Jews and Muslims. In fact many would assert that the Jews flourished more under Muslim rule than in Christian states, whose citizenry historically regarded Jews with contempt as the murderers of Christ.

Tables have indeed turned, setting the stage for the final conflict as described in apocalyptic literature. The historical enmity between Jews and traditional Christians has changed into support for the state of Israel. While in theory many governments have attempted to broker peace in the Middle East, the most promising of these attempts, representing Ehud Barak's offer to Palestinians in 1999 under the Clinton administration, was nonetheless rejected. The radical forces on either side have prevented the formulation of a peace plan that would be acceptable to both parties. The stumbling blocks to any peace process are the status of Jerusalem, important to both Jews and Muslims, the right of return for Palestinians and the question of Israeli settlements. Ehud Barak's offer to the Palestinians might have been accepted had the forces of moderation prevailed over extremism, but this was not the case. Ariel Sharon's government merely offered an extremely fractured Palestinian state on 48 percent of the occupied territories. Moreover Gaza and the presence of Jewish settlements in the West Bank will prevent a territorially contiguous state from ever coming into being, a scenario which most Palestinians will reject, especially with the election of Hamas as their representatives.

While Israel has withdrawn its settlements from Gaza, it will most likely keep them in the West Bank, as the area is geographically and historically more relevant to Jewish tradition and culture. Again, ultra-orthodox Jews would most likely refuse to leave their positions due to biblical prophecy and what they see as its fulfillment. Many wish to rebuild the Temple of Solomon on the site of Islam's third holiest mosque, all in the hope of fulfilling the prophecy of the Temple being rebuilt before Christ's second advent. Just as Sharfi above says, "Jews will be destroyed," Gershon Solomon asserts that once the Temple is built, "Islam is over."[5] In this the Jews have unflinching support from the evangelicals, many of whom choose to demonstrate solidarity with Jews by going so far as to adopt Jewish religious practices. Hamas, Islamic Jihad and Hezbollah, on the other hand, wish to see Israel completely wiped out from the face of the earth. In their religious zeal, these extremists are guided by words attributed to the Prophet when he said, "The day of resurrection will not arrive until you make war on the Jews, until a Jew will hide behind a rock or tree, and the rock or tree will say: O

Muslim servant of Allah, here is a Jew behind me, kill him" (Bukhari: Muhammad Muhsin Khan, Vol. 4, no. 177).

Tension over the latest Israeli incursion into Lebanon escalated, causing an outcry in the Islamic world. Its leaders, particularly those who believe in the apocalyptic truth of coming events such as Iranian president Ahmadinejad, warned of the war expanding all over the Islamic world as an "explosion." Addressing a crowd of thousands of protesters on July 7, 2006, Ahmadinejad said, "They [Israelis] should not let things reach a point where an explosion occurs in the Islamic world."[6]

The "explosion" that Ahmadinejad speaks of is also a hint towards the growing cooperation between Hezbollah, a Shiite terrorist organization, with Hamas which is Sunni and now the ruling majority in the Palestinian territories. Hezbollah, it is alleged, is being funded by Iran, whose president, Mr. Ahmadinejad, wants to see Israel destroyed. Ahmadinejad and his demonstrated apocalyptic zeal will wish to see his vision through. These militants and the inspiration they draw from apocalyptic literature will continue to fuel the jihadist apocalyptic ideology whose ultimate aim is the destruction of Israel. Even if these groups are destroyed militarily by Israel, the ideology will not die until the apocalyptic vision is seen as being fulfilled.

Indeed the situation is explosive and contagious and certainly not confined to Middle East politics. While Israel and the United States fight their own terrorists, Russia tackles its own brand of radical Islam. When the Soviet Union ceased to exist in 1991, many republics declared their independence from Russia. Chechnya was one of them. But whereas the others were allowed to secede because they were signatories to the new Federation Treaty, Chechnya refrained from signing the treaty, and consequently remained under Russian control.

A tiny country of 1.5 million Muslims situated in the Caucuses, Chechnya is rich in oil. Chechens understandably want control over their own resources but the Russians will not relinquish theirs. A Jihad has therefore unfolded, breaking out in an all-out war in 1994 which Chechnya, despite its inferior military strength, won through a series of guerrilla campaigns. This, however, would not result in Chechnyan independence. The intransigence of both parties in the conflict has manifested itself as pogroms, ethnic cleansing and torture of Chechen civilians on the part of the Russians, and terrorist reprisals from Chechen rebels. Thus far the conflict has taken the lives of close to one hundred thousand Chechen civilians.

There is also evidence that Al-Qaeda militants are helping the Chechen cause against the Russians. Al-Qaeda's global Jihad has also taken Chechnya in its fold, although Chechen rebels only have designs on their own land, at least in the short run. Terrorism is their tool. Apart from smaller routine terrorist strikes, the 2002 takeover of a Moscow theater and the 2003 takeover of a Russian school in Beslan, killing 300 people, mostly children, caught the attention of the world for the sheer brutality of the acts.

But many will argue that the siege which resulted in the killings of 150 schoolchildren pales in comparison with the Russian army's reign of terror on Chechen masses, since an estimated 200,000 Chechens have been tortured, imprisoned or killed by the Russians. Putin's government has also led a systematic campaign to hide its atrocities from the rest of the world by allegedly putting to death journalists who might wish to expose them. The recent death of veteran journalist Anna Politkovskaya is being vigorously attributed to the Kremlin.

Although this is largely a contained problem with Chechen forces targeting Russian interests, many rebels wonder why George W. Bush argued for Ukrainian sovereignty while ignoring the plight of the Chechens. Again oil is cited as a possible cause and again, the "crusaders" are united against Islam, the Muslims conclude as they expound their eschatological literature. A fundamentalist website called Party for Islamic Renewal recently posted an article by Prof. Francis A. Boyle in its issue of June 22, 2006, stating, "The imperial government of the United States of America is stealing hydrocarbon empire from Moslem States and peoples."[7] Putin and Bush they believe are united in this mission.

Of the Muslim nations of the world, Pakistan has sophisticated nuclear capability thanks to its most eminent scientist, Dr. Abdul Qadeer Khan. Also, Dr. Khan was very generous in sharing his knowledge with other Muslim nations and jihadist groups. But Pakistan's nuclear arsenal does not pose a threat to Israel. It is more of a deterrent against India, its longstanding political rival and neighbor in using its nuclear capability against Pakistan.

In recent months, both India and Pakistan have made strides towards improving relations with each other, but the terrorist groups who are fighting a Jihad in the disputed territory of Kashmir wish to subvert prospects of any long term rapprochement.

The Jihad in Kashmir began in earnest after the Afghan jihadists ousted the Soviets from Afghanistan. The collapse of the Soviet Union was only a mixed blessing for America. True, an identifiable superpower with whom America had both ideological and military rivalry was no more and America emerged as the only Superpower. On the other hand, before the collapse, the "balance of terror" between two equal and identifiable enemies had resulted only in a "cold war." Both parties were engaged in preserving their influences in various parts of the world; they met indirectly through the

Korean and Vietnamese wars and other skirmishes, but they never came in direct confrontation with each other.

Communism, though, would soon be replaced by Islamism in such former Soviet republics as Tajikistan, Uzbekistan, Tatarstan. This ideology was far more powerful because it claimed its authority from God. A much more elusive enemy that attacked the very values that America has always cherished would emerge. This ideology was in fact freed up from the clutches of Communism and became united against any perceived enemies of Islam whether in Afghanistan, Chechnya, Kashmir, Palestine or the "Great Satan," the United States.

A picturesque valley located in Northwest of the Indian subcontinent, Kashmir is roughly 70 percent Muslim. It has experienced a long history of war and conflict, but it is only in recent times that the conflict in Kashmir has posed a threat to international peace, as the two rivals laying claim to it both boast of nuclear capability.

When the Indian subcontinent became independent from British rule in 1947, a few states and provinces were asked to accede either to Pakistan or India. While the Dogra prince of Kashmir was Hindu, the population, being largely Muslim, rebelled against his rule, prompting the Pakistani army to invade a part of Kashmir in October of 1947. At that point the Dogra ruler acceded to India, who brought its own army to repel the Pakistani onslaught. The two countries now hold areas of Kashmir under their control divided by what is known as the "line of control." Every since the beginning of the modern Jihad there, the two sides have resorted to ethnic cleansing and human rights violations. Many Hindus have fled the Muslim areas into Jammu, the majority Hindu area of Kashmir. Many Muslims have been victims of brutality by the Indian army. Terrorism too has increased, supported by many small and large terrorist groups such as the former Lashkari Tayyaba and its two modern factions. These jihadist groups act under a single United Islamic Front in Kashmir. Their recent brutality was manifested in the Mumbai train blasts of July 11, 2006, killing two hundred commuters and wounding several others. The United States has tried to appease both neighbors. Donald Rumsfeld made a trip to both nations in mid–2006 in order to bring them both together. Pakistan is an ally of the U.S. in its war against terror. For this reason the Musharraf regime has at least tried to crack down on militants, but Musharraf's own position is extremely vulnerable in a country where Islamism is growing in leaps and bounds. India of course has also been a longtime U.S. ally, being the largest democracy in the world. Any tensions between the two neighbors will also spell horror for America. Who will it side with? How will a nuclear showdown be prevented if terror attacks by Islamic militants continue eroding any efforts towards peace? Will humanity be completely annihilated as predicted in scripture?

It is noted that Pakistan's nuclear capability is more sophisticated than India's. Pakistan has close to 48 nuclear warheads whereas India is said to have 35. Also, Pakistan's ability to launch a nuclear attack excels India's in how the weapons are delivered. In the event of a dreaded nuclear showdown between India and Pakistan, an estimated 12 million people will perish, though the fallout will not be of global proportions.

The nuclear threat is not unique to India and Pakistan. The autocratic regime of North Korea fired seven ballistic missiles into the sea of Japan on July 6, 2006, to demonstrate its military might. A bankrupt nation of starving millions, Kim Jong-il's North Korea spends the bulk of its revenue on developing its military, including nuclear arms. It has done so after refusing to sign the nuclear nonproliferation treaty five years ago.

There are many serious ramifications of North Korea acquiring nuclear arms. There is for example a great danger of the rogue nation selling its technology to terrorist groups across the world. In fact unconfirmed reports suggest this may have happened already. If George W. Bush's "axis of evil" is working together against U.S. interests, then Iran and North Korea are well equipped in terms of military arsenal.

North Korea also has a long history of rivalry with Japan. In this respect Japan also comes in direct confrontation with China, the emerging superpower, as the communist regime does not wish to see its tiny neighbor to the South destabilized. That would mean an influx of millions of North Korean refugees into China — a scenario the People's Republic is ill-equipped to deal with. So far it has helped sustain the North Korean economy by giving two billion dollars in aid to North Korea annually.

The U.N. response to the North Korean ballistic missile testing is an indication of how future conflicts may unfold in the region. While Japan and the U.S. drafted a very strong condemnation imposing sanctions on North Korea, China vetoed it, providing a much softer alternative to the original draft. A potentially explosive situation with the possibility of two superpowers at odds with each other, coupled with the threat of nuclear war, is a frightening scenario reminiscent of doomsday prophecies in scripture.

China has come a long way as a nation. Many already consider it a superpower, not one that is poised to be a superpower at some future date. Political analysts also predict that China will surpass the U.S. as a superpower by the year 2020. India too is making strides toward economic and political influence in the world. Bilateral relations between these two emerging superpowers have never been ideal. China on the other hand has been a longstanding ally of Pakistan, India's arch-rival. China's ties with the Muslim world are also crucial as its eastern province is predominately Muslim, though one of the poorest in the nation. The changing demographics in the region will also determine the course of political alliances which will tip the balance of power.

In order to comprehend the nuanced politics of China and South Asia, it is important to determine the nuclear status of these nations. China has been a longtime supporter of Pakistan's nuclear program, sharing its know-how with its populous Muslim neighbor to its southwest. Although when Pakistan finally tested its nuclear capability in 1998, China showed dismay, it did not impose any sanctions on Pakistan and continued to have warm relations with the country. India, on the other hand, justified its nuclear development based on the Sino-Pakistani cooperation, suggesting it needed to counter the nuclear threat from Pakistan and China with whom India has had long standing territorial disputes. China's close ties with Muslim nations may very well give hope to Muslim apocalypticists that their dream of seeing Islam triumphant in the world is indeed plausible, if the superpower of the future is on their side.

Added to this dynamic is the recent nuclear cooperation treaty signed by India and the United States in March of 2006. A superpower signing a nuclear treaty with an emergent superpower has put Pakistan in a vulnerable position. For its part, all it has achieved with China is a "friendship treaty" which guarantees economic cooperation and defense. Seeing it cannot rely on Pakistan's strength, China has also recently moved to strengthen its ties with India and is pushing ahead to resolve their longstanding border dispute. China is also greatly worried about the recent deal between India and the United States. In order to position itself as India's well-wisher, China has therefore increased trade with its southern neighbor. Both countries, which up until recently vied for the same markets for their energy needs, have mutually decided to give each other latitude in their various spheres of influence. India's recent rapprochement with China, however, does not spell China's abandonment of Pakistan as its ally. It has continued to maintain the balance of power with India by propping up Pakistan. China has also recently strengthened ties with Bangladesh and other smaller countries such as Nepal in order to expand its influence in the region.

The fourth player in this equation, the United States, is seen by China as its arch-rival in terms of superpower status. They are also economic rivals as China has lured jobs away from the U.S. by offering cheaper labor. The two global powers also do not see eye to eye on the status of Taiwan, and tensions between the two nations continue over it. Conflict can erupt anytime between the People's Republic of China and the Republic of China (Taiwan), as the latter does not wish to give up its booming economy for the austere standards of living associated more with mainland China.

In this regard, Taiwan recently conducted public military drills to show off its military strength in order to avert the prospects of invasion from mainland China, who wishes to assert its historical claims on the island. Taiwan also has a treaty with the United States which guarantees defense of the tiny island in the eventuality of an attack from China. Such a scenario would bring the two superpowers in direct confrontation over the island. The United States, on the other hand, does not want to forgo its influence on the island. There is informal talk that the island is its fifty-first state, and it is used as a naval base for the U.S. Taiwan and Japan are traditional foes of China with the United States on their side. On the other side, there is China and North Korea.

If China continues to feel threatened by the United States, or if it emerges as the next superpower, tensions will increase, particularly if the Muslim world's relationship with China, which has traditionally been much friendlier than its relationship with the United States, continues to grow. One sees the emergence of two great world alliances in these political trends. The Bible predicts an army of 200 million men that will ignite a global conflict in the end times (Rev. 9: 15, 16). Which other country in the world could boast of such an enormous army in terms of manpower, and whose side will it be on?

Thus far China has not exerted much influence in the Middle East other than the sale of its conventional weaponry to Arab nations. It has not been a key player in Middle East politics. If its relations with the United States remain tense, China may find more allies in the Middle East. Also, if its relationship with Muslim nations continues to strengthen, they may push China to assume a more powerful role in the highly volatile and troubled Arab world. A scenario where two superpowers will emerge divided over the Middle East conflict is worrisome, to say the least.

The Chinese foreign minister visited the Middle East in the fall of 2004 and expressed greater interest in the affairs of the region. He presented four proposals towards a speedy settlement of the conflict. As a prerequisite, he suggested the rebuilding of trust between the Palestinians and Israelis. He also called for a faster implementation of the "Roadmap to Peace" which would see the creation of a Palestinian state while guaranteeing Israel the right to security and the right to be recognized as a nation. The Chinese foreign minister also suggested the convening of the Security Council to discuss a comprehensive solution for the ongoing crisis. He also urged the international community to play a more active role in resolving the 58-year dispute.

China's approach to the Middle East conflict is seen as balanced by the moderate forces among Muslims who wish to see a resolution to the conflict. It is the militants and the radical Islamists who will not accept anything short of a one-state solution where Jews will end up being the minority. The die-hards are insisting on the Palestinian right of return to the area. But the very idea of Jews being the minority in Arab states is incongruous to the concept on which the state of Israel was built. Israel is meant to be a Jewish state for the Jewish people where they can live without having to endure the harassment they suffered as diaspora communities living all across the world.

China, with its much better reputation among Islamic nations, can broker a solution to these longstanding rifts and roadblocks to peace; however, this mighty nation of over a billion also tends to cower under U.S. pressure whenever violence erupts in the region.

Russia also has economic interest and influence in the Middle East. It has of late reasserted its role as an ally of the Arab nations along with the European Union, with Germany and France spearheading Mideast policy. Both Germany and France vehemently opposed the war in Iraq, much to the chagrin of Americans. In the 2006 violence between Hezbollah and Israel, France again called the actions of Israel a disproportionate reaction to the offense caused by Hezbollah in capturing two Israeli soldiers. The rest of the world continued to condemn the actions of the Hezbollah as igniting the conflict. The loss of life inflicted on the Lebanese people as a result of Israeli air strikes caused fresh resentments in Muslims, who were barely recovering from the devastation in Iraq. Why did the world not condemn this? Did the capture of two soldiers warrant the destruction of an entire country? Muslims by and large surmised that the Israeli war machinery was unleashed on civilian populations deliberately, so as to turn their opinion against Hezbollah. Many Muslims hence consider the Jewish state a terrorist state. "The United States and Israel are the real terrorists, not us," is the sentiment often echoed in Muslim circles.

The Sudan is yet another hotbed of conflict. More than one million of its citizens live as refugees in their own country and a humanitarian crisis looms. The entire Muslim world appears to be in disarray, but that is what Hadith predicted would happen in the end times. Where there is a semblance of democracy, there is political unrest and turmoil; where there is autocratic rule, there is the threat of terrorism, as Osama and his jihadists see these regimes as puppets of the United States. Sudan is also of strategic interest to the economic powers. It is rich in oil but divided along ethnic lines. Conflict often erupts between the Baghara and Non-Baghara Africans of the Sudan. The rebels are fighting for greater control of resources and more political representation in a government that is mostly of Arab stock. That government is arming the Janjaweed militia who have tyrannized the Darfuri population through rampage, rape and murder. The government notes that the United States has supported the rebels against the Islamic government in the North and that it arms the southern non–Muslim Sudanese against the Islamic regime, once again reinforcing the notion among Muslims that the U.S. is fighting Islam as a faith and a global force. Again the eschatological belief in Muslim versus non–Muslim in the end times resurfaces.

World politics today is closely linked not only to ideologies but to economic interests — not so much the economic interests of nations as of the affluent and influential few who control the decisions and polices of elected governments. The real power lies in business conglomerates, who influence the policies of democratically elected governments. The economic wealth of the world is concentrated in a few hands, 50 percent of which are American — Japan and France trailing behind as second and third in this economic race.

These multinational corporations are vying for influence in the various markets of the world. For this reason, the desire for access to the world's resources as well as its markets instigates wars of control. The war in Iraq is cited as the perfect example of a recent conflict to gain control. The main reason was the control of Iraqi crude. Halliburton, the huge corporation formerly headed by U.S. vice-president Dick Cheney, was marketing jobs in Iraq and "digging oil there twenty-four seven," according to one Muslim observer and sympathizer of the Iraq resistance.

Resolution 1441 of the Security Council of the United Nations clearly authorized force if it became evident that Saddam Hussein of Iraq possessed the dreaded weapons of mass destruction. Initially Russia and France opposed such a blatant permission for the U.S. to take up arms against Baghdad, but the two nations finally capitulated under pressure from the U.S., who had at any rate declared the United Nations irrelevant.

George W. Bush also claimed to fear clandestine links between terrorist organizations and Saddam. Although it was well known that Saddam was supporting Palestinian suicide missions against Israel, Bush said his main fear was Al-Qaeda. On September 12, 2002, he told the U.N., "Our greatest fear is that terrorists will find a shortcut to their mad ambitions when an outlaw regime supplies them with the technologies to kill on a massive scale."[8]

It is widely believed that these fears could have been allayed if negotiations had been allowed to run their proper course. It is also widely believed that the U.S. was going to attack Iraq anyhow — oil being the main reason. Also, giant corporations like Raytheon who manufacture weapons were to receive a great deal of business from going to war.

According to Ignacio Ramonet:

> The war in itself, with its squandering of "intelligence" and "precision" weapons, was already a great deal for certain U.S. weapons manufacturers. There are six participants who have been the greatest beneficiaries of the destruction of Iraq. United Technologies, which sold weapons worth €4 billion to the Pentagon (such as the Black Hawk and Sea Hawk helicopters); General Dynamics, €9 billion (aircraft carriers, battleships, F14 Tomcat and F18 Hornet fighter planes, unpiloted Global Hawk aircraft); Raytheon, which also sold $12 billion (Patriot and Tomahawk missiles, BLU 109 penetrator bombs); Boeing, €18 billion (Apache and Chinook helicopters, Wawacs, B52 and F22 Raptor fighter planes); and Lockheed Martin, €25 billion (F117 invisible aircraft, U2 spy-planes, C130 Hercules).[9]

But was it indeed all economics that dictated the decision to go to war with Iraq, as Ramonet suggests in his thesis on globalization? Evangelical Christians believe George Bush is a Christian man and can never inflict death and destruction on other human beings without good reason. Indeed the causes may have been economic, but what justified the massive killings was the notion that this was in some way a tussle between good and evil. Evil had to be eradicated whether it was in the form of a tyrannical ruler, his terrorist alliances, or the population that may have supported them. In the end, consciences can be appeased by invoking notions of good and evil in this fight, which has definitely acquired an apocalyptic religious zeal in the last few years.

For globalization, on the other hand, "free trade" is the mantra of the day. Any policies of democratically elected governments that may conflict with this phenomenon of gargantuan proportions are promptly scrapped and rejected by economic giants. The casualties in terms of social services provided to the citizenry may include labor laws, health care and the environment. The World Trade organization with the U.S., E.U. and Japan as its key players, controls the larger and smaller markets of the world. They accomplish this goal by pushing for even more mergers, which result in an almost continuous birth of mega-corporations reaping astronomical profits. Competition is obviously eliminated through the big companies' eating up the smaller ones by buying them out and hence bringing them under their control. In order to further maximize their profits, these conglomerates slash jobs, creating further social and economic inequities. And unemployment rates continue to soar in the developed world; twenty million unemployed Europeans languish in despair and poverty. Why, when the European Union is an essential player on the world economic scene, would its citizenry suffer in this manner? The answer is simple: The states and their citizens are not the beneficiaries of these policies. Wealth is concentrated in the hands of a few who own the mega-corporations.

The gap between the rich and poor widens. In fact the conglomerates earn more than the GNPs of nations. Toyota, for example, earns more than the GNP of Portugal.

Ignacio Ramonet, social democrat and author of the book *Wars of the 21st Century*, notes, "Of the six billion inhabitants of the planet, barely half a billion are comfortably off, while 5.5 billion suffer hardship."[10]

Ramonet also equates the conglomerate economic supremacy with a new type of colonization and conquest of the world. He states that the process of globalization has such far-reaching implications that "the world is experiencing a new period of conquest comparable with the colonial period. If, however, the leading actors in the previous victorious expansion were states, this time around the would-be conquerors of the world are private enterprises and industrial and financial conglomerates."[11]

The world according to the above analysis seems to be abdicating democracy for de facto oligarchies if the crucial decisions affecting ordinary citizens are made by the extremely rich. The world is aware of the growing inequities between rich and poor individuals and rich and poor nations and has undertaken some brain storming to reduce its effects. The World Social Forums have done this very thing. The problem lies mainly in whether solutions will ever be acceptable to those who really control the reins of power.

The aforementioned Ramonet suggests three possible solutions. He first points out that serious tax evasions are being committed by the mega-corporations by depositing their profits in countries like Gibraltar and Liechtenstein. These "tax havens," he suggests, must be eliminated through a financial boycott of these countries. He further suggests the imposition of the capital gains tax. The third solution to this ominous trend is mass education.

There is little social consciousness among the masses about the disparity in resources. The poorest of the poor live oblivious to the luxuries that are taken for granted in wealthy societies. The quest for daily survival keeps these individuals in a perpetual state of ignorance about what they might be missing. The poor in countries such as Pakistan are, however, painfully aware of the disparity between their personal resources and those of their rich countrymen. It is in these countries that revolutions may germinate, while Africa struggles for its very survival on a daily basis.

Ancient prophetic literature predicted world government, with the Antichrist spearheading the movement. The shape it has taken in the form of globalization, however, was perhaps beyond anyone's wildest dreams. On the political front, China's role remains to be seen with respect to its ultimate alliance with either Muslim or non–Muslim nations, or to whether it aligns itself with America or its enemies. America's enemies are increasing. If the Muslim nations, North Korea and China unite, it will form a powerful bloc against American imperialism, enough to form an army of 200 million predicted in the Bible.

CHAPTER TEN

Conclusion: Beyond Prophecy

To suggest that prophecy about apocalyptic political events plays a role in the determination of geopolitics in some small measure would not be far-fetched — though it is by no means the only force shaping our world today. Globalization and its ravenous agenda continues unabated, at times rendering powerless the elected representatives of countries. With the growing disparity in world resources, that disparity's effects on the common man, and the burgeoning numbers of child laborers and disenfranchised of the world, much of the developing world continues to swim down the spiral of poverty to abysmal despair.

And along with poverty come all the countless problems such as lack of education, religious fanaticism, and widespread resentment against the powerful. Despite its technological and industrial advancement, the world has become a much more inhospitable place for the bulk of its inhabitants. It is ruthless, anarchic and destitute, and many see its destruction imminent, consistent with eschatological literature.

The power of the state has declined due to the effects of globalization discussed in the previous chapter. This decline in turn has given rise to fanaticism, which manifests itself in autonomous groups and entities that often act independently of state authority. Perhaps the most telling example of this phenomenon was reflected in the July 2006 conflict in the Middle East between Hezbollah, the militant Shiite organization, and Israel. The terrorist group acted of its own accord when it took two Israeli soldiers hostage, sparking massive reprisals from Israel supported by the United States. With the devastation inflicted on the Lebanese people and Hezbollah's terrorist strikes on Israeli civilians through firing of the Katyusha rockets, the people of Lebanon came to repose more trust and confidence in the militant group and its ability to defend its citizens, rather than in the democratically elected Lebanese government. While states in the West are subject to pressure from the conglomerates and must relinquish their control on the decision making capabilities, countries in the developing world are seen by their citizenry as ineffectual to begin with — the proverbial "failed states" (including Pakistan, despite its nuclear capability). Those who have been able to provide their citizens a measure of stability are precisely the ones perceived by the masses as U.S. puppets and stooges.

Nuclear arms proliferation also continues covertly and overtly. Longstanding territorial disputes have yet to be resolved. Ethnic fights and "mininationalism" continue to grow as resources and wealth slip away from the poor into the hands of those who already enjoy comfort and luxury. The question then for the contemporary world is: how do we make it a more safe and peaceful place for posterity?

Prophecy tells us that peace and stability will eventually prevail, but at what cost? Will mankind destroy everything it has built and achieved? Will the bulk of humanity be destroyed through its own folly and will the few who remain be able to carve a new world out of its ashes? With its life-sustaining ecosystems successively destroyed, will human beings be able to survive on the ruins of this planet and for how long? More importantly, will mankind learn from its mistakes or is the earth doomed?

One of the pressing concerns facing the world is today is nuclear arms proliferation. The global destruction predicted in prophecy appears more plausible with the presence of weapons that can kill by the millions. Of the newer countries in this race, North Korea, Iran and Pakistan are increasingly seen as the greatest proliferators of nuclear technology. And all three have recently stepped up efforts to increase their nuclear capability. Pakistan is in the process of developing a new nuclear reactor, North Korea tested seven ballistic missiles over the sea of Japan, and Iran continues defiant in its construction of a "civilian" nuclear program. With the 2006 conflict between Israel and Hezbollah, speculation was rife that Iran might be building a nuclear bomb under cover that will be delivered someday to Hezbollah. Tehran insists its country's objective in building nuclear technology is only to defend itself, as Iran remains threatened as a nation and must never give up its aspirations to build nuclear weapons. Iran also insists it is under no obligation to stop its uranium enrichment program as the Nuclear Proliferation Treaty allows for such development programs that benefit civilians.

As for accusations that Iran is the main inspiration behind Hezbollah, the country has repeatedly denied charges that it supplied "Fajr" missiles, which have the capability of penetrating deep into Israel, to the militant Lebanese group.

Neighboring Pakistan continues building its nuclear arsenal as well. In the July 24 issue of the *Washington Post*, the story erupted that Pakistan was now building a new nuclear reactor with a capacity to produce plutonium for fifty bombs annually. This has again raised concerns about the nuclear arms race in a highly volatile and troubled region of the world. Pakistan wishes to keep pace with its longstanding rival India, who recently signed a nuclear deal with the United States. Pakistan, had previously requested similar treatment from Washington, but Washington refused, again contributing to the view among Pakistanis that the United States is no friend of the Muslims and that an apocalyptic conspiracy against Pakistan and Islam is under way. Pakistan's nuclear might is expected to increase twenty times its current capability with the construction of its new nuclear reactor. Pakistan has admitted to sharing information with North Korea, Libya and Iran during the years 1989 and 2003, with Dr. Abdul Qadeer Khan as the chief supplier of this information. Neither Pakistan not India has signed the Nuclear Non-Proliferation treaty, and both continue to develop more sophisticated technology.

China, however, recently joined the Nuclear Suppliers Group, which restricts member nations from sharing nuclear technology except for peaceful means. This was seen as a welcome move, as historically China has been implicated in the nuclear arms race in South Asia, particularly in its efforts to beef up Pakistan against India. The other members of this prestigious group are of course the nuclear giants such as the United States, France, the United Kingdom and Russia. Under the new agreement, China will share technology only for peaceful purposes, which would be a relief to many apocalypticists. If, according to apocalypticists, prophecy is to be fulfilled in China's 200 million-man army along with its nuclear arsenal, the country surely presents the potential of being a formidable global force.

North Korea, the third player in George W. Bush's infamous axis of evil, has also stepped up its rhetoric and efforts on its nuclear ambitions. Its defense minister announced the country's determination in pursuing its nuclear program on the Korean Central News Agency on Wednesday, July 26, 2006. He stated that North Korea will bolster its program "in every way by employing all possible means and methods." He further stated that his country would respond to any acts of aggression with "all-out-do-or-die resistance and unprecedented devastating strikes."[1]

What is telling about future events is the following statement made in the same broadcast. Kim Il-chol, North Korean defense minister, stood up to America by stating that this move was necessary for his country because of America's "extremely hostile act and the irresponsibility of the U.N. Security Council." Rebuffing the U.N. resolution to impose sanctions on North Korea, the defense minister said, "North Korea can survive without sweets, but not without bullets."

It is worth examining the role of these "rogue states" and non-state entities such as Al-Qaeda and Hezbollah as additional voices of defiance against American hegemony. There is speculation that the giant superpowers' hegemony or supremacy in the world is finally on the decline. Bible scholars will attest to the view that America does not have a role to play in the final resolution between good and evil. Though American might and influence as it stands today would certainly prove any Bible prophecy wrong, it is worth asking whether America's influence in the world is on the decline or if this is merely a fanciful claim on the part of its many detractors.

American credibility in the world —certainly in the Muslim world and North Korea — is definitely on the decline. Some would surmise it is at an all-time low. Each time there is a new conflict and America demonstrates its unequivocal support for Israel, the perception is further reinforced that America is no friend of the Muslim nations. Certainly the Bush administration has proven to be a disappointment, even to the American public itself, particularly over the issue of the Iraq war.

America has certainly slipped with respect to education and employment as well. Many of America's leading educators believe that recent reforms such as the "No Child Left Behind" act resulted in failure as teachers are now more preoccupied with procedures than with the learning process. Meanwhile, America's jobs are being exported through what is known as outsourcing for cheap labor.

Political rifts are more evident. The 2000 election was a classic example of such a rift when Al Gore won the popular vote and George Bush won the Electoral College vote. The election results were hotly debated right up to the Supreme Court level, but Bush emerged triumphant. Political schisms have also surfaced within an equally divided Congress between Democrats and Republicans. Are these trends grave enough to sound a death knell for America?

Actually, the United States has many years ahead of it in terms of maintaining its hegemony and influence in the world. In the Rome conference of July 26, 2006, to discuss prospects of a cease-fire between Israel and Lebanon, America emerged triumphant in delaying such an action, even though there were calls for an immediate cease-fire by other nations, France included.

Also, America refuses to talk to Iran or Syria even though these countries are now considered regional powers.

The forces of disintegration are becoming more apparent, but they are not strong enough to deal a fatal blow to American might. Also, planning by American politicians goes a long way, and America is not willing to loosen its grip on its influence in the world.

The collapse of the Soviet Union in 1989 and its subsequent dismemberment in 1991 gave America virtual dominion over the world. While Russia struggles to maintain its hold on its former republics and secessionist Chechnya, the United States not only expands its political and strategic influence, but also its military influence all across the world. It has strengthened its influence in the North Atlantic Treaty Organization by admitting into its field the Czech Republic, Poland, and Hungary, who supported the United States in its invasion of Iraq in 2003 and formed part of George Bush's "coalition of the willing." Ignacio Ramonet, in his book *Wars of the 21st Century*, makes trenchant observations regarding how the U.S. plans to expand its economic influence as the chief framework for globalization. He says that apart from the political and military influence,

> in the era of neoliberal globalization, the United States wants to transform NATO into the military wing and the security apparatus of the globalization, in order to reinforce its logic and to cut its risks, with the United Kingdom, Germany and France as its main allies among the remaining NATO countries (with the hope of including Japan and South Korea in a second phase). As a result, the United Nations has been thrust aside and diminished to a kind of moral reference point (rather like the Council of Europe with regard to the European Union, or some kind of lay Vatican), with no capacity to intervene in case of crisis.[2]

As the world sinks deeper into a state of anarchy, the United States tries to find ever more creative ways to maintain its longstanding hegemony well into the twenty-first century. But according to Tahir Qazi, a writer on geopolitical affairs, America's designs on the world date as far back as the Monroe Doctrine

> The Monroe Doctrine, which is about 180 years old, provides first glimpses of U.S. ambitions in the Northern Hemisphere. The Monroe Doctrine laid out a vision for trade interests.[3]

He further points out that in order to see its economic interests through, America has of late revived that vision, and the first one to do so was not a Republican president, but the Democrat Jimmy Carter.

And it was Jimmy Carter who also first thought of the doctrine of preemption. Qazi quotes Carter's January 23, 1980, address to the Congress:

Let our position be absolutely clear: Any attempts by any outside force to gain control of the Persian Gulf region will be regarded as an assault on the vital interests of the United States of America, and such an assault will be repelled by any means necessary, including military force.

Qazi also quotes the reinterpretation of that doctrine by Dick Cheney in a June 23, 1998, address at the Cato Institute:

The Good Lord didn't see fit to put oil and gas only where there are democratically elected regimes friendly to the United States. Occasionally we have to operate in places where, all things considered, one would not normally choose to go. But we go where the business is.

It is understandable why Dick Cheney would not want to visit these places as they are particularly inhospitable to any notion of American expansionism. According to Tahir Qazi, "The only obstacle in the way of building the pipelines is that religious oriented violent mindset in Afghanistan has not given in yet."

The notion of preemptive strikes to suppress any future threats to America's hegemony, economic interests and political influence was also engineered by Richard Perle, Dick Cheney, Donald Rumsfeld and Paul Wolfowitz during Bush senior's administration in what is known as the PNAC Mission statement or the infamous "Plan for a New American Century." The document drafted by the hawks of the Bush administration states at the outset that one needs something of the magnitude of Pearl Harbor for the United States to have a premise to go to war. September 11 was seen as the new Pearl Harbor, justifying a "global war on terror" and thus providing a ready-made moral justification to bombard countries rich in oil resources. Coincidentally they are Muslim countries such as Afghanistan and Iraq. The U.S. reluctance to call for an immediate cease-fire in the July 2006 conflict between Lebanon's Hezbollah and Israel also reinforces the perception among Muslims that the "Crusader-Zionist alliance" is most definitely out to destroy the world of Islam, or at least reduce it permanently to a state of subjugation so that it will never pose a threat to U.S. or Israeli hegemony.

This perception further fuels the jihadist zeal to counter the imperialist forces because according to its eschatological goal, Islam must prevail over these forces. The insurgency in Iraq is a manifestation of this unrelenting jihadist campaign to sabotage any efforts for moderate forces to take root in the country, as these are seen as agents of the "Crusader-Zionist alliance." What is often cited as the main reason for America's invasion of Iraq, i.e. the control over Iraqi crude, has been greatly undermined as Iraq's daily oil production is considerably low — an estimated half a million barrels fewer than what it was before the war started. Damage to pipelines is the major cause of this diminished oil production, a campaign undertaken with might and zeal by the jihadists.

There is growing popularity of radical Shia Islam in south Lebanon. Radical Sunni Islam in Iraq is a direct response to invasions by the "Crusader-Zionist alliance," according to political pundits. Despite the military strengths of America as a global power and Israel as a regional power, both countries face countless obstacles in maintaining their strongholds in the region. The "religious oriented violent mindset" of which Tahir Qazi speaks has taken over in Iraq and elsewhere — wherever American dominance wishes to reassert itself.

According to Professor Francis Boyle, professor of law at the University of Illinois, American imperialism dates even further back than the Monroe Doctrine to the time of America's birth as a nation. At a special 2006 session of the Perdana Global Peace Forum in Kuala Lumpur, Malaysia, Boyle stated, "Little has changed in the imperialist tendencies of American foreign policy since the founding of the United States of America in 1789." He says America's imperialist campaign started with "ethnic cleansing " of the native peoples. According to the professor, the current invasion of Muslim countries also has its roots in the Arab Oil embargo of 1973. In order to prevent such an embargo, which almost brought western economies to a screeching halt, the U.S. Central Command was established "to steal and control and dominate the oil and gas resources of the Persian Gulf and Central Asia."[4]

Prof. Boyle further asserts that the wars in Afghanistan and Iraq had been planned well in advance:

> This war had been planned against Afghanistan. And armed, equipped, supplied, trained and war gamed and ready to go. They just needed the pretext and that was September 11. Why? The United States wanted access to the oil and natural gas of Central Asia."

Now the question remains about the religious Muslim zeal and whether it has the capability of uniting all its warring factions and sectarian division into a unified force. Ideologically there are two powerful forces within the Muslim world, Saudi Arabia and Iran. Both currently espouse a fundamentalist version of Islam, but the former is uncompromisingly Sunni and the latter, fundamentally Shia.

Saudi Arabia began exporting Wahabism, its fundamentalist version of a strict and punitive understanding of Sunni Islam, as an antidote to the revival of Shia fundamentalism after the Iranian revolution under Ayatollah Khomeini. The spread of Wahabism has acted as a unifying force among

Sunni Muslims because of its pan–Islamic vision. Muslims who have embarked on the Wahabi worldview feel solidarity and affinity with Muslim peoples all over the world whether they live in populous Indonesia or impoverished Nigeria. This renewed commitment to religious identities is also evidenced in diaspora communities of Muslims who regard themselves as Muslims first and Canadian, American, British or French second. Many devout Muslims believe this assertion of their primary identity as Muslims is essential if Islam's *Nishat Saani*, or prophesied second and lasting glory, is to be realized.

In concordance with this sentiment, Mubin Shaikh, one of the informants for CSIS (Canadian Special Intelligence Service) in the seventeen arrests in connection with a foiled terror plot in Toronto in 2006, said in an interview with the Canadian Broadcasting Corporation that when he informed the authorities of a suspected terror plot his primary loyalty was to Islam and Muslims: "I was thinking about the interests of Islam and Muslims, over and above Canadian interests."[5]

It is often stated that common enemies and threats can unite otherwise fragmented communities, but the Shia and Sunni versions of Islam have traditionally gone their separate ways, and the recent surge in sectarian violence in Iraq and Pakistan shows no signs that the two sects will reach a compromise in an effort to combine their resources against foreign domination. At the political, social, and military levels, there seems to be no movement towards unity except in July 2006 when Lebanon's Hezbollah was fighting Israel. Syria, although a Sunni nation, provided safe passage of arms and ammunitions purportedly from Iran to the Hezbollah. Also, Hezbollah's standing ground in the war with Israel enabled its popularity to soar even among Sunni populations.

But at the same time, the rifts are also becoming far more unbridgeable. Muslims are becoming more and more doctrinaire about their particular view of Islam being the only correct one. Although Wahabism has united a segment of the Muslim population throughout the Islamic world as an ideology that promotes an apocalyptic pan–Islamic vision, it has also caused schisms in the Muslim world that have manifested themselves in ways that are often violent and brutal. The founder of the movement, Mohammed Abdul Wahab, sought to restore the pristine doctrinal purity of the faith by expunging many of the idolatrous practices that had crept into both the thought and action of Muslim laity. These included shrine worship or a reverence for relics from early Islamic times such as belongings of the Prophet Mohammed, including strips of his hair and other personal items. Abdul Wahab declared this unislamic. He advocated a reversal to the Quran and Hadith as the two most authentic sources of Islamic teaching.

Page after page of the Quran describes the nature of God as a unity in what has resulted in an uncompromising monotheism. Therefore no one can be joined as "partners with Allah" or they have committed the gravest sin — the only one God will not forgive. This radical monotheism as opposed to the softer monotheism of Christianity, Sikhism or Hinduism must be defended at all costs. Thus invoking Christ or other prophets including Mohammed, God's angels and saints, is regarded as a heresy. Similarly, asking the deceased for assistance in worldly matters, wearing amulets to ward off evil, practicing witchcraft or even challenging the orthodox narrative of Islam as interpreted by the early generations known as the *Salaf–Sahih*, is deemed blasphemous — in some cases punishable by death.

According to the puritanical understanding of monotheism as a doctrine, Shiite Muslims, who revere Imam Ali, Sufi Muslims, who have a pantheistic understanding of God, and even some Sunni denominations such as the Barelvis, with their excessive reverence and adoration for the Prophet, no longer qualify as Muslims because they have abandoned Islam's central doctrine of unadulterated monotheism. They stand at risk of being excommunicated by the proponents of Wahabism.

The Ahmadiyah movement in Islam has already suffered this fate. Although staunch believers in Islam's pristine monotheism, the Ahmadis do not regard the Prophet Mohammed as God's final messenger; they consider Mirza Ghulam Ahmad, who declared himself Mahdi or Christ the Messiah, as the latter day apocalyptic prophet — though subservient in status to Mohammed.

The deep doctrinal schisms have plagued Muslim communities from Indonesia to Morocco with sectarian violence as an almost daily occurrence. Though doctrinal differences abound in their faiths as well, among Christians, Jews and other faith traditions there seems to be a greater "live and let live" policy that does not result in the defense of the doctrine with the ferocity with which Muslims of various stripes and persuasions have come to defend dogma.

Much has been made recently about a potential "alliance of terror" between Sunni extremists such as Al-Qaeda and the Shia Hezbollah. It must be stated that the two brands of Islamism are faced with irreconcilable doctrinal differences. They are also fundamentally different in what they hope to accomplish. The Hezbollah wishes to defend Lebanon's borders and introduce Shariah law in the country; Al-Qaeda has global ambitions to establish a worldwide caliphate.

The sectarian and ideological schism has also penetrated the masses, who engage in violent activity, wreaking death and destruction on their opponents. The ideological splinter groups have become so numerous in their differences

over the minutest details over dogma that they have created further opportunity for friction and conflict, which among the poor and illiterate masses
often spells violence. The Prophet had predicted that his followers would
divide into seventy- three sects in the end times. While there is no account
of just how many sects and denominations there are among Islam's adherents, the divisions nonetheless run deep.

The Shia-Sunni divide has been deep historically, and is exacerbated
now because of Wahabi insistence on "correct" doctrine. Although masses
of Sunni and Shia both rallied in large numbers behind the Hezbollah in the
July 2006 conflict between Israel and Hezbollah, Osama bin Laden's supporters promptly dissociated themselves from the Shia Lebanese militia, one
cleric issuing a fatwa from Cairo saying that the "party of God" (Hezbollah) was actually a party of the devil. Safar Al Hawali, the cleric, also urged
Sunnis not to pray for the Hezbollah.

These doctrinal schisms and divisions are so profound among Muslims
that in this current climate of hostility, they have come to assume an even
more fiery dogmatic tenor. Perhaps because dogma was defended militarily
in the early days of Islam, it becomes important enough to defend it militarily now as well. The differences may seem minute, but feelings run deep
nonetheless. In his book *Islam and Emirs: State Religion and Sects in Islam*,
Fuad I. Khuri states that 35 percent of Lebanon is Shia of the Asna Ashri
variety, meaning they believed in twelve anointed imams. Iraq has the largest
population of Shia outside Iran, forming 57 percent, with Bahrain a close
second at 54 percent. The Zaidis, a Shia denomination who choose to follow Sunni jurisprudence, have the largest concentration in Yemen at 51 percent. The Alawites, who also believe in the continuation of the divine message
through "babs," form a sizable majority in Syria.[6]

The Sunni majority thus wishes to apostatize the Shia sects, having
excommunicated the Ahmadis already. Recently there was a move to excom-
municate Ismailis in Pakistan as well. According to Khuri, the Sunnis regard
the Shia as being guilty of *tawil,* meaning they focus unnecessarily on the
hidden meanings of the Quran in preference to its obvious and clearly stated
injunctions. But these divisions are more obvious to local populations and
therefore the conflicts and sectarianism are regional and tend to occur in
pockets. A Sunni Muslim in Pakistan, for example, would not be aware of
the tiny sects living in Syria or Lebanon. Moreover tragedy seems to unite
the masses against outside threats. Predominantly Shia Iraq, although
embroiled in sectarian conflict, has nonetheless received much sympathy
from the Sunni masses as well, judging by the size of demonstrations and
rallies against the U.S.–led invasion of Iraq.

The United States and Israel have recently both attacked Muslim countries. When Muslims as a whole begin to perceive this as a common threat to Islam, they may let go of their internal differences to resist a common enemy. There are signs this may have already begun to happen in some segments of Muslim society. Muslims of all stripes and persuasion appear to be united in their hatred of Americans and Jews. The question remains of political unity. With Saudi Arabia and Iran both vying for regional and ideological influence, it does not seem at all likely. Moreover, governments in most Muslim countries are not democratically elected and therefore do not represent the sentiments of the masses who identify more with Muslims all over.

Niall Ferguson, in his book *The War of the World* nonetheless comes to the startling conclusion. He says:

> As a religion, Islam is of course far from monolithic. There are deep divisions, not least between the Shiites who predominate Iran (and Iraq) and the Sunnis who predominate in the Arab countries. But "Islamism" was a militantly political movement with an anti–Western political ideology that had the potential to spread throughout the Islamic world, and even beyond it.[7]

In other words, according to the author, Islamism transcends Islam itself and will act as the force uniting the diverse Muslim populations of the world to fight common foes. And if Islamism continues to be embraced by the masses, public opinion in Muslim countries will be of utmost importance, particularly when political succession has had a violent history whether there is democracy or dictatorship. Riots and unrest cause upheavals in Muslim countries where often the military has stepped in to topple popularly elected governments in order to quell the unrest. The present Musharraf regime is one such example of a military coup in recent Pakistani history. Although Musharraf has time and again attempted to institutionalize his idea of "enlightened moderation," promising reforms to certain laws of Pakistan that discriminate against women and minorities, he has met with fierce opposition from the Islamist parties who have thus far been able to thwart his efforts considerably. Musharraf is also regarded as an ally in the U.S. war on terror, which once again makes him a target of the radical forces in the country. If Islamism as a philosophy transcending sectarian differences takes hold of Muslims, they will indeed become a force to be reckoned with, at least when it comes down to resisting occupying armies.

Public opinion matters when it comes to world affairs. The countless polls taken by CNN on a daily basis are designed to check the pulse of the electorate because ultimate power rests with the masses. Governments make and implement policies in democracies, but the people elect them. Even in "quasi-democracies" like Pakistan, public opinion is of paramount concern. If the people are alienated too much from the government, there is inevitable unrest. Mass rallies are organized to protest government policies. Rallies to expedite an Israeli-Hezbollah cease-fire put pressure on Prime Minister Tony Blair of Britain to urge George W. Bush to pressure Israel into an early cease-fire. Public opinion certainly influences politicians to at least soften their rhetoric on their various stances.

As an example of such softening of rhetoric, Canadian prime minister Stephen Harper took an extraordinary move to appease the Canadian Muslim community over his July 2006 comment that the Israeli response to Hezbollah's provocation was a "measured response." He was forced to seek alliances with liberal MP Wajid Khan as his special advisor on Mid-Eastern affairs so as to deflect criticism from his government onto a liberal MP — and that too a Muslim!

Intra-religious differences among Muslims are likely to remain — but should that matter? More importantly, even if Muslims were to unite and combine all their resources, would they as a block still be able to pose a threat to America's global hegemony and Israel's regional hegemony? Would Muslims have to develop stronger alliances with Russia or China? What about the European Union and its somewhat different stance from America's unwavering support for Israel.[7] Would world alliances emerge exactly as predicted in scripture?

Muslims live in large numbers in various European countries, the largest concentration being in France at roughly 6 million. Their population is expected to double from its current 15 million to 30 million by 2025. Diaspora Muslim communities live in poverty and conditions of social and economic marginalization in Europe, breeding further resentment against the more prosperous and influential Christian majority. But the resentment is mutual. Fear of a cultural invasion drives the European media outlets to mount propaganda campaigns against Muslims and their beliefs. While Fox News in the U.S. and the *National Post* in Canada are considered particularly hostile to Muslim interests, what sparked the greatest ire among European Muslims in early 2006 was caricatures of the Prophet Mohammed published in the Danish newspaper *Jyllands-Posten*. The cultural divide between Muslims and westerners was evident in the responses to what came to be known as the "cartoon controversy." Flemming Rose, the culture editor of *Jyllands-Posten*, was described by an Islamist Web site (of the Party for Islamic Renewal) as "crusading." While most westerners are accustomed to satire as a legitimate form of expression which may often include the caricature of religious beliefs — Islam therefore being no exception — Muslims revere religious personalities, particularly their own prophet, to the extent of not even taking his name without adding the deferential adjunct "peace be upon him" to it. From early childhood Muslims are taught that the person of the Prophet is inviolable in every respect. They are taught to love him more than their own kith and kin, otherwise their faith in Islam would not be complete.

The cartoon controversy took a heavy toll, with rioting on the streets of Indonesia, Pakistan and other Muslim lands. Danish products disappeared from the shelves of Saudi grocery stores. An explanation by Flemming Rose which fell far short of an unequivocal apology finally put an end to the month-long riots and protests in the Muslim world, but the controversy had already sent ripples in the Atlantic ocean all the way to Canada.

A leading spokesperson for the Muslim community and founder of the Islamic Supreme Council of Canada, Prof. Badi-ud-din Soharwardy, felt compelled to demand that Canada tighten its blasphemy laws to include caricaturing of all religious personalities as an act of blasphemy. Needles to say, his move did not resonate with the Canadian government or other interest groups, who uphold freedom of speech as a basic democratic right that must be considered sacrosanct.

The cultural divide between Europe and its Muslims widens as more turn to Salafism as a reaction to western "laxity" in moral standards. Perhaps the most extreme and telling example of this divide and things to come was the murder by Mohammed Bouyeri of Theo Van Gogh, a film producer Bouyeri accused of "disrespecting" Islam. After shooting Van Gogh eight times, Bouyeri left the body with a five-page note attached to it by a knife stuck into the torso. The note included the following lines:

I surely know that you, O America will be destroyed
I surely know that you O Europe will be destroyed
I surely know that you O Holland will be destroyed
I surely know that you O Hirsi Ali, will be destroyed

Much of the above apocalyptic zeal is echoed frequently among Muslim masses, perhaps as a consolation for their sorry plight in countries where they occupy the lowest rung of the current political ladder. But regardless of the internal conditions for Muslims living in Europe, on the political front, the European Union, Britain excepted, has shown sympathy towards the issue of statehood for Palestine. (Britain of course has traditionally aligned itself more with the United States in its Middle East policy). In addition to recognizing the two-state solution with Israel and Palestine living side by side, the European Union has also offered financial aid to facilitate the transition to peace, as it recognized the Palestinians' rights to economic self-development. According to a press release of January 16, 1998, the European Union's position is that a prosperous Palestine would be less of a threat to Israel's security. The European Union is one of the four major parties, along with the U.S., Russia and the U.N., to broker a final settlement in the region. According to the prophets, one group of Christians will side with the Muslims while the other will oppose them. These soothsayers interpret differences in the political strategies of America and Europe as a fulfillment of that prophecy.

What needs to be acknowledged in this day and age is the new concept of asymmetrical warfare in the ongoing conflict in the Middle East; and how widespread and variegated the mechanisms may be in the region; and what the global jihadists can achieve with guerrilla warfare at their disposal. In the 2006 conflict between Hezbollah and Israel, for example, it became quite evident that a traditional army, no matter how powerful, was not able to dislodge the guerrilla militia of some three thousand Hezbollah rag-tags who continued to fire their Katyusha rockets into the northern cities of Israel.

Generally understood as forces made of indigenous peoples who are not part of a regular army, guerrillas operate in small groups called cells. The tactics of guerrilla warfare include lying in ambush, staying mobile and avoiding all-out combat . These tactics can change as the situation demands. The command and control is not followed meticulously, hence guerrilla strategy allows for much greater flexibility in responding to changing fortunes of the army. Military equipment is usually provided by outside sources; in the case of Hezbollah, both Iran and Syria remain implicated for providing the guerrilla group with the Katyushas as well as the Fajr rockets with capability to reach Tel Aviv.

Usually guerrilla warfare occurs when territories come under occupation. A similar situation has arisen in Iraq where the insurgency has taken a heavy toll on American forces. The Hezbollah, too, were created after the occupation of Lebanon by Israeli forces in 1982, though even after the Israeli withdrawal from Southern Lebanon in 2000, the Hezbollah have continued to operate in small numbers, instigating border clashes. With respect to Muslims and guerrilla warfare, author Scott Piraino suggests, "Conventional warfare is dead. More precisely, wars with national armies fighting across opposing lines will be the exception in the future, not the rule. Instead the twentieth century has seen the rise of guerrilla warfare and its vicious stepchild, terrorism."[8] Both actions have been called the warfare of the poor. These paramilitary tactics are increasingly being employed by vanquished Muslim peoples either as a resistance to occupation or as part of a terrorist strategy. They have erupted all across the Islamic world from Indonesia to Morocco in attempts to resist occupying forces as well as to dislodge governments seen as supporting foreign interests. As seen in the 2006 Mid-East conflict, guerrilla warfare can prove to be an effective resistance to conventional warfare. Also, on August 9, 2006, radical Islamist guerrilla forces took control of a town near the Somali-Ethiopian border. The Taliban, too, recently recaptured small townships in Afghanistan.

While the guerrillas act as autonomous groups waging a Jihad against imperialism, Muslim countries strive to forge ties with more powerful neighbors. Crucial to the debate over apocalyptic events is whether China will have a role to play in Middle Eastern politics. While the U.S. continues to demonstrate an obvious bias in favor of Israel, China is determined to have a balanced approach towards solving the sixty-year-old Arab-Israeli dispute, though it may rarely get the chance to assert its stand other than through its membership in the Security Council of the U.N., as it is not part of the quartet composed of the U.N., Russia, U.S. and E.U.

Even so, China has consistently expressed a desire to facilitate peace in the troubled region. In this regard it has made the following proposal to the two parties. At the very outset, China recognizes the need for building mutual trust as a fundamental imperative. This would be followed by the birth of a sovereign Palestinian state, which for its part will recognize Israel's sovereign right to peace and security. The U.N. Security Council must meet as early as possible to discuss a comprehensive peace in the region. Lastly, the world community must be actively engaged in seeing that peace is maintained in the region after the proposed peace plan is implemented.

China's proposal bears a striking resemblance to the Russian position on the Middle East over the years. Both are opposed to Palestinian violence and terror tactics but nonetheless recognize the urgency of implementing the peace plan. They are also both highly critical of Israel's construction of a defensive wall around the Palestinian territories.

But an increasing number of people are asking why China, as a permanent member of the Security Council, is not forceful enough to present its vision for a lasting peace in the troubled region of the world, often referred to as the "black hole" of geopolitics. As an emerging superpower, China can do much more to broker a peace in the region that will be seen as being fair to both sides, but it chooses not to.

Though China has vast strategic interests in the region, Fareed Zakaria, senior editor of *Newsweek*, suggests China has thus far "used soft power in the sense that it has exercised its power softly. It does this to show that it is not a bully, unlike guess who."[9] Other pundits and analysts suggest China is still only a remote second to American economic and global might and is governed more by an isolationist policy till such time as it perceives actual threats to its sovereignty.

Prophecy says that a 200 million man army from the East will rise to combat evil at the final battle of Armageddon fought in the Middle East, the aforementioned black hole of politics. Only time will tell whether prophetic pronouncements have any merit, or which side the gargantuan army will align itself with. Meanwhile, Pat Robertson traveled to Jerusalem in August 2006 to provide moral support to Ehud Olmert, suggesting Ezekiel prophesied that Israel will be attacked by Russia, Iran, Libya, and Sudan but will emerge triumphant. In an interview with Wolf Blitzer on CNN, he said this is because "the Jewish people are the people of God."[10] But as Armageddon unfolds, or at least the scenarios leading to Armageddon unfold, it is crucial to ask if the United Nations will play any role at all in preventing a war that is prophesied to wipe out two thirds of humanity.

During the deliberations on whether to go to war in Iraq to disarm Saddam's weapons of mass destruction, George W. Bush declared the U.N "irrelevant." Also, on November 10, 2002, the general secretary of the White House, Andrew Card, in a press conference stated that the United Nations could convene, but that the U.S. did not need its permission. The fact of the matter is that the United States was able to impose its will on the others, mainly a reluctant France and Russia. They had opposed military action based on Resolution 1441, which called for going to war with Iraq only upon discovery of WMDs by U.N. weapons inspectors.

According to Ignacio Ramonet, the role of the United Nations has therefore been reduced to one of "arbiter under the influence of its most powerful and demanding member state. In many parts of the world, respect for the United Nations has hit rock bottom. It is accused of measuring a world's problems according to whether one is an ally or an adversary of the United States."[11] Quite in line with Ramonet's conclusion is the recent statement of a fundamentalist Islamic website which called the United Nations an "agent" of the United States in the Israeli-Hezbollah conflict of summer 2006. One fundamentalist website described the U.N., World Bank and IMF as a manifestation of the machinations of the Dajjal, who would appear as the corrupt and powerful Antichrist of the apocalypse.

Whether or not it is fair to characterize the U.N. as a U.S. agent or "Dajjal," it was evident during the month-long bloody conflict that the U.N. was unable to enforce a speedy cease-fire despite Secretary General Kofi Annan's pleas and mounting world pressure. The general impression created was that Israel wished to fight for a stated period of time and the United

States kept stalling any efforts towards peace by making disingenuous statements about peace not being desirable unless it was "sustainable."

Although peace was finally brokered by the U.N., the timing, conditions and terms were spelled out by the U.S. Israeli prime minister Ehud Olmert in a telephone conversation with President Bush on August 11, 2006 even thanked President Bush for "watching out for Israel's interests" as reported by *CNN Headline News.*

But has the role of the U.N. been truly as abysmal as some international affairs analysts suggest? Certainly the fifty-one founding nations of the United Nations had high hopes that the international body would provide a forum for diplomacy to always replace the prospects of armed conflict after having witnessed the massive destruction of World War II. The ideal that inspired the ideals of the United Nations was collective security. But would such cooperation be really possible when the militarily dominant powers of the world — China, the United States, the United Kingdom, Russia and France — would have veto over decisions?

Yet what actually gets accomplished does not make headlines the way failures and disruptions to world peace do. According to the *Human Security Report* 2005,[12] the U.N. sent many peacekeeping missions to various trouble zones from 1990 to 2002 in places where peace remains fragile. In that respect it has prevented many armed conflicts. Its failure has largely been in the realm of not being able to enforce its resolutions, particularly where Israel has been asked to dismantle settlements in Gaza and the West Bank. Skirmishes therefore continue to erupt in that area. Also, in recent times it was not able to prevent genocides such as the one in Rwanda and the ethnic cleansing of Muslims that took place during the Balkan wars. One can therefore legitimately ask if the United Nations is indeed worth keeping or not.

Despite its many failures and shortcomings, the U.N. as a body needs to remain in place as a forum for diplomacy even when conflicts have emerged in troubled regions of the world. On the plus side, the world body has responded promptly to many conflicts where strategic interests are not of vital importance to the major world players, such as the conflict in East Timor. As an independent voice, the United Nations has at least kept the vision of world peace alive and has contributed towards the alleviation of poverty, arms control, children's welfare and other humanitarian efforts. It has also funded the United Nations University for Peace as an institution to foster world harmony and cooperation. In the absence of such ideals, the world would most definitely sink into a "war of the worlds" with catastrophic consequences.

Recently, Global Action to Prevent War and Armed Conflict, a movement which strives to empower the United Nations as a force for world peace, has moved to introduce a United Nations Emergency Peace Service whose job it will be to prevent genocide and crimes against humanity even when a war has erupted. This proposed contingent will be made of volunteer forces who will be deployed urgently in war-torn areas to prevent the excessive use of force against weaker parties. This is an idea that has been supported by many U.N. stalwarts such as Sir Brian Urquhart, former U.N. Undersecretary General for Special Political Affairs. As an independent center of international justice, the U.N. is in dire need for reform, but to dispense with it is precipitating "Armageddon" and the large-scale global destruction it will cause.

Whether we are living in the apocalypse remains to be seen. Many devout Christians and Muslims appear to agree that we are indeed living in the "end of times." The Quran, Hadith and the Bible as religious texts paint a gory picture of the scenarios that will lead us into the end of times, but they all predict the ultimate victory of good over evil, of harmony over bigotry, of peace over hatred and anarchy. But "good," "evil" and "peace" have all come to acquire connotations in our present age that defy traditional definitions. What is good for the jihadist is anathema to the evangelical. What is "peace" is now a nebulous concept too. Is it just the absence of war? Is that what we will achieve in the Middle East at best: a "cold" peace?

More importantly, would the peace-loving peoples of the world let the radicals, jihadists, crusaders, neo-imperialists, and conglomerates define the world we live in, or would they wake up to the realities and begin to take matters into their own hands?

The time has now come to take a hard look at these questions.

Appendix 1.
The Lesser Signs of the Hour

(1) **The Splitting of the Moon:** In 1969 three American astronauts landed on the moon and dug up soil from its terrain. The Quran purportedly makes a reference to such an event as occurring in the end of times (Quran, 54: 1).

(2) **War and Anarchy:** Wars, bloodshed and anarchy will prevail in the world during the end times. According to one authentic Hadith, "Near the establishment of the Hour, there will be the days of Al-Harj, and the religious knowledge will be taken away [vanish, i.e., by the death of religious scholars] and general ignorance will spread." Abu Musa said, "Al-Harj, in the Ethiopian language, means killing." Ibn Masud added: "I heard Allah's Apostle saying: [It will be] from among the most wicked people who will be living at the time when the Hour will be established" (Bukhari: *Muhammad Muhsin Khan*, Vol. 9, no. 187).

(3) **The Fire:** "The Hour will not be established till a fire will come out from the land of Hijaz, and it will throw light on the necks of the camels at Busra" (Bukhari: Muhammad Muhsin Khan, Vol. 9, no. 234). There are various possible interpretations of the prediction of a fire that will emerge from the Arabian Peninsula. One possibility is that it refers to the great fire of 654 a.h. ("after Hijra," or migration of the prophet to Medina), which lasted for months according to Abu Shama, an early historian. Modern possibilities of the fulfillment of this prophecy point to the fires in Kuwait lit by Saddam Hussein when he burned the oil fields of Kuwait. The reference to Busra in Iraq gives credence to this view. That fire lasted for months as well.

(4) **Sanctions Against Iraq, Syria and Egypt:** "Iraq will be denied its Dirham and Qafiz, Syria will be denied its Mudd and Dinar, and Egypt will be denied

its Irdab and Dinar. You will return to where you began, you will return to where you began" (Muslim: 7/137).

(5) **Earthquakes:** The earth will rock many times before it is finally destroyed (Quran, 99: 1–8). Recent times have seen massive earthquakes such as the one in Kashmir, Pakistan, on October 8, 2005, and the Asian tsunami which killed over two hundred thousand people in 2004.

(6) **Power will come to be vested in immoral people.** "The Hour will not be established till a man from Qahtan appears, driving the people with his stick" (Bukhari: Muhammad Muhsin Khan, Vol. 9, no. 233). Nowadays corporate greed and the quest for political power determine who runs political office. Although this has always been the case, the phenomenon appears to be much more pervasive now than before.

(7) **The general collapse of moral values:** The threshold of tolerance will be lowered for adultery, fornication and other vices. Women will imitate men and vice versa. Homosexuality will come to be more widely accepted as "normal" behavior. There will be a prevalence of open sexual intercourse (Bukhari: Muhammad Muhsin Khan, Vol. 9, no. 232).

(8) **The religion of Islam will come under much censure from both within and without.** September 11, 2001, became the catalyst for much debate over the religion of Islam. Many Muslims have since renounced the faith. Its precepts are being questioned more and more even by those who do not reject it outright. The following quote from the Quran carries a prophetic message: "My lord, my people treat this Quran as something to be ignored" (Quran, 25: 30)

(9) **Family values will diminish.** "Verily these events will occur before the hour, greetings of peace will be extended only to specific people, trade will spread to the extent that a woman will help her husband in his business, ties of family relations will be cut off, false testimony will be given on widespread scale, truthful testimony will be kept hidden and the pen will become widespread" (Ahmad: 1/408). Many Muslims will find concordances between the contents of this Hadith and the present-day erosion of family values.

(10) **Shopping Malls?** "The hour will not come until tribulations become widespread, lying increases, marketplaces come near to one another, time converges and Al-Harb occurs frequently" (Ahmad: 2/519). Does the expression "marketplaces come near to one another" indicate the presence of malls with stores in close proximity to each other?

Appendix 2.
The Greater Signs of the Hour

(1) **The Appearance of the Mahdi:** See references to the Mahdi in Chapters 1–5.

(2) **The appearance of Gog and Magog:** They will wreak havoc on earth and all its inhabitants, killing and destroying as they plunder across the earth (Quran, 21: 97).

(3) **There will be an attack on the Kaaba.** The Kaaba, which is the old shrine dedicated to the worship of the one true god, will be attacked. When the Kaaba is destroyed, a treasure from underneath it will be revealed. Narrated by Aisha, the Hadith states that an army will attack the Kaaba. When it reaches a desert it will be swallowed up by the earth (Muslim: 41/6890).

(4) **The emergence of a strange beast from the earth:** This beast will be able to speak to human beings. "And when the word of torment is fulfilled against them, We shall bring out from the earth a beast for them, to speak to them because mankind believed not with certainty in Our signs" (Quran, 27: 82).

(5) **The sun will rise from the West** (Quran, 6: 158).

(6) **Atheism and apostasy will grow.** Apostasy will be rampant and appear to grow. In a Hadith reported by Abu Huraira, "the Hour will not come to pass until tribes from my nation will go and join polytheists and until they worship idols. And indeed there will be among many nations thirty liars. Each one of them will claim that he is a Prophet though I am the seal of the Prophets — there is no Prophet after me" (Tirmidhi: 2219).

(7) **The war fought over "mountains of gold":** Hadith states: "The hour will not come until the Euphrates lays bare a mountain of gold. People will fight over it and from every 100 people, 99 will be killed. Every man among them will say, "Perhaps I will be the one who will be saved" (Muslim: 41/6918).

(8) **Jews and Muslims will fight.** Abu Hurrairah narrates: "The Hour will not come to pass until the Muslims fight the Jews and the Muslims will kill them. A Jew will hide behind a rock and a tree. The rock and tree will say: O Muslim—O Abdullah, this is a Jew behind me, so come and kill him. The only exception is the Ghraqad tree, for it is the tree of the Jews" (Muslim: 41/6985).

(9) **The trumpet will be blown.** The world will come to an end. There will be a great fire that will drive people to gather in one place for final judgment (Quran, 18: 98–99).

Glossary: Explanation of Islamic Terms Used in the Book

Adhan Islamic call to prayer.

Allah The Arabic name for the deity.

Ansar "Helpers." A term used for the host community of Medina when early Muslims migrated to the city to seek refuge there from pagan persecution.

Asharah A word used to denote the number ten.

Baitul Muqqaddus Literally the sacrosanct house, but used for the Al-Aqsa mosque in Jerusalem.

Basharah Good News.

Bayaan Narration.

Caliph The spiritual and political head of the entire Muslim nation.

Dajjal False messiah; literally, "the Liar." Similar to Christian idea of the Antichrist.

Dawah The call to Islam.

Fajr The morning prayer.

Fitan Tribulations.

Hadith Compilations of the sayings of the Prophet Mohammed.

Hajj The annual pilgrimage to Mecca.

Harb War, killing.

Hijrah The migration of Mohammed from Mecca to Medina. The Islamic calendar begins with the year the migration took place.

Imam A leader. A title commonly used for those who lead Muslims in prayer.

Injeel Arabic word for "Gospel."

Israiliyat The traditions attributed to the Jews of Medina who converted to Islam.

171

Jamaat Party; group.

Jihad Personal struggle or fighting in Allah's cause.

Jizya Tax required of non–Muslims in a Muslim state.

Kaaba The cubical structure at the center of the grand mosque in Mecca. Muslims believe it is the first shrine dedicated to the worship of the one true god, built by Adam when he arrived on earth after being banished from paradise.

Kafir One who rejects faith; a non-believer.

Khalifa Arabic for caliph or the political and spiritual ruler of the entire Muslim world.

Kitab Book.

Madrassah A religious school.

Mahar Dower. The husband's gift to the wife at marriage.

Mahdi The "rightly guided" one. The expected redeemer of Islam.

Masih-ud-Dajjal The false Messiah. Same as Dajjal.

Miraj The Prophet Mohammed's night journey. He is said to have traveled from Mecca to Jerusalem and then to the highest heaven for a meeting with God in the span of one night, riding on a magical white horse.

Mubashar The conveyer of good news.

Mujahideen Plural of Mujahid, or one who undertakes Jihad.

Mullah Islamic clergy.

Nabi Prophet.

Qital Warfare.

Quran The holy book of the Muslims, said to be the verbatim word of God dictated to the Prophet Mohammed through the angel Gabriel.

Ramadan The month of fasting and atonement.

Sadiq "The truthful." One of the titles of Mohammed.

Shahadah The declaration of faith that there is no God but God and Mohammed is the messenger of God.

Shaheed A martyr in the cause of Islam.

Shariah The code of public and private conduct of a Muslim.

Tablighi Missionary.

Tajdid Renewal. A philosophy which strives to replicate pristine Islamic society founded under the Prophet.

Taliban or tulaba. Both plurals of Talib, which means student.

Zam-zam Holy water which has supposedly flowed since Ishmael quenched his thirst when he and his mother were abandoned in the valley of Paran by Abraham.

Chapter Notes

Chapter Two

1. In a broadcast on the Christian Broadcasting Network (CBN), 11 Nov. 2002.
2. Abdur Rauf, *Illustrated History of Islam* (Lahore, Pakistan: Ferozsons, 1994), p. 240.
3. Tim LaHaye, *The Merciful God of Prophecy* (New York: Warner, 2004), p. 212.
4. Maryam Jameelah, *Islam versus the West* (Toronto: Al Attique, 2000), p. 45.
5. Jameelah, p. 46.
6. Abdullah Ibrahim, "The Trinity Explained to Muslims." Retrieved Nov. 2006 from *Christian Doctrine Explained*, www.arabicbible.com.
7. Jameelah, p. 25.
8. Rauf, p. 112.

Chapter Three

1. David Cook, "The Beginnings of Islam as an Apocalyptic Movement," http://www.bu.edu/mille/publications/winter2001/cook.html.
2. M. Yasin-Owadally, *Emergence of Dajjal: The Jewish King* (Pakistan: Talha, 2003), p. 17.
3. Yasin-Owadally, p. 42.
4. Hadith as quoted in Yasin-Owadally, p. 30.
5. Owadally, p. 74.
6. Hadith as quoted in Yasin-Owadally, p. 54.
7. Imran Hosein, "Explaining Israel's Mysterious Imperial Agenda." Retrieved March 2007 from www.imranhosein.org.

Chapter Four

1. Ibn Kathir, *The Signs Before the Day of Judgement* (London: Dar al Taqwa, 1994), p. 18.
2. Ibn Babuya al-Suduq, as quoted in Shaukat Ali, *Millenarian and Messianic Tendencies in Islamic History* (Lahore, Pakistan: Publishers United, 1993), p. 25.
3. Kathir, p. 23.
4. Moojan Momen, *An Introduction to Shia Islam* (New Haven: Yale University Press, 1983), p. 231.
5. "The Báb, Forerunner of Bahá'u'lláh." Retrieved Dec. 2005 from *Bahá'í Topics*, http://info.bahai.org/the-bab-forerunner.html.
6. Quoted by John Alden Williams in *Themes of Islamic Civilization* (Berkeley: University of California Press, 1971), pp. 243–244.
7. Williams, p. 238.
8. Text of Ahmadinejad's 2005 U.N. address. Retrieved Dec. 2005 from GlobalSecurity.org.
9. Goinaz Esfandiari, "Iran: President Says Light Surrounded Him During UN Speech," *RadioFreeEurope*, http://www.rferl.org.

Chapter Five

1. Stephun Gaukroger, *The Book of Acts: Free to Live* (Grand Rapids MI: Baker, 1993), p. 15.
2. Harun Yahya, "The Signs of the Last Day in the Quran." Retrieved Jan. 2006 from www.signsofthelastday.com.
3. Douglas Harper, *Online Etymology*

Dictionary. Retrieved Jan. 2006 from http://dictionary.reference.com/browse/gospel.

4. *Good News: The New Testament and Psalms, Today's English Version* (New York: American Bible Society, 1970), preface.

Chapter Six

1. Dictionary.com, retrieved Jan. 2006.

2. Paul Merritt Bassett, "(Christian) General Information." Retrieved Jan. 2006 from http://mb-soft.com/believe/text/fundamen.htm.

3. Mary Beth Marklein, "Birth of Clean Town: Ave Maria," *USA Today Online,* July 18, 2007. Retrieved Sept. 10, 2007, at http://www.usatoday.com/news/nation/2007-07-18-ave-maria_N.htm.

4. Dwight L. Moody quoted in George M. Marsden, *Fundamentalism and American Culture* (New York: Oxford University Press, 1980), p. 14.

5. George M. Marsden, "Defining American Fundamentalism: A Response," in Norman J. Cohen (ed.), *The Fundamentalist Phenomenon* (Grand Rapids MI: William B. Eerdmans, 1990), p. 49.

6. Retrieved April 2006 from Liberty University Website, http://www.liberty.edu/index.cfm?PID=6899.

7. Liberty Website.

8. As reported by CBS News, June 5, 2003. Retrieved April 2006 from CBS News Web site, http://www.cbsnews.com/stories/2003/06/05/60minutes/main557187.shtml?source+search_story.

9. "Quotes from the Religious Right." Retrieved Aug. 2006 from http://www.geocities.com/CapitolHill/7027/quotes.html.

10. Pat Robertson, *The New World Order* (Nashville: Thomas Nelson, 1992), p. 218.

11. Chris Mitchell, "Jerusalem Dateline: Dec. 23, 2005," CBN.com. Retrieved Sept. 12, 2007, from http://www.cbn.com/blogs/chrismitchell/051223.aspx.

12. "Robertson Suggests God Smote Sharon," CNN.com. Retrieved Sept. 12, 2007, from http://www.cnn.com/2006/US/01/05/robertson.sharon.

13. Retrieved Sept. 12, 2007, from http://mediamatters.org/items/200508220006.

14. Bill Sizemore, "Pat Robertson's Right-Wing Gold Mine," *Ms. Magazine Online.* Retrieved Sept. 12, 2007, from http://www.msmagazine.com/sept03/sizemore.asp.

15. Both quotes retrieved Jan. 2006 from Bob Jones University Web site, www.bju.edu.

16. Bob Jones III on *Larry King Live,* March 3, 2000. Retrieved Sept. 2007 from http://transcripts.cnn.com/TRANSCRIPTS/0003/03/lkl.00.html.

17. Michael Northcott, *An Angel Directs the Storm* (London: I. B. Tauris, 2004), p. 1.

18. U.S. president George W. Bush, Inaugural Address, Jan. 20, 2001.

19. Stephen Mansfield, *The Faith of George W. Bush* (Lake Mary FL: Charisma House, 2003), p. 85.

20. Samuel Huntington, *The Clash of Civilizations and the Remaking of World Order* (New York: Simon & Schuster, 1996), p. 28.

Chapter Seven

1. Amir Ali, "Jihad Explained." Retrieved July 2006 from the Web site of the Institute of Islamic Information and Education, http://www.iiie.net/node/33.

2. Retrieved Oct. 2007 from http://ibnayyub.wordpress.com/2007/04/10/the-meaning-of-jihad/.

3. Sheikh Abdullah Bin Muhammad Bin Humaid, "Jihad in the Quran and Sunnah." Retrieved Sept. 14, 2007, from http://www.islamworld.net/jihad.html.

4. "Jihad," *Islamic Glossary Home,* USC-MSA Compendium of Muslim Texts. Retrieved July 2006 from http://www.usc.edu/dept/MSA/reference/glossary.html.

5. Ibid.

6. Sayed Qutb, *Milestones* (India: Islamic Book Service, 2006), p. 62.

7. Hadith as quoted in "Hadith Prophecy on World Wars." Retrieved March 2007 from http://www.mail-archive.com/ahli_sunnah_vs_anti_hadith@yahoogroups.com/msg00238.html.

8. Table as it appears in Saleem Hassan Ali's *Islamic Education and Conflict: Understanding the Madrassahs of Pakistan* (unpublished manuscript, 2005). Data from Ministry of Religious Affairs (1979 data) and Ministry of Education (1988–2000 data), Islamabad.

9. David Montero, "Westerners in Madrassahs," *Christian Science Monitor,* April 5, 2006. Retrieved July 2006 from Web site of World Wide Religious News, http://wwrn.org/sparse.php?idd=21058.

10. Noah Feldman, *After Jihad* (New York: Farrar, Straus and Giroux, 2003), p. 7.

11. Feldman, p. 8.

12. "Taliban, Pakistan and Modernity," *Daily Times,* March 29, 2006. Retrieved July 2006 from Daily Times Web site, http://www.dailytimes.com.pk.

13. Quoted in Saleem Hassan Ali, p. 70.

14. Charles Krauthammer, "Today Tehran, Tomorrow the World," *Time*, March 26, 2006. Retrieved July 2006 from http://www.time.com/time/magazine/article/0,9171,1176995,00.html.

Chapter Eight

1. Yossef Bodansky, *The Man Who Declared War on America* (New York: Random House, 2001), p. x.

2. Bodansky, p. x.

3. Bodansky, p. x.

4. Osama bin Laden, "A Letter to the American People." Retrieved July 2006 from http://observer.guardian.co.uk/worldview/story/0,,845725,00.html.

5. Paul Williams, *Osama's Revenge* (Amherst NY: Prometheus, 2004), p. 69.

6. Williams, p. 60.

7. Williams, p. 61.

8. Bin Laden, interview with *Time*, December 23, 1998.

9. Daniel Benjamin and Steven Simon, *The Next Attack* (London: Hodder & Stoughton, 2005), p. 18.

10. "Jihad against Jews and Crusaders," World Islamic Front statement, Feb. 23, 1998. Retrieved September 28, 2007, from http://www.fas.org/irp/world/para/docs/980223-fatwa.htm.

11. Clifford D. May, "Bin Laden Speaks," *National Review Online*, Feb. 13, 2003. Retrieved July 2006 from http://www.nationalreview.com/comment/comment-may021203.asp.

12. Daniels and Simon, p. 27.

Chapter Nine

1. Samuel P. Huntington, *The Clash of Civilizations* (New York: Free Press, 2002).

2. Abul Ala Maudidi, quoted on the back cover of *Did the Prophet Mohammed Predict the Second Coming of Jesus and World War II?* by Zakiuddin Sharfi (Brooklyn: Saut-us-Salam, 1983).

3. Sharfi, p. 13.

4. Sharfi, p. 4.

5. Louis Sahagun, "End Times Religious Groups Want Apocalypse Soon," *Los Angeles Times*, June 22, 2006.

6. Full transcript of Ahmadinejad's address retrieved Sept. 2006 from The Liberal Avenger (www.liberalavenger.com).

7. Retrieved June 2006 from the Web site of the Party for Islamic Renewal.

8. U.S. president George W. Bush, address to the United Nations General Assembly, Sept. 12, 2002. Retrieved Sept. 2006 from http://www.whitehouse.gov/news/releases/2002/09/20020912-1.html.

9. Ignacio Ramonet, *Wars of the 21st Century* (Melbourne: Ocean, 2004), p. 147.

10. Ramonet, pp. 162–3.

11. Ramonet, p. 2.

Chapter Ten

1. Retrieved July 2, 2006, from the Web site of the North Korean News Agency, http://www.kcna.co.jp/.

2. Ignacio Ramonet, *Wars of the 21st Century* (Melbourne: Ocean, 2004), p. 104.

3. Tahir Qazi, "Corporate War on Terrorism," July 31, 2006. Retrieved Sept. 2007 from http://www.chowk.com/articles/11033.

4. Francis A. Boyle, "The Middle East Agenda: Oil, Dollar Hegemony and Islam," lecture delivered June 22, 2006, at the Perdana Global Peace Forum. Retrieved Sept. 2007 from http://www.informationclearinghouse.info/article13864.htm.

5. Mubin Shaikh, interview on CBC News, July 13, 2006. Retrieved Sept. 2007 from http://www.pbs.org/frontlineworld/stories/canada602/shaikh.html.

6. Fuad L. Khuri, *Imams and Emirs: State, Religion and Sects in Islam* (London: Saqi, 1990).

7. Niall Ferguson, "The March of Islam," extract from *The War of the World* (London: Allen Lane, 2006), published in the *Daily Telegraph Online*, May 21, 2005. Retrieved August 2006 from http://www.telegraph.co.uk/arts/main.jhtml?xml=/arts/2006/05/21/svniall21.xml.

8. Scott Piraino, "The De-Evolution of Warfare." Retrieved October 2007 from http://www.leatherneck.com/forums/showthread.php?t=7583&highlight=scott+piraino.

9. Fareed Zakaria, "The U.S. Can Out-Charm China," *Newsweek*, Dec. 12, 2005. Retrieved July 2006 from http://www.FareedZakaria.com/articles/newsweek/121205.html.

10. "The Situation Room," CNN.com, August 9, 2006. Retrieved October 2007 from http://transcripts.cnn.com/TRANSCRIPTS/0608/09/sitroom.03/html.

11. Ramonet, p. 138.

12. Human Security Centre, *The Human Security Report 2005* (Oxford: Oxford University Press, 2005).

Bibliography

Primary Sources

'Ali, 'Abdullah Yusuf. *The Meaning of the Holy Quran: New Edition with Revised Translation, Commentary and Newly Compiled Comprehensive Index*. Beltsville MD: Amana, 2002.

Al-Qur'an: A Contemporary Translation. Trans. Ahmed Ali. Princeton NJ: Princeton University Press, 1993.

Asad, Muhammad. *The Message of the Quran* Gibraltar: Dar-al Andalus, 1980.

The Glorious Quran. Trans. M. Marmaduke Pickthall. First US edition. Elmhurst NY: Tahrike Tarsile Qur'an, 2000.

The Holy Bible: English Standard Version. New York: HarperCollins, 2002

Holy Bible: New King James Version. New York: American Bible Society, 1982.

The Holy Quran: Arabic Text and English Translation. Trans. Sher Ali Mualvi. London: Islam International Publications, 1989.

Khan, *Muhammad Muhsin*, the translation of the *Meanings of Sahih Al-Bukhari*, Kazi Publications, Lahore, 1979.

The Inspirational Study Bible. Ed. Max Lucado. Dallas: Word, 1995.

The Koran Interpreted. Trans. Arthur J. Arberry. London: Oxford University Press, 1964.

Sayings of the Holy Prophet Mohammed (Agreed upon Ahadith). Comp. Syed Maqbool Hussain. Salam Trust, 2000.

Secondary Sources

Aftab, Shahryar. *Dajjal: The Final Deception*. New Delhi: Islamic Book Services, 2005.

Ahmad, Mirza Ghulam. *Jesus in India*. London: Islam International Publications, 1989.

Ali, Saleem Hassan. *Islamic Education and Conflict: Understanding the Madrassahs of Pakistan*. Unpublished manuscript, 2005.

Ali, Shaukat. *Dimensions and Dilemmas of Islamist Movements*. Lahore, Pakistan: Sang-e-Meel, 1998.

_____. *Millenarian and Messianic Tendencies in Islamic History*. Lahore, Pakistan: Publishers United, 1993.

Armstrong, Karen. *Islam: A Short History*. New York: Random House, 2002.

Benjamin, Daniel, and Steven Simon. *The Next Attack: The Globalization of Jihad*. London: Hodder and Stoughton, 2005.

bin Bayyumi, Muhammad. *Smaller Signs of the Day*. Houston: Dar-us-Salam, 2004.

Boadt, Lawrence. *Reading the Old Testament: An Introduction*. New York: Paulist, 1984.

Bodansky, Yossef. *Bin Laden: The Man Who Declared War on America*. New York: Random House, 2001.

Cook, David. *Contemporary Muslim Apocalyptic Literature*. Syracuse: Syracuse University Press, 2005.

Esposito, John. *The Oxford History of Islam*. New York: Oxford University Press, 1999.

Feldman, Noah. *After Jihad: America and the Struggle for Islamic Democracy*. New York: Farrar, Straus and Giroux, 2003.

Ferguson, Niall. *The War of the World: Twentieth-Century Conflict and the Descent of the West.* London: Allen Lane, 2006.

Gladney, Druc. *Dislocating China: Reflections on Muslims, Minorities and other Subaltern Subjects.* London: C. Hurst, 2004.

Goldstein, Jonathan. *China and Israel, 1948–1998: A Fifty-year Retrospective.* New York: Praeger, 1999.

Graham, Franklin. *The Name.* Nashville: Thomas Nelson, 2002.

Human Security Centre. *The Human Security Report 2005.* Oxford: Oxford University Press, 2005.

Huntington, Samuel. *The Clash of Civilizations and the Remaking of World Order.* New York: Simon & Schuster, 1996.

Iqbal, Mohammed. *The Reconstruction of Religious Thought in Islam.* Chicago: Kazi, 1999.

Islamic Council of Europe. *Jerusalem: The Key to World Peace.* London: Islamic Council of Europe, 1980.

Jameelah, Maryam. *Islam versus the West.* Toronto: Al Attique, 2000.

Kathir, Ibn. *The Signs before the Day of Judgement.* London: Dar al Taqwa, 1994.

Keppel, Gilles. *Jihad: The Trail of Political Islam.* Cambridge MA: Harvard University Press, 2002.

Khan, Shahrukh Rafi. *Basic Education in Rural Pakistan: A Comparative Institutional Analysis of Government, Private and NGO Schools.* New York: Oxford University Press, 2005.

Khuri, Fuad. *Imams and Emirs: State Religion and Sects in Islam.* London: Saqi, 2006.

LaHaye, Tim. *The Merciful God of Prophecy: His Loving Plan for You in the End Times.* New York: Warner, 2002.

Lewis, Bernard. *The Crises of Islam: Holy War and Unholy Terror.* New York: Random House, 2003.

Lindsey, Hal. *The Late Great Planet Earth.* (1973.) Grand Rapids MI: Zondervan, 1998.

Marsden, George M. *Fundamentalism and American Culture.* New York: Oxford University Press, 1980.

Momen, M. *An Introduction to Shia Islam.* New Haven: Yale University Press, 1983.

Naipaul, V.S. *Beyond Belief: Islamic Excursions Among the Converted Peoples.* Boston: Little, Brown, 1998.

Rahman, Tariq. *Denizens of Alien Worlds: A Study of Education, Inequality and Polarization in Pakistan.* New York: Oxford University Press, 2005.

Ramonet, Ignacio. *Wars of the Twenty-first Century: New Threats, New Fears.* Melbourne: Ocean, 2004.

Rashid, Ahmed. *Jihad: The Rise of Militant Islam in Central Asia.* New Haven: Yale University Press, 2002.

_____. *Taliban: Militant Islam, Oil and Fundamentalism in Central Asia.* New Haven: Yale University Press, 2000.

Rauf, Abdur. *Illustrated History of Islam.* Lahore, Pakistan: Ferozsons, 1993.

Sardar, Ziauddin. *Desperately Seeking Paradise: Journeys of a Sceptical Muslim.* London: Granta, 2004.

Shichor, Yitzhak. *The Middle East in China's Foreign Policy, 1947–1977.* Cambridge: Cambridge University Press, 1979.

Small Wars Manual. United States Marine Corps, 1940.

Sonn, Tamara. *A Brief History of Islam.* London: Blackwell, 2004.

Stark, Rodney. *For the Glory of God: How Monotheism Led to Reformations, Science, Witch-Hunts, and the End of Slavery.* Princeton NJ: Princeton University Press, 2003.

Thomson, Ahmad. *Dajjal: The Antichrist.* London: Taha, 1997.

Williams, Paul L. *Al Qaeda, Brotherhood of Terror.* Indianapolis: Alpha, 2002.

_____. *Osama's Revenge: The Next 9/11: What the Media and the Government Haven't Told You.* New Delhi: Viva Books Private, 2005.

Yahya, Harun. *Palestine.* New Delhi: Islamic Book Services, 2005.

Index